FREEDOM AND CATHOLIC POWER
in Spain and Portugal

FREEDOM AND CATHOLIC POWER

in Spain and Portugal

An American Interpretation

By PAUL BLANSHARD

BEACON PRESS   BOSTON

Published simultaneously in Canada by
S. J. Reginald Saunders and Co., Ltd., Toronto

Library of Congress catalog card number: 62-9368

Second printing, June 1962
Printed in the United States of America

For Mary, as always

PREFACE

My preparation for the writing of this book might be described as intermittent and sporadic. I am not a professional scholar in the field of Spanish and Portuguese institutions or history, but I have had the opportunity, as an occasional, roving professional journalist over a period of almost forty years, to see a great deal of fascism and political Catholicism in the course of eight periods of residence and study in Europe. I was fortunate to get more than a casual glimpse of Republican Spain when I visited the country in 1933 at the height of the rule of its troubled social-democratic regime. Then I went on to Nazi Germany to see how German fascism worked. I had lived for a time in Mussolini's Italy when Italian fascism was taking shape, and I had lived long enough in Ireland to produce a book about Catholicism there. During four years of service in the U. S. State Department, I had been able to make some observations about Latin America and European colonial systems. Later I lived in Rome and elsewhere in Europe, studying political and labor Catholicism.

This was all background preparation. Then in 1959, in a small French car, my wife and I trundled to almost every corner of Spain and Portugal, spending four months in the most intensive interviewing I have ever attempted in my life. If this were a travel book, I could fill many pages with tales and descriptions of the beauties, the glories and the delights of two of the world's most fascinating countries, of which the greatest delight is the cordial hospitality of the Spanish and Portuguese people to visiting Americans.

In both countries we had much assistance, professional and otherwise. My wife, Mary Hillyer Blanshard, was throughout the whole project an indispensable collaborator.

I found that the Spanish and Portuguese people talked and talked quite freely—behind closed doors. Since I came with im-

vii

peccable credentials from Iberian revolutionists in Paris and elsewhere, I was able to reach the most secret sources of the anti-
Franco and anti-Salazar opposition. Since I came with equally
impeccable credentials from important leaders in American
Protestantism and Judaism, I was able to reach the Protestant
and Jewish minorities. My former State Department connections
helped to open government doors. Without any Catholic credentials, I found that Catholic priests, high Jesuits and many of the
nation's most important Catholic laymen were also willing to
talk quite frankly.

So, on our idyllic itinerary through these two romantic and
hospitable countries, I talked to people of every class, priests,
Catholic editors, Protestant clergymen, industrial leaders, Falange
and Union Party leaders, librarians, university professors, American diplomats, Socialists, government officials—everybody except
Communists. The Communists had to live so far underground
that they did not dare to risk conversation with a non-Communist
stranger.

An author of a book like this, which borrows so many
background facts from other authors, should acknowledge those
authors if possible even when he suspects that they might totally
disagree with his conclusions. Every author in this field should
acknowledge first the indispensable journalism of the *New York
Times,* which year in and year out has handled the facts about
Spain and Portugal realistically through its distinguished correspondents. Equally valuable and even more voluminous in its
Spanish coverage is the anti-Franco magazine *Iberica,* published
in New York in both Spanish and English. It is a mine of accurate information about both Spain and Portugal.

Among historical works about Spain, none has covered
recent developments more adequately than Salvador de Madariaga's 1958 book, *Spain: A Modern History.* In the appropriate
places I have mentioned also those excellent recent books by
American and English writers about the Spanish Republic and
the Spanish Civil War—by Hugh Thomas, Gerald Brenan, F. Jay
Taylor, Emmet J. Hughes, Herbert L. Matthews, Lawrence Fernsworth and Charles Foltz Jr. The most important and scholarly
recent work on Spain and American policy was published after I
had completed most of this book, *Spain and Defense of the West*
by Arthur P. Whitaker. An equally important work about Portugal
is *Portuguese Africa* by James Duffy.

For the story of Protestantism in Spain I owe much to a scholarly book published in England but almost unknown in this country, *Religious Freedom in Spain* by J. D. Hughey Jr. Dr. Hughey did the basic research for this book in a Ph.D. thesis for Columbia University. A most valuable and up-to-date short treatment of Spanish church-state conditions is *Church and State in Franco Spain* (Princeton University, 1960) by Professor William Ebenstein of Princeton.

I must confess also that, although I totally disagree with the major conclusions of Richard Pattee's *This Is Spain* and *Portugal and the Portuguese World*—and I say so in this book in no uncertain terms—I have found his works immensely stimulating and his extensive research very valuable. For those who share his Catholic point of view, continuing sustenance may be found in the temperate analyses of Spain and Portugal in the Jesuit magazine *America*. In a somewhat different class are the three distinguished works of the late Professor E. Allison Peers of the University of Liverpool, listed in the Notes, the most valuable for the purposes of this study being *Spain, the Church and the Orders*. Professor Peers seems to me to be too charitable to Catholic policy in Spain, but no one questions his outstanding scholarship.

To the countless and nameless friends in Spain and Portugal who, sometimes late at night in secret meetings, risked their professional careers to tell an American journalist what inconsistent juveniles we are for cooperating with Franco and Salazar, my thanks and my hope that this book will help to strengthen and sustain them.

CONTENTS

CONTENTS

Paul Blanshard has had a varied career as journalist, lawyer, public official and author. Under Mayor La Guardia he was head of New York City's Department of Investigations and Accounts for four years. During World War II he was a State Department official in Washington and the Caribbean. Among his books are *Democracy and Empire in the Caribbean; American Freedom and Catholic Power; Communism, Democracy and Catholic Power; The Irish and Catholic Power;* and *The Right to Read.*

Two of Mr. Blanshard's books on the problems of Catholic power in American society were national best sellers for many months.

Motif

Catholicism is the fascist form of Christianity. . . .

> —Richard Coudenhove-Kalergi
> in *Crusade for Pan-Europe*

. . . it is vital for Americans to keep in mind that the enemy in our century is totalitarianism, whether it take the form of communism or fascism. We fought the Second World War with communism as an ally, only to find at the end that the threat to world democracy was greater than ever. It would be extraordinarily shortsighted if now we fought communism with fascism as an ally.

> —*New York Times* editorial,
> August 3, 1950

1. PERSONAL PROLOGUE:
An American Issue

Perhaps the first question an author should face in beginning a book like this is: Why should America be interested in freedom and Catholic power in Spain and Portugal today?

One general answer is that in this troubled and interdependent world no suppression of human freedom is irrelevant to our own future. The bell that tolls for the death of freedom in Spain and Portugal may be tolling for us.

A more specific answer is that both fascism and Catholicism in Spain and Portugal have a direct and almost personal relationship to American foreign policy and to American Catholicism. The United States is a military ally of the Spanish and Portuguese dictatorships, and America's largest church, the Roman Catholic Church, is a religious and political ally. On both sides of the Atlantic, the significance of one cannot be discussed without considering the other. More than half the world's Roman Catholics speak the languages of the Iberian peninsula, and, simultaneously, the Catholic people of the United States constitute the chief source of financial power for the expansion of their Church.[1]

The Iberian peninsula is not, as some people might suppose, a minor backwater in the critical struggle between Communism and democracy. It is, rather, a crucial testing ground for the West's philosophy of freedom. In this southwestern corner of Europe, partially cut off from the rest of the Continent by the Pyrenees, are two of the most fascist nations in the world, which claim also that they are the two most Catholic nations in the world. They are ruled by Catholic and fascist dictators who have the official blessing of their Church.

That Church is both the largest church organization operating on American soil and the chief propaganda agency within the United States for support of our alliances with Spain and Portugal. Partly as the result of Catholic pressure, our government is the

1

only major military ally in the world today which supports the Spanish dictatorship, and this unique American position has been attained at the very moment when we are attempting to convince a suspicious Latin America, Asia and Africa that we are the world's purest apostle of freedom.

The anomaly of this position is something that we must face even at some risk of misunderstanding and misrepresentation. The easy answer to the question of why we are in alliance with two fascist dictators is that they constitute a bulwark against Communism. In the prevailing mood of America that oversimplified answer is usually accepted without analysis. The person who questions it is likely to be charged either with softness toward Communism or a deliberate desire to fan the flames of religious discord. Actually, our very survival in this century may depend upon facing the realities of clerical fascism as a reactionary force independent of any Communist threat. Unless we can demonstrate that we understand and oppose all threats from both the right and the left, it is not likely that we can hold the friendship of the great masses of Asia, Africa and Latin America in our campaign against the threat of the Soviet left.

This foreboding has had particular significance since the Castro revolution in Cuba and the African convulsions in the Congo and Angola. One reason why the United States has failed to win general Latin American sympathy for its anti-Castro policy is that we have had no consistent anti-Franco and anti-Salazar policy. We have appeared to condone fascist dictators and grant them billions for defense and progress while simultaneously proclaiming undying hostility to dictators—if they happen to be Communist. Our foreign critics have noted that in the present climate of American opinion it is considered uncouth even to suggest that the Roman Catholic Church itself is a dictatorship of the right whose long record of alliance with dictatorial regimes entitles it to classification as a reactionary political force.

The Iberian peninsula achieved a new importance for America in 1961 when the violent wave of black nationalism in Portuguese Africa brought the United States into sharp conflict with the Salazar regime at the United Nations. Spain entered the picture indirectly because Franco stood with Salazar in claiming that the tiny remnants of Spanish African territory were still an "integral" part of the homeland. Portugal challenged both the United States and the United Nations by attempting to deny any international guardianship rights over its gigantic African colonies.

The capture of the Portuguese cruise liner *Santa Maria* in January 1961, and the subsequent uprisings in Angola, illuminated the whole imperial landscape like a flash of summer lightning. The United States, under the new Kennedy administration, voted with the UN majority for an honest inquiry into Portuguese tyranny in Africa. With honorable exceptions among liberal Catholics, Catholic power lined up on the other side in defense of Salazar and his "quiet" dictatorship. Thus, a new international issue was created between Catholic Spain and Portugal on the one hand and the United States on the other.

Long before the 1961 Portuguese incidents, we had become deeply involved in an unholy alliance with Franco which had cost us more than $2 billion[2] and the respect of European and Latin American liberalism. Four great air and naval bases had been built by American taxpayers on Spanish soil from Cadiz to Saragossa, with a Spanish flag flying over them, and their very availability in time of war subject to Franco's whim.

Religion had become, willy-nilly, an important factor in that aid-to-Franco program. The American Catholic Church had become a primary promoter of the alliance as a necessary defense measure against Communism, with the ardent and undiscriminating support of the Pentagon. Some of the anti-Protestant and anti-Jewish practices of the Catholic kingdom of Spain had been imported even into our bases, although the great majority of servicemen in our armed forces were Protestants and Jews. This applied not only to mixed marriage but even to Protestant picnics—while in Spain I was able to document the story of a Protestant Sunday School picnic, composed entirely of American armed forces personnel, which had been broken up by Franco police in a Madrid park in June 1959 simply because it was an illegal "public manifestation" of a non-Catholic faith.[3] To this day, the Protestant chaplains in our armed forces are forbidden to make any contacts with Spanish Protestant congregations for fear it will upset the "religious unity" of Spain.

These are miniscule items in an alliance which has worldwide religious as well as political significance. In some ways it is quite a unique alliance. There are many political dictatorships in the world with which the United States cooperates, but Spain is different from all the rest. Spain fits most precisely into that rather ill-defined classification, "a clerical fascist state." It has all the ingredients associated with that classification: political rule by a single dictator, the control of capital and labor by state syndicates, a single political party which is rabidly nationalist, a completely controlled press and the collaboration of a state church. Its middle and lower classes are impoverished and its upper class is panic-stricken about Communism. It is the last unreformed nation in Europe whose government was spiritually a part of the fascist Axis in World War II.

Most significant for the purposes of this study, the American alliance with Spain brings together two nations which lie at opposite ends of both the democratic and the religious spectra. The most advanced democracy in the world is allied with the most fascist nation in the world in such a way that our strength and prestige are being used to sanction not only political tyranny but religious discrimination and suppression as well. That nation among all the nations which has most Protestant strength, and which believes in the separation of church and state most consist-ently, has become the strongest military and economic partner of that nation which practices the union of church and state with the most savage discrimination against non-Catholic Christians and Jews.

The paradoxes and inconsistencies in that Spanish-American alliance seem to justify the description I have used at the head of this chapter, "An American Issue." They might even justify a stronger description, "An American Absurdity."

Some Qualifications and Hedgings

The very inclusion of the word "Catholic" in the title of this book raises certain fundamental questions. Are the political dic-tatorships of Spain and Portugal essentially Catholic dictatorships, or simply reactionary and semi-fascist dictatorships whose rulers happen to be Catholics? Is the Catholicism in these dictatorships incidental or organic? Is the cooperating relationship between the dictatorial states and the dictatorial Church an accident of his-tory or a fundamental partnership of affinities?

A large part of this book is taken up with an answer to these questions. The answer, of course, is not simple or unequivocal. Although the Roman Catholic Church is monolithic in its central structure of power, and although it claims that its basic doctrines are unchanging and unchangeable, it is a sufficiently dynamic and adjustable institution in practice to adapt its working policies to national conditions. Spanish Catholicism is not American Catholicism—at least in day-to-day execution of political and social policy. Roman Catholicism is not necessarily fascist, nor is fascism necessarily Catholic. On both sides of the Atlantic millions of devout Catholics are sincerely opposed to the Franco and Salazar tyrannies.

Nevertheless, because of the weight of the evidence, the answer points definitely to a fundamental partnership. And the evidence for the affirmative, as well as for the negative, will be marshaled in this book. Catholicism and fascism both operate on the authoritarian leadership principle, in sharp contrast to the practices of democracy. In Spain and Portugal that common and deadly characteristic has resulted in two societies which, through the union of state and church power, deny free enterprise in politics, economics and religion. In spite of protests within the Catholic world, the Church has become, with the full official sanction of the Holy See itself, a part of the warp and woof of the Franco and Salazar dictatorships. The systems of political and religious power are interwoven and interdependent. The thousands of heroic young priests and laymen in both Portugal and Spain who oppose the church-state partnership would be the first to admit that, as of the present time, the partnership is organic rather than incidental.

That use of the phrase, "as of the present time," leads me to interpolate a face-saving and precautionary paragraph. During the process of writing this book, I have picked up my morning paper each day with increasing trepidation to see whether (1) Franco and/or Salazar is/are dead; and whether (2) he/or they has/have been superseded by a conventional king, a military junta, a Christian Democratic committee, a Communist dictatorship, and/or chaos. Dictators aged seventy years or more—Franco was born in 1892 and Salazar in 1889—are likely to be very thoughtless about dying or retiring at moments which are convenient for authors writing under a date line. Some learned journalist predicts the fall of Franco and/or Salazar almost every day in some sapient and vague prophecy. In spite of the uncertainties, I am compelled to write about them in the present tense.

Actually, not much of this analysis would be out of date if Franco should go to his Valley of the Fallen and Salazar to his plain and modest grave before these words reach the public. The forces which would dictate the future of a post-Franco Spain and a post-Salazar Portugal are the same forces that I have attempted to analyze in this volume. An understanding of a new Spain and a new Portugal would require some comprehension of the present social factors in Spanish and Portuguese life, especially those factors involving collaboration between church and state which have not been so extensively described in any other recent volume. Whatever happens to Franco and Salazar, Spanish and Portuguese, as well as American and Roman, Catholicism will remain. They will have their interlocking systems of power and they will continue to promote their programs for the world and for the Iberian peninsula.

2. FROM THE INQUISITION
TO FRANCO

"Do not forget, gentlemen, that in my country freedom of worship and the separation of church and state do not date from 1776, as in your country. They were born yesterday."

The speaker was Fernando de los Rios, ambassador of the Spanish Republic to the United States, one-time Foreign Minister and Minister of Education for his government, and one of the foremost anti-clerical leaders of the Republican regime. The place was Washington and the time was October 1936, a time of crisis in the Spanish Civil War when Franco was about to begin that long siege of Madrid which would finally end in 1939 in the total defeat of the Republican forces in Spain. Senor de los Rios was defending the anti-clerical policies of his government as embodied in laws that he himself had written. He was stating his case against a Catholic Church which had become the instrument of clerical oppression while using the slogans of religious freedom.

He summed up in that single sentence the reason why Spain and the United States stand at opposite ends of the church-state spectrum. For 173 years, since the Bill of Rights was written into our Constitution, the American people have lived under a system of church-state separation which has given every sect equality and freedom. During that same period Spain has been the living symbol of church-state union as expounded and advocated by the Roman Catholic Church.[1]

The historical distance between Madrid and Washington cannot be measured merely in geographical and political terms. It is also a religious span. When I say "religious," I do not refer to the mere creedal difference between a predominantly Catholic country and a predominantly Protestant country. I wish to include the whole sweep of church-state relations and the fundamental attitudes of governments and peoples toward religious freedom and the separation of church and state.

7

In historical terms the difference between the American and the Spanish outlook in respect to church and state is almost as sharp as the difference between our democracy and Communism. In religious matters we have grown up in freedom, while Spain has developed under an authoritarian rule which is as arbitrary as that of the Kremlin—and almost as political. For centuries the Spanish people have been accustomed to thinking of Catholicism and political power as so closely intertwined that they are parts of the same amalgam. No one can tell where the power of the church leaves off and the power of the state begins. Since the American people adopted the First Amendment in 1789, we have been accustomed to thinking of the state as independent of clerical control and the churches as independent of political tyranny.

One basic reason for the union of church and state in Spain is that the country was born out of a religious conflict against a religious enemy, the Moorish invaders. The Spanish Inquisition, spectacular as it might have been, was not the beginning of church-state association but only its bloody culmination. It was the fruit of eight centuries of history in which the religious and political forces in the Iberian peninsula were welded together in opposition to the religious-political power of the Moors.

The Spanish Inquisition

The last heretic to be killed by the Spanish Inquisition was strangled by hanging on July 26, 1826.[2] He was a schoolteacher named Cayetano Ripoll who was actually a deist, willing to teach his pupils the principles of the Ten Commandments and faith in God, but unwilling to teach them some other items in the Catholic creed.

By that time the Inquisition had been operating in Europe almost six hundred years, and the custom of burning heretics alive had begun to pall a little. The screams of the dying had invaded the nightmares of both bishops and executioners. Gradually a new code of "mercy" had been developed. If victims were docile and manifested some signs of repentance, especially after the extraction of their fingernails, they were granted the favor of being strangled in advance and their dead bodies burned for the pleasure of the crowd without any public display of personal agony. That is what had happened to Savonarola in Italy in 1498 to the great disappointment of the multitude. In the case of Cayetano Ripoll the crowd seemed to be satisfied to have him buried in a barrel with flames painted on the outside, symbolizing both the lost bonfire and the descent of his soul into hell. Then the members of the crowd pulled his body to pieces. Earlier crowds in Spain, Italy, the Netherlands and France witnessed more complete performances.

The impression is quite widespread that the Spanish Inquisition was unique, and that Torquemada somehow embodied qualities which no other human monster had ever possessed. Actually, the reputation of Torquemada and the Spanish Inquisition is based partly on timing. Although Spain had the dubious honor of killing the first victim for heresy in A.D. 385, its chief orgy of roasting, flaying and strangling came a little later than the similar orgies in Italy, France and other countries. So the Spanish events were somewhat more conspicuous. In practice the procedures of the Inquisition were quite similar throughout Europe and Latin America. There is no reason to believe that Spanish inquisitors were personally any more cruel than Italian, French or Dutch inquisitors. The Church, with its monks as investigators, searched out the victims, produced the "evidence," convicted the culprits of mortal sin, and then, washing its hands of political guilt, turned them over to the state for execution. Nominally the state decided upon the method of killing or torture. Actually the monks knew exactly what they were doing when they exposed a victim to the charge of heresy. Franciscan and Dominican friars served as chief investigators. They rarely lit a faggot themselves or turned the screw on a rack, although it is said that they sometimes suggested torture before conviction in order to guarantee "complete" evidence.

Although the methods of the Spanish Inquisition were, by present standards, approximately on a par with genocide, it should be remembered that the methods of ordinary criminal justice in medieval times were just as bad. Confessions could be extracted legally in civil courts from men charged with petty crimes by the use of red-hot pincers or the water cure, and no Civil Liberties Union was in existence to protest. It was a savage world and Spain was part of that world.

Even after the Reformation, Europeans, both Protestant and Catholic, continued to believe in and to practice cruelties that no citizen of the present day would consider civilized. Michael Servetus was a native of Spain, and his death in 1553 symbolized the common villainy of both Catholics and Protestants. He was burned alive at the stake in Geneva with the blessings of both priests and Calvinists because he was essentially a Unitarian. Lest we feel self-righteous about American superiority, it should be remembered that nineteen residents of Salem Village, Massachusetts, were hanged for "witchcraft" in 1691.

The thing that made the Spanish Inquisition most distinctive and enduring was that, beginning in the fifteenth century, it was made into an organic part of Spanish church-state power as it expanded throughout the world. Spain, at the very moment Columbus was discovering America, mobilized church and state in a joint drive against all enemies, political and religious. It used spiritual as well as temporal tests to identify its enemies, and it coupled the glory of the faith with the glory of an empire which became for a short time the largest empire in the world.

Ferdinand and Isabella, who brought Castile and Aragon together by their marriage, received a papal bull in 1478 authorizing them to set up a special Spanish Inquisition, nominally under the Pope but in practice almost independent of Vatican control. The two "Catholic sovereigns"—they are always called that—proceeded with the help of the Dominican friar, Torquemada, to unite most of the territory now known as Spain in a "holy crusade" against the infidels—the Moors and the Jews. The campaign reached its successful climax in 1492 in the official expulsion from the country of those Jews who insisted on preserving their faith. From that time onward Spain was officially committed for more than three hundred years to the maintenance of "religious unity" by force. Although the Church publicly asserted that it disbelieved in conversion by force, in practice the fate of an unbeliever who stood firm for his heresy was often worse than death. In 1525, Pope Clement VII officially permitted Charles I of Spain to issue a decree of forced conversion against the Moors.

When Protestantism was born in the sixteenth century, the Inquisition was used against a few Protestants, and there is no doubt that it prevented the development of Protestantism by punishment, threats and persecution. But the Spanish Inquisition was never primarily an anti-Protestant device. It was primarily a church-state device for combining spiritual loyalty with patriotic fervor in support of a Catholic state. The Spanish government was Catholic and the Catholic Church in Spain was Spanish, and they were never politically separated except during the two brief periods of the First Republic in 1873 and the Second Republic in 1931-1936.

This concept of a combined church and state, with compulsory loyalty enforced by the Inquisition, was carried by the conquistadors to the New World and used against both natives and non-Spaniards—although it never attained the importance in the New World that it had at home. Lima had an *auto de fe* in the seventeenth century that was particularly savage; the Inquisition burned several "infidel" non-Catholic Englishmen in Mexico in 1567; Mexico's greatest early hero, the priest Miguel Hidalgo of Dolores, who led the anti-Spanish revolt of 1810, was shot as a rebel and denounced to the Mexican Inquisition as an atheist. Morelos, his successor and also a priest, was the last heretic to be sentenced to death by the Mexican Inquisition. "The union of altar and throne was much more intimate in America than in Spain," says the American historian, J. Lloyd Mecham.[3] One of the charges brought against Morelos by the Inquisition was that "he sent the oldest of his three sons to study in the United States, desirous that he learn the maxims of Protestantism."

The Rise of Anti-Clericalism

"Clericalism," says the Spanish historian, Salvador de Madariaga, is "a disease of Catholic societies." Similarly, it may be said that anti-clericalism is the antibody developed within Catholic societies to resist the infection of clerical tyranny. It existed in Spain long before the Catholic press had the opportunity to pin upon it the oversimplified label, "Communism."

Anti-clericalism has not been as uniformly and consistently powerful in Spain as in France, but it has been intermittently in evidence for the last one hundred years. During that stormy century the Church has again and again been humbled by its political opponents, its buildings burned by anti-clerical mobs, and its leading religious orders expelled from the country. The nation which claims to be the most Catholic nation in the world has probably murdered more priests and nuns and burned more convents and schools than any other nation in the world, far more than Communist Hungary or the Soviet Union. These anti-Church demonstrations have not been demonstrations against religion as such or against Christianity in particular. The Church has been victimized because the Church has been regarded as a part of the ruling structure of political power. For almost two hundred years the advocates of political democracy in Spain have been automatically anti-clerical, and the defenders of dictatorship have tended to be pro-Catholic.

Even before the Inquisition came to an end, the Spanish Church began to pay the price for its own greed. Part of the anti-clerical opposition was based not on doctrinal skepticism but upon economic jealousy. Partly through priestly pressure upon the dying for bequests, the Church had become the largest landlord in Spain. Pope Alexander III had decreed in 1170 that no will was valid unless drawn up in the presence of a priest. In the sixteenth century half of the entire income of the country came from Church-owned land.[4] Some of this income went to hospitals, schools and the poor; perhaps one-fifth went to the sixty-four archbishops and bishops of the Church itself who lived in such conspicuous grandeur that they were branded as the economic royalists of their time. In spite of many adverse comments against them, they tried to hold this privileged position down to the twentieth century—and failed.

Almost as conspicuous as the bishops in land ownership and income were the great male religious orders of Spain, those semi-secret religious communities whose members take the tripartite oath of poverty, obedience and chastity. (The oath of personal poverty has never prevented the orders themselves from becoming rich.) In early years these religious orders not only monopolized education at home but also extended their enterprises far afield into the world of business enterprise in the colonies. They retained enough wealth and power to become the targets of almost every Spanish revolutionary movement from the middle of the eighteenth century to the present time.

The Jesuits particularly have always been the most hated religious group in Spain. I found this to be true in 1933 when the attacks upon them came from the heads of the Republican regime, and equally true in 1959 when they were officially sacrosanct under Franco's protection. Beginning in the eighteenth century, they have been expelled from, or suppressed within, Spain six times for excessive ambition, greed and political manipulation. They were expelled from the country in 1767 shortly before the Papacy temporarily abolished the order altogether—in the period from 1773 to 1814. They were dissolved later by the Spanish liberals in 1820, and again in the revolution of 1868. They were the first to be condemned and dissolved by the government of the Second Republic early in 1932.

Many historians believe that the Jesuits did not deserve all this punishment. They had rendered some service to Spanish children by establishing the only halfway acceptable secondary schools in the country. But when a religious order stands, as the Jesuits have stood, for church-state dictatorship, the order's power only increases the bitterness of the reprisals. In a sense the Jesuits have been the victims of their own success. In fact, almost all the Spanish religious orders have been the victims of political animosity because the state has underwritten their privileges and given them quasi-political status. Their fortunes have gone up and down with the fortunes of their political patrons.

This hatred of the religious orders has been revealed throughout the world wherever the Spanish flag has been raised. In the Spanish-American War the American people were given a special exhibition of this attitude in the Philippines when the United States temporarily took over the Philippine government.[5] Catholic friars had accompanied the conquistadors to the Far East and had appropriated for themselves some 400,000 acres of the best land in the archipelago. The Spanish government had appointed the friars tax collectors and administrators in many districts. In 1,200 Philippine villages they were the only Spanish residents. They charged the natives high fees for the sacraments and they dominated and censored the teaching in the pathetically underprivileged schools. In the end their cruelty and their rapacity, plus their conspicuous wealth, led to their destruction. When the Filipinos rose in rebellion, the friars were forced to leave.

Action and Reaction

During the entire period when the American people were achieving and practicing self-government and the separation of church and state, from the middle of the eighteenth century down to the present time, the Vatican was cooperating with Spanish authoritarian rulers in the maintenance of its own particular type of authoritarian rule. The cooperative church-state pattern was written into political treaties or concordats, which were agreed upon by political ambassadors who used all the shrewd bargaining techniques of conventional diplomacy.

In general, these concordats between Spain and the Vatican were not the product of genuine democratic choice by the Spanish people. They were essentially bargains between dictators. In all the bargaining, a religious monarch in Rome and a political monarch in Madrid scorned the techniques of democracy as well as the democratic principle of religious freedom. All the concordats gave to Catholicism a privileged and monopolistic position in the state, which was quite inconsistent with any policy of equal protection for all faiths. No representatives of any other faith except Roman Catholicism were ever consulted in the negotiations.

Since the first concordat in 1757 there have been several violently anti-clerical regimes in Spain. The most famous early one was that of Prime Minister Mendizabal, who decreed in 1836 the sale of all land belonging to Catholic religious orders in order to pay off the Spanish national debt. From the point of view of church and state the most important revolution in the nineteenth century came in 1868, when Isabel II was dethroned and a new Constitution was written guaranteeing a slight increase in religious liberty. But this small guarantee was secured only after a great outburst of violence had frightened both the bishops and the government. The anti-clericals burned churches and monasteries in Madrid, Barcelona, Seville and other cities.

"The nation," said the new Constitution, "binds itself to maintain the cult and the ministers of the Catholic religion." No ministers of any other cult were guaranteed support, although they were nominally assured the right of "public or private observance." Even this small concession brought prolonged attacks on the "revolutionary" concept of religious equality and freedom from Catholic leaders in the new Cortes and from the Vatican itself. The papal secretary of state protested vehemently against any departure from Catholic standards.

Almost one hundred years after the American Revolution a Spanish Catholic leader of the opposition in the Cortes was proclaiming: "The Catholic Church can approve of tolerance of other religions only when this is necessary in order to prevent a greater evil, and no such greater evil faces Spain. The Spanish people ought to maintain Catholic unity for patriotic as well as religious reasons. . . . If Spain should reject religious unity for religious freedom, the great Spain of the past would die." [6]

In the twentieth century, during the long reign of Alfonso XIII (1902 to 1931), the liberals and conservatives oscillated in power, with the Church always on the conservative side and the liberals always in opposition. The image of the Church as pro-monarchical, pro-capitalist and pro-censorship was so clearly established that republicans, socialists and advocates of freedom of thought were almost automatically anti-clerical. The Church frequently defied Spanish laws which the bishops regarded as disadvantageous to their interests. Although the anti-clericals usually lacked the political power to compel enforcement of these laws, they did not hesitate to practice violence against a Church which they regarded as an organic part of the national tyranny. During one week in Barcelona in 1909, sixty-three churches and religious houses were burned down.

Gerald Brenan in his classic, *The Spanish Labyrinth,* places the blame for the reactionary clericalism of this period largely on the religious orders, many of whose members had been displaced in France by the secularizing of the schools of that country. "The Church in Spain," he says, "was ruined by its inability to react intelligently to the ideas of the French Revolution." French ideas poured into Spain, but they were the defeated ideas brought in by intellectual exiles. The members of religious orders, Mr. Brenan says, tried "to save at least one country in Europe from 'liberal atheism.' Within a few years the Peninsula was studded with almost as many convents, colleges and religious foundations as it had seen during its palmiest period." [7]

The Republic and the Church

When the Second Republic came into existence after the flight of Alfonso XIII in April 1931, it would have been a miracle if it had not been anti-clerical. The Church had opposed it from the beginning, branding the Republicans as Communists in the election campaign of 1931. One reason for the Church's anger was that the Provisional Government during its first month in office proclaimed complete religious freedom, the abolition of compulsory Catholic teaching in the nation's schools, and the end of compulsory attendance at mass by prisoners in the nation's jails. Officers in the armed services were forbidden to attend religious services in their official capacity. The Concordat with the Vatican was repudiated.

Pedro Cardinal Segura, the fiery Primate of Spain, did not even wait to see what kind of government the new Republic would produce before rushing into print with a pastoral letter, two weeks after the regime had been established, praising Alfonso and referring to the triumph of "the enemies of the Kingdom of Jesus Christ." He called for a political movement in defense of the Church under the aegis of Catholic Action.[8] The majority of the bishops were more tolerant of the new regime, but the words of the Cardinal attracted more attention—and vengeance. A wave of violence against the churches immediately followed. Although Segura was virtually exiled, and was supplanted by a more tractable prelate, the anti-church violence continued—at the very moment that the deputies of a new Constituent Cortes were discussing a new Constitution.

Under such circumstances the constitutional debates on church-state relations were not wholly temperate. The Church was always on the defensive. The new Republican Constitution, when it was finally drafted, contained many anti-church features which most Americans would regard as discriminatory. But it should be remembered that the anti-clericalism of the period was the fruit of a Catholic political policy which had made the Church a partner with the tyrannical state. The anti-clerical liberals regarded a Catholic bishop as belonging in the same class with a captain of the secret police. The powerful Anarchist movement was openly anti-God as well as anti-government.[9]

The animosity against the Church broke out in eloquent anti-clerical orations on the floor of the new Cortes while the Republic's Constitution was being drafted. Almost immediately everybody agreed that Spain should have "religious freedom" and "the separation of church and state." Clerical and anti-clerical factions disagreed completely as to what the two concepts meant in practice, but they all agreed—some under protest—that Catholicism was no longer the official state religion. They wanted a nation in which the Catholic Church should be displaced as an arm of the state.

Alcala Zamora, president of the provisional government and a devout Catholic, vainly attempted to block punitive anti-clerical measures. He advocated a new Concordat with the Vatican which would achieve the separation of church and state gradually. When the majority scorned his moderation, he resigned in protest and was succeeded by the most outspoken of the anti-clerical leaders, Manuel Azana, who was later to become prime minister.

Azana's speech at the end of the debate on the religious clauses was a devastating attack on the Church.[10] The church-state issue, he said, was primarily political rather than religious. Spain was no longer a Catholic nation even though millions of its people were Catholic individuals. "Catholicism has ceased to be the expression and the guide of Spanish thought," he said. When he came to the religious orders and their privileged position in Spanish life, he declared that he thought the Jesuits should go, but in any case and above all they should not be permitted to teach, even in their own schools.

This was extreme gospel for an advocate of civil liberties, but Azana backed it up with reasoning that had a great appeal to those Spaniards who had suffered under conservative clerical rule. "I tell you," he said, "that, in the sphere of the political and moral sciences, the Catholic religious orders are compelled, by virtue of their dogma, to teach everything that is contrary to the principles which are the foundation of the modern state."

Azana thought that the new Republic could not survive if large numbers of Spanish young people were being indoctrinated in anti-democratic philosophy by the Jesuits. He said:

The continual influence of the religious orders on the consciences of the young is precisely the secret of the situation through which Spain is now passing and which as Republicans—and not only as Republicans but as Spaniards—we are in duty bound, at all costs, to prevent. Do not tell me that this is contrary to freedom; it is a question of public health. Would you who oppose this measure in the name of Liberalism, permit a university professor to lecture on Aristotle's astronomy and to say that the stars are fastened to spheres which make up the heavens? Would you permit sixteenth-century medicine to be taught from a Chair in a Spanish University? You would not; in spite of the professor's right to teach and in spite of his freedom of conscience, such a thing would never be permitted.

After an all night sitting, the article on religious orders passed by a vote of 178 to 59.

The famous Article XXVI of the new Constitution completely abolished government subsidies to the clergy and nationalized the property of every religious order which required its members to take the "special vow of obedience to any authority other than the legitimate authority of the state." This was aimed particularly at the Jesuits, who were alleged to require from their members this special, extra oath—although they denied it vociferously.

In the heat of the debate over this suppression of the chief religious orders, other sweeping religious reforms were almost overlooked. These included complete freedom for non-Catholic cults, the secularization of the national schools, civil jurisdiction for all cemeteries, freedom for divorce and provisions for civil marriage for everybody. The government was directed in the near future to stop paying the annual state grant to the clergy, to dissolve the convents and take over their property, and to close all the religious schools except the seminaries. However, ordinary Church activity was not to be interrupted or impeded. Even in the violent triumph of anti-clericalism the Church was granted more freedom for ordinary activities than it had granted to Protestantism.

When I interviewed Azana in Madrid in 1933, he was in a desperate position, but he seemed to have no regrets about the severity of his church-state policy. It was in the critical period when his new educational law was about to displace more than 300,000 children from Catholic schools, and he had only five months to provide places for the displaced children. Actually, his government fell late in 1933 under rightist assaults before his school program could be completed. The Republic, under pro-clerical pressure, even restored two-thirds of the salaries of the priests. Azana came back into power in 1936 in spite of the fact that Cardinal Goma had directed Catholics to vote against him. But it was too late then to carry out his full program before his government was challenged by rebellion.

Was Azana wise in attempting to nationalize schools so abruptly and in ordering out the Jesuits when the new nation had so few replacements? Should he have permitted the Jesuits and other religious orders to operate their schools a little longer to ease the transition? I confess that at the time I thought Azana was reasonably justified because it was a war situation, and the ordinary principles of civil liberties did not apply. In retrospect, I realize that the moderates may have been right. Catholicism was more deeply rooted in popular affection than Azana realized and his anti-clerical policy produced a great wave of hostility against his government. Salvador de Madariaga was later to say that the government's religious policy was its "gravest error," and that "Spain will continue to be a Catholic nation."

The abruptness of the Azana program gave the priests the opportunity to complain of persecution and martyrdom, particularly when some were murdered in cold blood by the anarchists. The bishops, who had practiced the suppression of intellectual freedom for centuries, now had the opportunity to use the shibboleths of civil liberties for their own advancement.

Although Azana started to dissolve the Jesuit institutions in February 1932, the full program of his Law of Religious Congregations and Confessions was never carried out. The government reduced the state subsidy to the clergy very gradually, awarding the Church 75 million pesetas in 1931, and scaling it down to one-third of that amount in 1933. The plan was to stop subsidies altogether in 1934, but it was never completed.

The Church and the Civil War

The years of the Republic were disorderly years. The government was constantly assailed by rightist and leftist forces more anxious to realize their own ambitions than to make democracy work. The anti-clerical left held power for the first two years; then lost it to a right coalition for about two years; then recaptured control of a shaky regime for about six months in 1936. Then came the deluge of civil war, launched by Franco and his associates in July 1936. Before it had ended the Church had become one of the primary participants and victims of the war.

Nobody knows how many priests and nuns were murdered, and how many churches and convents were destroyed—and how many priests and nuns acted as spies and soldiers for the Franco forces. Spanish Catholicism was not entirely united behind Franco, since the devoutly Catholic Basques of the north were pro-Republican, and their priests remained loyal to them during the war. But by and large it was a war of liberals, socialists, anarchists, republicans and anti-clericals—the classifications often overlapped —against the army, the Church, the monarchists, the great landowners and the conservatives generally. The values were mixed and the loyalties confusing. The issues divided almost every family in Spain. Altogether, at least 192 cities, towns and villages in Spain were more than 60 per cent destroyed.

The Italian fascists and the German Nazis entered the picture early, and in reply to their intervention came the Communists with their direct Russian support. However, the war in the beginning was not primarily either fascist or Communist. It was a war of self-preservation by a not very competent, strife-torn, left-of-center government which finally accepted extremist left-wing support for reasons of self-preservation. There was no other support available. The United States could have saved the government by lifting the arms embargo, but it was prevented from doing so largely by Catholic pressure on Washington.[11]

It is difficult to justify in terms of Western democratic standards the methods used by either of the two sides in the Spanish Civil War. The Republicans came nearer to representing the struggle of man for a free society, and they certainly constituted the duly chosen government of Spain. But their savagery in the conflict will always be held against them, even though it was counter-savagery.

Herbert L. Matthews of the *New York Times* echoed the opinion of many independent journalists when he said that there was little to choose between the two sides in the matter of atrocities. The Republicans made no attempt to maintain religious freedom for Catholics in the Republican zone. Outside of the Basque country they shut down virtually every Catholic church in their territory which was not converted into a munitions depot or a market. Although they created a Commissariat-General of Worship in 1938 and guaranteed religious freedom on paper, they found it either impossible or disadvantageous to grant religious freedom during hostilities to that Church which was regarded as an ally of the rebels.

In the course of the struggle thousands of priests, nuns and bishops were murdered, and hundreds of churches and convents were burned.[12] Some of the clericals were killed as soldiers in action; many more were murdered in cold blood. In 1954 official church estimates put the total of deaths of priests and members of religious orders during the civil war at 7,287, including indirect losses of life. A pro-Franco Madrid newspaper estimated that 13 bishops, 5,235 priests and 2,669 nuns were executed. The number may be slightly exaggerated, but the totals are appalling in any case.

On Franco's side the murdering—usually by firing squads—

was even more extensive, and priests often acted as security observers and finger men in identifying the culprits. Both sides in entering a region often captured the "disloyal" suspects and executed them wholesale. In many parts of Spain the mere fact of being a priest was enough to guarantee execution.

De Madariaga, who thinks that this persecution of the Church was one of the most unpardonable mistakes of the revolutionists, puts his finger on one basic cause, that "the Church almost infallibly espoused the worst causes in our national life." [13] He quotes a Catalan priest as saying: "The Reds have destroyed our churches, but we priests had first destroyed the Church." As to the distribution of guilt for atrocities, he says that "the tale of terror is equally bad on both sides. All attempts at distinction are futile."

Charles Foltz, formerly chief of the Associated Press in Spain, is far more severe in judging Franco and the Church. He believes that Franco's forces during the war executed at least five times as many as the government executed, and that Franco's postwar executions ran to half a million.[14] Foltz, in fact, estimates the postwar executions by Franco forces as greater than the total killed on both sides in action during the entire war.

Communism was so small a factor at the beginning of the war that Franco did not even include it in his first manifesto calling for rebellion. At the height of its prewar strength in 1936, the Communist Party had only 16 members in a Cortes of 473. But today Spain hears only the orthodox, anti-Communist interpretation of the war. The Spanish people are told that it was a conflict of atheistic Communism against God and civilization, when, as a matter of fact, the Spanish Republic did not even have diplomatic relations with the Soviet Union at the beginning of the war.

On March 29, 1939, Franco's troops made their final, triumphant entry into Madrid, exacting from their defeated enemies unconditional surrender. On April 1, Pius XII telegraphed to Franco:

LIFTING UP OUR HEARTS TO THE LORD, WE GIVE SINCERE THANKS WITH YOUR EXCELLENCY FOR SPAIN'S DESIRED CATHOLIC VICTORY. WE EXPRESS OUR HOPE THAT YOUR MOST BELOVED COUNTRY, WITH PEACE ATTAINED, MAY UNDERTAKE WITH NEW VIGOR THE ANCIENT CHRISTIAN TRADITIONS WHICH MADE HER GREAT. WITH AFFECTIONATE SENTIMENTS WE SEND YOUR EXCELLENCY AND THE MOST NOBLE SPANISH PEOPLE OUR APOSTOLIC BLESSING.[15]

Since then, the Spanish bishops and the Vatican itself have sedu-lously promoted a version of the Civil War which places virtually all the guilt on the Republicans.

The Catholic Dictator

The pudgy little man—five feet, four inches—who entered Madrid in triumph in March 1939 is one of the great accidents of world history. Not that he is entirely devoid of talent—even his most bitter enemies would give him some credit for courage and sagacity as an army officer. But he owed his ascent to power not only to the foreign intervention of Mussolini and Hitler but to the accidental removal from his path of promotion of three senior of-ficers who were considered by many to be more logical choices to lead a counterrevolution. General Jose Sanjurjo, General Emilio Mola and General Manuel Goded lost their lives by accident or execution in 1936. When the rebellion broke out in that year, Franco was actually no higher than sixth in rank among the gen-erals who organized it.[16] Apparently the generals who made him their chief in the early days of the rebellion intended that his directorship should be temporary and provisional. They ex-pected the monarchy to be restored when the immediate crisis was over. They did not view Franco as a potential, permanent dictator.

By fate, the third—some say the fourth—choice among the rebel leaders became the first. And even after Franco had backed a European fascist bloc that was discredited in World War II, he was saved again by chance. The Western powers were so busy with other problems after the Spanish Civil War was ended, and so panic-stricken, first about the Nazis and then about the Com-munists, that they failed to remain united in their postwar op-position to Franco.

Francisco Paulino Hermenegildo Teodulo Franco Bahamonde was born in Galicia in northwestern Spain in 1892, the son of a naval paymaster. Although he graduated from a military academy near the bottom of his class, he developed military qualities quickly, and at thirty-three it is said that he was the youngest full general in Europe. He attained some military eminence before he became a counterrevolutionist. It should be remembered that he

originally supported the Republic and rose to a position of Chief
of General Staff under its regime.

Many legends have sprung up about his military skill, including the legend which may be apocryphal that he won a Nazi prize
for devising a military plan for the protection of Berlin. He has
such iron nerves that he is able to sit through seven-hour committee meetings which even his hardiest officers cannot face. He
does not smoke and rarely drinks. His unruffled temper is, on
the surface, notorious, as is his basic cruelty in dealing with anyone
who challenges his power.

The most famous story about Franco's personal qualities in
circulation in Spain—I heard it from several sources in several
forms, and Herbert Matthews of the *New York Times* has
published it—is the story about the desperately angry soldier who
once threw a little soup in Franco's face in protest against bad army
food.[17] It was in the days when Franco commanded a section of
the Spanish Foreign Legion, and its members had gone on a virtual strike in protest against their bad food. Franco ordered an assembly, and when the soldiers fell in line with their tins of thin
stew, Franco walked down the line. One angry soldier threw some
of the soup in his face. Franco did not blanch or flinch. He
ended the review with perfect poise, and ordered the officer who
was responsible for the bad food to be arrested. Then, the next
day, he assembled the soldiers in line again, singled out the soldier
who had thrown the soup in his face and said: "Execute that man."
The man was immediately shot.

Officially Franco is a very pious man. He is faithful in attending Mass and he is said to kneel and repeat the rosary every mid-
night with his wife. At appropriate moments he honors the alleged bones of St. James at the famous shrine in Santiago de Com-
postela, not far from his birthplace. He has frequently used this
shrine to rally Catholics to his support at critical moments, allowing the Spanish newspapers to fill their pages with photographs
of Franco the devout, wearing the decoration of the Supreme Order of Christ, conferred upon him by Pius XII.

How much of this official piety is sincere devotion no one can
tell. Most observers in Spain seem to think that Franco is a genuine and devout Catholic and that his wife, who is not only a devout
Catholic but a wealthy financial manipulator, shares his rather
wooden, rather peasant-like attitudes of devotion. At times

Franco seems to be more eager to advertise his attachment to the Church than the Church is eager to advertise its attachment to him. He is constantly calling in bishops and archbishops to participate in public ceremonies in which their appearance implies the endorsement of the Church for his regime. At the present time the service rendered to each by the other is about equal. However, the Church is increasingly uneasy about a possible social revolution in which the pictures of Franco embracing cardinals may be used against it.

To one who has seen Italy under Mussolini and Germany under Hitler, the Spain of Franco offers an immediate surprise. Relatively few Franco pictures and statues are displayed. Although the Franco cult is not suppressed, it is muted. The Franco picture is on postage stamps and the Franco name is on telephone directories, and many streets have been named for the *Caudillo* (leader), but there is nothing like the organized adulation for Franco in Spain that there was for Hitler in Germany or for Mussolini in Italy. The Franco picture, of course, is displayed in public buildings and hotels; beyond that the signs of national adulation are not overwhelming. Franco himself has no genius for publicity and no talent for dramatics. He is accepted, not idolized. I met very few persons in Spain who expressed any strong admiration for the Caudillo. John Gunther's estimate in his *Inside Europe Today* seems to be reasonably accurate: "Probably, all in all, something between 80 and 90 per cent of the people as a whole oppose Franco, but they have no means of displacing him." [18] In the theaters of Barcelona and Madrid I never heard any crowd break into applause when the Franco picture was flashed upon the screen—and it flashes upon the screen quite frequently in government-controlled newsreels. A similar exhibition of Mussolini on the screen when I was living in Italy in 1923, or of Hitler when I was visiting Germany in 1933, would always have resulted in minor ovations.

On those rare occasions when Franco appears in public for photographic and parade purposes—usually with high dignitaries of the Church—the police must take extraordinary precautions to prevent assault and assassination. The houses near his point of appearance are searched carefully for possible sources of ambush, and the names of all strangers are checked against the police lists. When Franco greeted President Eisenhower in Madrid in 1959 during a brief and unfortunate visit, the streets leading to the place of meeting and the houses surrounding the public drama were carefully scoured for blocks. In spite of the artificial pump-priming, the whole celebration seemed wooden and synthetic. When Franco went fishing near San Sebastian in the summer of 1959, all the regular fishermen's boats were ordered out of the area in order to guarantee that he would get plenty of fish and that there would be no attack upon him. When he landed without any cheers from the sullen fishermen, the landing area for blocks around was cleared of all spectators.

There is nothing highly intellectual, or spectacular, or warmly personal about Franco. Even the most skillful tailoring can not rescue his pudgy little figure from the commonplace. His pedestrian speeches, delivered in a high-pitched monotone, remain pedestrian even with the best ghost writers.

Perhaps the government that Franco has created is not exactly the kind of government that Pius XII wanted after the Civil War, but the old Pope was glad to accept it because it represented a return to Catholic power. The new Pope, John XXIII, is less enthusiastic but he also is part of a system, and Franco is the foremost lay representative of that system. The Church accepts him as a breakwater against both Communism and anti-clericalism, and in return for that acceptance Franco gives the Church a cultural and religious monopoly.

Under the Franco scheme of control, the Cortes is a mockery of democracy. Two-thirds of its members are appointed by the Caudillo directly or indirectly, and the rest gain power through his controlled syndicates and municipalities. No law can even be considered by the "people's representatives" unless they are given permission to consider it by the Council of State, which is completely directed by Franco. There is no guarantee of public debate on any controversial issue.

In governing the Spanish people with the help of the Church and the army, Franco resorts to only a few, slight pretenses of democratic rule. There has never been a genuine election in Spain since he came into power in 1939. No opposition political party may legally be organized. No opposition public meetings are permitted. No opposition pamphlets, books or even handbills are allowed. And no one may say in a public meeting that the Spanish people have been denied their basic democratic rights.

There is, however, a considerable amount of what may be called "coffeehouse opposition." Franco is shrewd enough to allow the people to whisper even if he will not allow them to speak or write or print. So they talk and talk and talk, expressing privately a bitterness which would never be allowed to appear in the censored newspapers.

Although Franco uses the phrase "organic democracy" to describe his regime, Spain actually has no government in the sense that Americans use that word. The will of one man prevails regardless of the will of the people. The institutions of information and opinion are so closely controlled by that one man that there is no reality of consent in the whole governmental process.

In 1945, Franco went through the motions of establishing freedom by proclaiming a Spanish Charter which contains many of the standard guarantees of liberty and due process that are taken for granted in western democracies. In Franco's own charter the guarantees were all subject to so many exceptions that today they are meaningless. In the words of Madariaga:

> The Charter of Rights is the most mendacious document ever penned. It guarantees every right which the government tramples upon daily: freedom, when any man is at the mercy of any official and never knows whether his day will not end in jail; property, when any man's property may be confiscated and sold over his head at the behest of any official; honor, when any newspaper may insult any man without hope of redress on his part; justice, when none is administered unless it suits the regime; opinions, when none are allowed but those that please the dictator.[19]

Only once since he came into power has Franco made any attempt to get popular sanction for his status and then the process was so completely fraudulent that it evoked an almost unanimous jeer from the foreign press. This was the so-called referendum of July 1947 in which the Spanish people were asked to vote on the Law of Succession after a subject Cortes had passed it.[20] If the majority of the votes favored the "choice," Franco was to be given tenure for life as Chief of State at his own option, with power to turn over the government of Spain to a king. Nominally the law created a throne; actually the throne was only a shadow to be left vacant at Franco's option.

No opposition movement or party was permitted at the time of this referendum. It was said that of the 45,000 prisoners in Spanish jails at the time virtually every opposition leader of any importance was included, and 1,750,000 former Republicans were barred from the polls because of their war records. The question on the ballot read: "Do you ratify with your vote the Law of Succession to the post of Chief of State as approved by Parliament on June 7, 1947?" Franco, of course, won—or said he won—by a ratio of about twenty to one. He brushed off the criticism in the foreign press by saying that "the press and radio of the world live under the tyrannical dictatorship of their proprietors."

The resultant Law of Succession declared that "Spain is a Catholic, social and representative state, which, in accordance with its tradition, declares to form itself into a Kingdom." But the kingdom is all in a hypothetical future. Francisco Franco Bahamonde became the actual ruler of Spain until such moment as the hypothetical monarchy was established. The year following the referendum Franco announced that he intended to hold on to his job for life.

The Church virtually instructed its people to vote for Franco in this referendum through an official letter of the bishops. After Franco's victory, the Cardinal Primate gloated: "It is an incontrovertible fact that practically all Spaniards voted, and that a very high majority voted in favor of the Law of Succession." The Cardinal had no word of criticism for the suppression of the opposition and the creation of a one-slate ticket. Instead, in an interview with the *New York Times,* he condemned those forces which "persecute the Church and her ministers" and endorsed those groups "which resort to the same force to re-establish order as was done in the Crusade of Spanish Liberation." (This is the Catholic label for the Spanish Civil War.)

The Cardinal's statements are typical of the official Catholic attitude toward Franco. On the twenty-third anniversary of his rule—the Franco newspapers always date that rule from the moment when he started the rebellion in 1936—the Catholic Action daily of Madrid, *Ya,* published a Franco portrait on its front page with the following reverent inscription:

This photograph of the Spanish Chief of State on the front page of an issue dated July 18th does not need an extended text below it. Neither the accumulation of adjectives nor the swift summary of unforgettable facts can match the simple contemplation of this historic portrait which has such singular significance, a photograph of the man who presides over and has directed Spanish life for twenty-three years. A triumphant leader in great national undertakings, of which the liberating war was the first, he remains to this day the leader of our destinies, determined, as he has put it in his own words, to confront new enterprises in every aspect in the economic, social and political spheres. The loyalty and trust which the Spanish people have given him since the very first day remain firm and solidified today, with purpose to accompany him in his task of stabilizing our political institutions, our economy, our social life and all that which will crown the great task which began with the National Uprising of 1936.[21]

Franco himself added one item to this thoughtful appraisal in a 9,000-word, year-end radio speech in 1960. His government, he declared, was the only government in the West that had defeated Communism thus far. He did not make it clear where he classed the government of the United States.

Meanwhile, Franco has tried to guarantee immortality for himself in stone, both as a Catholic and as a national hero, in his famous Valley of the Fallen, thirty-five miles west of Madrid in the Guadarrama mountains. It was dedicated in 1959 as a tomb for the dead on both sides of the civil war, but it is primarily a commemorative monument to Catholicism, to Jose Antonio Primo de Rivera, martyred leader of the Falange and, most of all, to Franco himself. It is surmounted by a 500-foot granite cross with arms 60 feet wide, and contains a basilica 200 feet high and six chapels carved out of the solid rock of the mountain, chiefly by political prisoners. Just above it stands a Benedictine monastery.

When Franco dedicated it, he declared: "We congratulate ourselves on our victory over Communism when we see what has happened to other Catholic countries. Our victory was not a partial victory, but a total victory for everybody. Our war was not a civil conflict but a true crusade, as it was then termed by the Pope."

3. A POLITICAL CHURCH AT WORK

It is usual for American defenders of the Catholic Church to describe Spanish Catholicism as something entirely different in kind as well as in degree from the relatively progressive Catholicism that exists in the United States. Neither the Vatican nor the leaders of Spanish Catholicism like this distinction. They admit to a difference in degree in matters of strategy and in the application to specific situations of certain social and ecclesiastical policies. They usually deny any fundamental divergence in doctrine and dogma.

When, in February 1951, Cyrus L. Sulzberger of the *New York Times* said: "The Church in Spain is less liberal than elsewhere," and "Roman Catholicism in Spain is a far different and reactionary force than in other nations," he was indignantly refuted by some Spanish Catholics. One of them, in a letter to the *Times,* said: "The Roman Catholic Church does not have one set of teachings for Spain and another for the United States and another for Latin America. This fact cannot be clouded by insulting the church in Spain and paying grudging tribute to the church outside of Spain. . . . The church is the same all over the world and Catholics are proud of it." [1] The Church, of course, is not "the same all over the world," but it has the same government all over the world and this government attempts to keep its basic policies uniform.

The central machinery of power in the Roman system is quite frankly designed to prevent substantial local variations. Uniformity and discipline are part of the teachings of the Church, and no power structure in the world is more centralized, not even the power structure of world Communism. Nominally every priest is appointed by his bishop and every bishop is appointed by the Pope. Spanish congregations of Spanish people have even less to say about the nature of central rule in their church than Catho-

29

lics in the United States, because they have no free press in which to debate the issues.

As we shall see later, Protestantism and Judaism are so weak in Spain that the average Spaniard can go from cradle to grave without ever seeing a Protestant church or a Jewish synagogue—and if he passed one on the street he would not recognize it, since both Protestant churches and Jewish synagogues are forbidden to look like Protestant churches and Jewish synagogues. The Spanish village has one church, the Catholic church, and one moral mentor in the public school, the Catholic priest. Probably the great majority of the Spanish people have never read any literature about Protestantism or Judaism except the carefully weighted and hostile descriptions contained in the catechisms of the national schools or in the Catholic journals.

The laws of the nation consecrate and legalize this pre-eminence of the one true Church, and exclude all other churches from official recognition. Even the selection of religious holidays is delegated by the state to the Church in the 1953 Vatican Concordat in such a way that Canon Law is supreme over civil law in regard to such holidays. (Key excerpts from that Concordat are printed in the Appendix.) "Civil authorities, both national and local," says the Concordat, "will see to it that these holidays are duly observed." The Church returns the compliment in the same Concordat by pledging every Spanish priest to pray for Franco every day.[2] Franco perpetuates the alliance in countless ceremonial ways, from the imposition of the biretta on the head of every new cardinal to the dragooning of adjacent prelates for government functions.

The first two articles of the 1953 Concordat with the Vatican read:

> The Catholic Apostolic Roman religion will continue to be the sole religion of the Spanish nation and will enjoy the rights and prerogatives which are due it in conformity with the Divine Law and the Canon Law.
>
> The Spanish State recognizes in the Catholic Church its character of a perfect society, and guarantees it the free and full exercise of its spiritual power as well as of its jurisdiction. It also guarantees the free and public worship of the Catholic religion.

It is not surprising that the most authoritative Church journal in Spain called this Concordat "a model Concordat between the Holy See and a Catholic state in the twentieth century."[3] The

Spanish Catholic statistics proudly support the monolithic religious character of the country and frequently describe the nation as the most Catholic nation in the world. Statistically this claim is true. According to the *National Catholic Almanac* of the United States for 1961, Spain has a population of 29,903,871; of these 29,814,-070, or 99.7 per cent, are Catholics. That makes a total non-Catholic population in the country of fewer than 90,000. Even this infinitesimal minority is four times the official total of Protestants and Jews, so it must include some atheists and Muslims.

The "Unity" of Church and State

From the American point of view the most striking feature of Spanish Catholicism is that it has never been actually separated from the state. As we have already seen, separation has been frequently threatened and attempted for short periods but never completely achieved. Spain entered the twentieth century with a government which still printed postage stamps containing pictures of the king and the Pope side by side. Today the great majority of the Spanish people see nothing inappropriate in a government calling itself a "Catholic Kingdom." In their experience, religion and the state have been intertwined so long that the intermingling is accepted as natural.

The chief cardinals of the nation have always been close to Spanish political rulers, and they have always been accepted as part of the ruling system of power. Their official titles as princes of the Church have been wholly appropriate. The nation's political rulers have participated with the bishops in the machinery of government of both church and state simultaneously.

This joint Spanish arrangement has always pleased the Vatican. When Pius XI condemned the separation of church and state in 1864 as one of the "principal errors" of his time, he was not only echoing standard Spanish and Vatican political philosophy but he was also by inference condemning as inferior the system of church-state independence which had developed in the United States. Many papal encyclicals have indicated that the Church has never accepted the American scheme as ideal; it has always preferred the Spanish scheme; it has always held that a partial union of the Catholic Church with Catholic political regimes is preferable to church-state separation.

As in most Catholic countries, the Papal Nuncio is the dean of the diplomatic corps; and since the sixteenth century the relations between the Spanish state and the Roman Catholic Church have, at almost all times, been sealed by political treaties or concordats. These concordats have been as much financial as spiritual. They have given the Church certain exclusive rights and certain financial claims upon the public treasury. In return the Church has given the state certain powers over ecclesiastical appointments.

The Church in seeking to carry out the concordats has participated in the pull and haul of Spanish political manipulation with all the hearty zest and adroit manipulation of an ambitious political party. But the analogy with political parties is somewhat misleading. The concordats have been essentially "deals" between dominant political rulers, lay and clerical, and dominant social classes. The Church has marshaled its obedient followers as a chess player moves his men on the board, allying them with the army, the great landowners and the great industrialists as a "force for stability" distinctly right of center in the political spectrum.

The rulers of the state have made use of this right-of-center bloc for their own conservative purposes. If ever there was a church which deserved Karl Marx's slur against religion as "the opium of the people," it is the Spanish church. Its conscience has been identified with the paternalistic and possessive conscience of the upper classes. Occasionally and reluctantly it has been prodded into advocacy of social justice, but the pressure has usually come from the outside. "There can be no doubt that the priest and the Catholic in general," says the distinguished Spanish philosopher, Jose Luis Aranguren (with whom I had a long talk in Madrid) "have remembered the working classes a little belatedly. Marx and his followers were many decades ahead. . . ."

At the present time the chief mechanism for state control of the Church is the participation of Franco in the selection of all bishops. Under Article VII of the Concordat of 1953, Franco nominally has the final selection in his own hands. He can eliminate any nominees for purely political reasons. His appointive power is much more than a veto power. When a vacancy occurs in a diocese, it is Franco who first names the six potential candidates; then the Vatican reduces the list to three, and Franco makes the final designation himself.

This arrangement is not new. It was essentially the same arrangement made between Franco and the Vatican in 1941. Of course, the Vatican has some protection against a completely objectionable slate of six first choices, since Franco is supposed to confer secretly with the Papal Nuncio concerning the qualifications of the original slate in order to guarantee some clerical fitness. If, thereafter, he should nominate an entirely unacceptable list of potential bishops, the Pope could reject them all and offer a counterproposal of three names. Pope John XXIII has done this twice in order to appoint Spanish-born bishops from his own staff, somewhat to the chagrin of ambitious local prelates. But the Concordat calls for the final choice of the individual appointee by Franco alone, and this establishes an initial political control over bishops which does not exist for the Catholic Church, or for any other church, in the United States. In fact, it does not exist in most other nations of the world, including Portugal. It gives Franco a practical way of guaranteeing that no bishop will be an active revolutionist.

Although the 1953 arrangement was worked out in negotiations with Pius XII, it is being perpetuated without public protest under Pope John XXIII. We shall see later how the Church, in return for this veto power over its bishops, has secured from the state discriminatory provisions against Protestants and Jews.

The political control involved in the appointment system is chiefly useful in blocking promotion for any priest who strongly opposes the Franco regime. The only avenue of promotion for a priest is through the favor of his bishop, and all bishops must have both Vatican and Franco approval. There is, of course, no assembly of Catholic members to interfere with this control formula, since there is no plenary assembly of Catholic members anywhere in the world. The machinery of power in the Catholic system is wholly sacerdotal. Although the Vatican permits the Spanish church to have a primate, or head bishop, a privilege which the Pope does not extend to the American church, the political control of appointments means that the primate is a creature of the state.

The Church and the Criminal Law

The criminal statutes of Spain are so written that Catholic priests are in a separate class from all other citizens. Under Title II, Sections 205 to 212, a chapter of the Penal Code is called "Crimes Against the Catholic Religion." To insult, or malign, or ridicule, or disturb a Catholic priest or a Catholic ceremony is a special kind of crime, quite distinct from a parallel offense against other persons and creeds. The sections of the criminal code protecting the Catholic faith are printed just above the provisions outlawing sedition and rebellion. The juxtaposition is quite revealing. The presumption of Spanish law is that someone who fights the Church is guilty of sedition.

This special treatment of Catholicism by the law of Spain is not described by the Church itself as favoritism or even as the union of church and state. It is promoted by the Church as a natural right in a Catholic country, and, because of the censorship, it is apparently accepted by the people with very little protest. The Church does not pretend to treat all religions with equal justice, and in this policy it has the backing of the Catholic government.

If a cardinal, papal nuncio, bishop, or abbot commits a crime —even murder—he may not be summoned before a Spanish court as a defendant without the Pope's special permission. This is in fulfillment of Canon 120 of Roman Catholic Canon law which applies to all nations where the Church has the power to enforce it. The law says:

> In all contentious or criminal cases clerics are to be summoned before an ecclesiastical judge, unless lawful provision to the contrary has been made for particular places. . . . What is forbidden is to summon the person as a defendant in a contentious case or as accused in a criminal case [to a state court] without the necessary permission. Summoning as a witness is not forbidden. The permission required is that of the Holy See or of the Ordinary [Bishop] of the place of trial, according to the dignity of the person summoned.[4]

In Spain a priest may not even be summoned by a magistrate as a *witness* in a criminal case without permission of his bishop. If a Catholic judicial officer ignores the rule requiring Church permission to bring a priest or bishop into court, he commits a serious sin. The Church is allowed to have its own apparatus for punishment of its own priests, even its own prisons. However, it agrees under Article XVI of the Concordat to permit priests to be tried by state courts for "non-canonical" crimes. Priests who are sent to prison for these non-canonical crimes are not imprisoned in the same place or treated in the same way as ordinary prisoners. They must be "treated with a consideration due their position and rank." This means that if they are not defrocked by their bishops in advance, they are confined in special quarters.

The Catholic Canon law affords some protection to the state against non-cooperating bishops by saying that they should not refuse permission for the arraignment of a priest "without a just and grave reason." But it is the bishop and not the Spanish judge who decides whether the reason for cooperation in prosecuting a priest is "just and grave."

This whole scheme of special treatment for priests is in accord with the ancient privilege of the Catholic Church which it demands in Catholic countries, under the title, *privilegium fori.* In Spain, under the *privilegium fori,* there are even some restrictions on *summoning* priests into state courts in *civil* cases. In this respect the status of a Spanish priest is something like that of a noble in the Middle Ages.

The state is also obliged wherever possible to protect any priest or Catholic religious order against the "scandal" of intra-church litigation. If an offense is charged which involves a violation of ecclesiastical law exclusively, the state will respect the decision of the Catholic court in the matter and will not permit an appeal to its own courts. This prevents the people from knowing about any internal scandal in the Church. Under some circumstances, lawsuits involving priests and bishops are allowed to enter the civil courts, but in that case the government guarantees under Article XVI of the Concordat that "necessary precautions will be taken to avoid all publicity." The local Spanish judge must ask the consent of the bishop before the case starts, and must send the bishop special information concerning the outcome.

In practice the power of the bishop in the judicial system is even greater than these rules indicate. In the country districts the priest has a moral rank at least equal to that of a judge, and the bishop is the superior of the priest. The special position of the Church affects court proceedings in many ways. If a Spaniard accused of a crime wishes to establish his good character for a local court, it is the recommendation of the priest that is most essential. As Professor Arthur Whitaker has put it in his book, *Spain and Defense of the West*: "The typical Spanish village lives under a kind of condominium of church and state, represented by a mayor appointed by Madrid and a priest assigned by a bishop who in most matters is responsive to the wishes of Madrid." [5]

It is Church law rather than civil law that governs most of the family relationships of Spain. This subservience of the civil law is written into the Concordat with the Vatican in such a way that, nominally at least, it cannot be repealed without Vatican consent. Even the state's own laws concerning the marriage of minors are dovetailed into Catholic Canon Law officially, since the Protocol of the 1953 Concordat says: "The civil norms relating to the marriage of children, whether minors or adults, shall be made to harmonize with Canons 1034 and 1035 of the Code of Canon Law." Under this rule Spanish legislators surrender their freedom to alter domestic relations law in perpetuity—or as long as the combination of church and state dictatorship endures in their country.

Oddly enough, there is no specific statute prohibiting ex-priests from serving as teachers and public officials, as there is in Italy under the 1929 Concordat with Mussolini. In Spain such a statute is deemed unnecessary. In general, a Spanish ex-priest is a leper, morally and socially, and the Church is so powerful that it does not need statutory supplements. Under Canon 2267 all Catholics are obliged to shun such a leper.

Spain, like Italy, has had for many decades criminal statutes designed to punish those who "insult" the dominant religion in any way. In Italy the statutes are almost a dead letter because of the powerful Communist opposition. In Spain all satire at the expense of the Church is suppressed under the censorship laws, and there are no Communists in the open to specialize in the journalism of derision. Accordingly, although Spanish cafe conversation may be full of anti-clerical jibes, the Pope, the Church, and the bishops are sacrosanct in the official press. No scandal may ever be printed about them. A Protestant clergyman who commits murder—or who does *not* commit murder—may be pilloried ad infinitum in the controlled press. A priest-murderer is protected under the Concordat and the statutes.

It is doubtful if the age-old Catholic policy of suppressing public criticism of the Church in Spain has actually strengthened it as an institution. Probably the suppression has contributed to the belief of many Spanish anti-clericals that violence is the only effective response to the Church's power. The anti-clericals are fond of an answer once made by Voltaire when he was asked: "What would you have done if you had been born in Spain?" He replied: "I would have gone to Mass every day; kissed the monks' robes; and set fire to their convents."

The Church and Public Money

The primary cohesive force that binds church and state together in Spain is public money. The state pays money for a Church which serves its interests; the Church receives the money as a natural right. Neither party sees anything wrong or extraordinary about this interdependent financial relationship. Each gets what it pays for: the state gets an obedient Church; the Church gets a pro-Catholic state.

The Spanish state has always contributed to the Church except during those few interregnums when anti-clericalism captured the government. The Vatican has always held that a Catholic state owes a duty to the Church to grant financial support to the best of the state's ability. The gospel of state support for Catholic enterprise is repeated over and over again in Catholic Canon Law and papal encyclicals. In Spain it is practiced as completely as in any nation of the world.

As for the bishops, they have always assumed that the payment of public money is part of the normal bargaining relationship between church and state. As early as 1753 the monarchy was given power to choose bishops in return for hard cash.[6] After the Civil War, Franco and the Vatican engaged in the same kind of financial and political haggling before a temporary agreement was finally worked out in 1941, followed by the permanent agreement in 1953. In each case Franco bought power over the bishops with cash and the promise of future cash support.

Here are the financial clauses of the 1953 Concordat which the Church extracted from Franco in return for giving him extensive power over its activities. It should be noted that they not only guarantee exclusive financial support for the Catholic Church, its priests, its seminaries and universities, but they also provide pensions for bishops, and they include an escalator clause to protect the church from runaway inflation.

The Church and the state shall study by common agreement means of creating an adequate Church fund which will provide for the maintenance of the clergy and of religious activities.

Meanwhile, the state, by way of indemnification for past confiscation of Church property, and as a contribution to the Church's work for the good of the nation, will provide the Church with an annual endowment. This will include, in particular, the apportionment of funds for diocesan Archbishops and Bishops, coadjutors, auxiliaries, general vicariates, cathedral chapters, collegiate chapters, collegiate churches and parishes, as well as funds for seminaries and ecclesiastical universities for the general practice of the [Catholic] religion. . . .

If, in the future, a marked change in the general economic situation should occur, the endowments will be adjusted to the new situation in such manner that support of religion and the clergy will always be assured.

The state, ever faithful to the national tradition, will award annual subsidies for the construction and repair of parish churches, rectories, and seminaries; the development of religious Orders, congregations and Church institutions devoted to missionary activities; and to the care of monasteries of historic value to Spain. . . .

The state will collaborate with the Church in establishing and financing social institutions for the benefit of aged, feeble, and invalid clergymen; also the state will provide an adequate pension to resident Prelates who, for reasons of age or health, retire from their posts.

All Spanish priests are exempted from paying income tax on that portion of their salaries which comes from the government.

No one except the hierarchy and Franco's financial henchmen, knows exactly how much public money the Church gets from the Spanish state because the money is distributed through many departmental and local budgets, and the meager statistics are given out in a most confusing manner. I tried in vain in 1959 to get a definitive government estimate of the *total* appropriations to the Church. There is a Department of Ecclesiastical Affairs which publicly appropriates some funds to priests, but its budget totals are not all-inclusive.

The Church itself, of course, never makes financial figures available to the public. It is an iron rule of the Vatican that the Church in all countries must abstain from making complete public reports of its financial condition. This rule applies equally in Spain, the United States and the Vatican itself. No national Catholic Church ever tells its own people how it stands financially, and the Holy See is equally silent.

The world was treated to a brief glimpse of Church finances at the highest echelon when the Vatican-Mussolini Concordat of 1929 was signed, and it became necessary for Mussolini and the Church to render some public accounting to the Italian people of the amounts involved in the agreement.[7] The published total of indemnities paid to the Church was about $100 million. This brief lifting of the Vatican's financial curtain in 1929 revealed a great empire of banks, holding companies and landed estates, but when the curtain finally dropped again, all the world knew was that the Vatican had considerable wealth. Its chief property holdings, which are in the hands of individual dioceses and religious orders, had never been fully disclosed either in Spain or in any other country.

In 1959 the chief budgetary payment of the Department of Ecclesiastical Affairs of Spain to the Church was 650 million pesetas or a little more than $10.8 million. This figure is not inclusive, since some welfare and educational grants are made directly or indirectly to the Spanish Church without being included in the reports of the Department of Ecclesiastical Affairs. Probably the most authoritative estimate of the annual Church grants of national tax funds is that of Professor William Ebenstein of Princeton in his monograph, *Church and State in Franco Spain;* he put the total in 1959 at 750 million pesetas, or about $12.5 million.[8] Franco, in one of his 1961 speeches commemorating the twenty-fifth anniversary of his rule, boasted that his government had spent nearly $53 million between 1939 and 1959 for Church buildings alone.

Although the accumulated property holdings of the Spanish Church are still enormous, it is certain that the proportion of the national wealth controlled by the Church has declined during the twentieth century. There is no parallel today to the Church's success in the sixteenth century, when it took half of the national income.[9] Government payments in 1959 were only about 1½ per cent of the national budget. Although this is an amount greater than the government's total appropriation for high schools and colleges, it is certainly not large by American standards. In fact, the direct allowance for priests in the departmental budget—553 million pesetas for some 33,000 priests and their assistants, or about 16,757 pesetas ($279) per year per priest—indicates that the typical Spanish priest cannot live in luxury if he relies solely on government appropriations. The average village priest is still pitifully poor, and the cash income of a Spanish bishop is a small fraction of that of an American bishop.

The low income of the priests is a factor in downgrading the priesthood as a profession for men of education. In order to secure priests at all, the Church usually must pay for their education from youth onward. Thus, automatically, this endowed education becomes primarily education for the poor. The great bulk of the priests come from poor country families, which cannot afford higher education for their sons without Church endowment. The wealthy and cultured families tend to send their sons into law, medicine, engineering and business.

Because of the Church's policy of financial secrecy, most of the Spanish people apparently believe that the Church is much wealthier than it actually is. Some of this belief has been produced by Communist propaganda; some goes back to the days of the anti-clerical Republic; some derives, no doubt, from the exhibition of jewel-encrusted relics in great cathedrals. Whatever its source, it inhibits giving to the Church in all parts of the country.

One factor which undoubtedly increases the public estimate of the Church's wealth is the relative absence of independent private charity. Welfare organizations are supported by the state, absorbed by the Church, or perish.

Professor E. Allison Peers of Liverpool, who was, for a non-Catholic, an extraordinarily sympathetic observer of Spanish Catholicism, carefully documented many of the exaggerated claims about the Church's wealth in Spain and came away with the conviction that they contained many elements of unverified propaganda.[10] It is not even certain that state subsidies have, in the long run, made the Church any richer than it would have been if Catholicism had adopted the American principle of voluntary financial support. The subsidy system has dried up the wells of private giving. Many of the Church's welfare enterprises are anemic because Catholics make no serious effort to support them. Most important of all, the Church, in accepting money from a reactionary regime, has mortgaged its whole future to that regime. If and when the dictatorship is superseded, the forces of the left may demand a fearful accounting.

How Strong Is Spanish Catholicism?

This naturally raises the question: How strong is popular support of the policies of the Church? The baptismal proportions of a nation which is 99.7 per cent Catholic cannot be taken as representative, especially in a nation where the public opponent of Catholicism can be ruined by social discrimination. Church attendance and Church contributions provide a somewhat more reliable index of Catholic strength, but here the statistics are meager. Surveys by scholars provide better clues.

Tourists who witness the relatively large crowds at masses in most parts of the country can usually justify a judgment that Catholicism is very strong among the Spanish people. Certainly it has survived many bitter anti-clerical campaigns with considerable success. Even so skeptical a historian as Professor Madariaga, in assessing the prospect of Spain's future, predicts a large and important place for the Church. "In broad outlines," he says, "the Left must yield to the Right in religious matters and the Right to the Left in economic matters."

Most of the anti-Franco liberals in exile in Europe and the United States seem to agree with him. Although they have little respect for the leaders of the Spanish Church, they believe that it is so basically and traditionally a part of Spanish culture that it will continue to be a major force in any future society. Hence, they are very reluctant to make their anti-Franco movement in any sense an anti-Catholic movement. Only the Communists and the remaining small fragments of anarchist groups attack the Vatican openly as a reactionary political force as such and even they are cautious in the attack. When they criticize the Church, most liberal Spaniards concentrate on its power, its privilege and its alliance with reaction, leaving Catholic dogma out of the discussion.

Several test checks and opinion polls in various regions of Spain in recent years have revealed what can only be described as shocking disloyalty to the Church in a Catholic country. As these surveys have been sponsored by Catholic agencies, their pessimistic findings cannot be charged to anti-clerical groups. The most famous survey was made in the Barcelona area in 1957 by HOAC—Hermandades Obreras de Accion Catolica (Workers Brotherhoods of Catholic Action). It was described for me in that city by a horrified priest a few years later. It showed that 90 per cent of the industrial classes in the area approached were, to use their own words, "anti-clerical"; 41 per cent were anti-religious; 55 per cent not interested in religion; and only 7.6 per cent attended Mass regularly.[11] Anti-clericalism, of course, is not a new phenomenon among Spanish industrial workers, but it should be remembered that this survey was made after eighteen years of uninterrupted favoritism to the Church by a Catholic-oriented regime.

I asked at least fifteen Catholic leaders, priests and laymen in all parts of Spain in 1959 to estimate the proportion of Spanish people who were reasonably faithful Catholics. I never received an estimate of more than 50 per cent. Most estimates ran nearer 25 per cent; some were considerably lower. It seems clear that if conversational returns can be accepted at face value, the majority of the Spanish people are not deeply attached to their Church, since regular attendance at Mass under Catholic law is obligatory for all members. The HOAC survey referred to showed that the industrial workers who were questioned did maintain some slight, formal connection with the Church through baptism, marriage and death, and 29 per cent of them attended Mass at least once during Lent. The other 71 per cent stayed away from the Church entirely.

The loyalty of university students to the Church does not seem to be much greater than the loyalty of the industrial workers, although classes in Catholicism are compulsory for those who want a university diploma. A 1954 survey of university students in Madrid and Murcia, summarized in Professor William Ebenstein's study, indicated that 74 per cent thought that official Catholicism breeds "pharisaism." This is not exactly surprising because the students see how their professors are compelled to pay lip service to the Church in order to gain promotion in a regimented cultural world.

Loyalty to the Church is very uneven in Spain's various geographical regions, partly because regional hostility to Franco is associated with anti-clericalism. Barcelona and its environs cherish anti-clericalism partly because of Catalan nationalism. Madrid has not forgotten that it was the heart of the Republic's defenses against both Franco and his associated Church. The Church remains strongest in rural regions, but there is no generalization that can apply to all of Spain. In many of the allegedly devout regions of the South, the peasants rarely go near a church except for baptism, marriage and burial. In the election of February 1936, under the Second Republic, the anti-clerical Popular Front carried not only Barcelona, Valencia, Seville and Madrid but almost all of the rural South.[12]

As in most Catholic countries, the great majority of the attendants at Church are women. The priests are deeply disturbed by the disproportion in the sexes. In July 1959 the Catholic Action daily of Madrid, *Ya,* carried a large and typical headline: "Catholic Religion Is Not Only For Women." The story summarized an address by the Spanish Primate, Cardinal Pla y Deniel, begging the men of Spain to recognize the Catholic faith as a religion for the manly and the virile.[13] The Primate mentioned the fact that years before Cardinal Mercier of Belgium, during a visit to Spain, had commented on the disproportion of men in Spanish congregations and had declared that the condition was so obvious and so evil that it would be difficult not to predict for Spain an anti-clerical and anti-religious revolution.

The decline of the Church's influence over Spanish men is reflected in the relative decline in the number of members of male religious orders. While the population of the country was going up 25 per cent from 1931 to 1958, the number of members in male religious orders actually declined. However, the Jesuits are confident and powerful, and the new male secular institute called Opus Dei has risen to great power in recent years. (Opus Dei will be discussed in the chapter on education.)

In relative mathematical terms, Spain is not a priest-ridden country. In fact, the leaders of the Church are constantly complaining that they cannot recruit enough priests for their ordinary needs. The proportion of priests to Catholic members is lower in Spain than it is in the Netherlands and the Irish Republic; it is even lower, by a slight margin, than the proportion in the United States. In statistical terms, summarized in a Spanish Church Guide early in 1961, Spain claimed 42,438 Catholic churches, about 35,000 Catholic priests, about 20,000 members of male religious orders, and 70,000 female members.[14] These figures are not impressive for a Church which has a virtual national monopoly of religion and which has basked in special government favor for more than twenty years. *Ya* revealed in 1959 that there were only 26,000 secular (non-religious order) priests in all of Spain for approximately 30 million Spaniards, and that Madrid and Barcelona were supplying only two such priests for each 10,000 persons in the population, a ratio which put them at the bottom of the ecclesiastical ladder in recruitment. *Ya* mournfully summarized figures to show that Spanish Catholics produced proportionately about eight times as many secular priests in 1769.

The Spanish Church, however, still maintains a considerable missionary establishment overseas. As we shall see, it has had great aspirations in Latin America, even in Cuba until recently, and it hopes to reclaim for Catholicism in the New World some of the evangelistic enthusiasm it has lost in the home country.

The Catholics Against Franco

In spite of the alliance of the Catholic hierarchy with Franco, there are thousands of Spanish Catholics who are opposed to him and his dictatorship. That was the most inspiring discovery of my visit to Spain in 1959. I met many of the leaders of the anti-Franco Catholic forces in all parts of the country, and I became convinced that they represented a very substantial bloc in the nation. This Catholic opposition is not confined to Basques and Catalans, who might be expected to oppose any strong central government because of their regional animosity to Madrid. In Madrid, Valencia, Seville and elsewhere I interviewed sincere Catholic critics of the regime who were equally opposed to Franco and to their own bishops' collaboration with Franco.

The almost universal comment by both priests and laymen when Franco was discussed ran something like this: "The younger Catholics are restless and want more freedom. It is the older Catholics and bishops who misrepresent the real sentiment of the Spanish Catholic people." And then the commentator would often complain bitterly of the savage persecution of Catholic dissidents by a regime which suppresses all freedom of the press and prohibits the formation of any political party except the Falange. The complainants were not united in advocating a remedy for the present situation; they were united only in hating Franco.

When I challenged them to name a single prominent clerical leader in Spain who had come out openly against the regime there was often silent embarrassment. One bishop was occasionally mentioned, Dr. Antonio Pildain, who had attacked the Falange syndicates in 1951. But I was told that he had been assigned to the Canary Islands. He was not wanted on the mainland.

No bishop within Spain could be discovered who had been aggressive or open in basic criticism. A few, very few, bishops had made public complaints about the poverty and suffering of the people, but they were careful not to couple such questioning with any fundamental challenge to the policy of dictatorship, or with a demand for any genuine democracy. The Abbot of Montserrat, Aureli Maria Escarre, was most frequently mentioned as anti-Franco, but he was banished by the Vatican at Franco's request. Angel Herrera, Bishop of Malaga, was also mentioned frequently. There is no doubt that he has tried to awaken the social conscience of the nation, but he is not by American standards a champion of either democracy or freedom. During the days of the Republic, he was editor of one of the newspapers most hostile to the Republic in Spain. He has not asked for self-government either in Spanish politics or within his own Church. He is head of Editorial Catolica, the private corporation which publishes Catholic Action journals.

The reason why no member of note in the Spanish hierarchy can be named as open and consistent opponent of Franco is quite obvious. The machinery of power gives no real opportunity for the appointment of bishops of genuine independence. Bishops are by definition prelates who have been rewarded for conformity by a regime which has described itself quite blandly as totalitarian.

The general policy of the Franco-controlled press in dealing with the Catholic opposition is to suppress the basic facts concerning that opposition. In recent years almost all news about this opposition has leaked out of Spain via the French press, through confidential sources of American and British correspondents, or through the New York magazine, *Iberica*. As we shall see, if any story about the Catholic opposition or any other opposition within Spain in a foreign newspaper is effective and hostile to Franco in its tone, the offending foreign journal may be stopped at the borders, or excluded from Spanish newsstands after arrival. The very existence of any Catholic opposition is known to only a small circle within Spain.

When, for example, forty-two Basque priests signed a strong letter of protest against the regime on May 30, 1960,[15] the fact never reached the Spanish people except through trickles of rumor coming from the foreign newspapers. The protest denounced police brutality and press censorship and demanded more civil rights for Spaniards. It was not only suppressed within Spain, but its signers were hunted out by the leaders of the Church and publicly condemned. The condemnation was even echoed in the United States by faithful Church journals like the Brooklyn *Tablet*. Four high Spanish prelates—an archbishop and three bishops—issued a statement saying that the Basque letter was "without any guarantee of authenticity"; and this slur was circulated in the American Catholic press by the National Catholic Welfare Conference. The Papal Nuncio to Spain joined in the denunciation by saying in the presence of Franco's Minister of Justice:

The soldier of Christ, when he has something to say to his bishop, should go to him. But he should never publish the text of his confidences nor still less place them in the hands of the enemies of religion. . . . The rights of a human being are a constant preoccupation of the Bishops, who will convey any complaints in this context to the proper quarters.

Six months after the event, a statement by the Bishop of San Sebastian was printed throughout Spain warning any "participating priests" engaged in intrigue against the regime that "if they persist, if only by favorable advice, they risk *ipso facto* the penalty of suspension *a divinis*." This phrase describes a condition in which a priest is forbidden to preside over a Mass, and often precedes complete excommunication.

The Catholic bishops, if they wish, can order the arrest and confinement in their own Church prisons of any priest who defies the political regime. On May 11, 1958, a Basque priest in the town of Campuzano in Santander—Father Carlos Martin Castaneda—preached a sermon in which he mourned the suffering of the unemployed, anti-Franco members in his parish. He started an unauthorized collection for them with a gift of thirteen dollars, and announced that High Mass would not be sung that day.

Now [he said], though I exceed my pastoral functions, I cannot fail to voice a protest from this sacred place whence all immoralities should be attacked, against the oppressions, violences and brutalities to which our various brother laborers have been subjected. No one who goes to confession and calls himself a Christian can employ evil means under the pretext of attaining good ends, as—let this be quite clear—this is reprehensible to and condemned by Christian morality.[16]

The priest was immediately suspended by his Vicar-General and ordered confined in the monastery of Cobreces.

The Underground Rebellion

Among the definitely rebellious underground forces working against Franco in Spain, none is officially Catholic; that is to say, none has the support of the hierarchy. The two nearest exceptions to this generalization are the HOAC, the Workers Brotherhoods of Catholic Action, an organization which has dared to stand up to the

Falange in mild protest against the Falange monopoly in the industrial field; and the few small, isolated journals with Catholic leanings that are published intermittently in Madrid and Barcelona by young Catholics. These journals are obliquely, but never directly, anti-Franco. If they dare to make any direct assault on the dictator, they are immediately suppressed.

HOAC has a journal which is allowed to print a few vague eulogies on freedom and a few mildly critical things about social conditions in Spain, but the government and the hierarchy will not permit its editors to give it general circulation. For a time the journal was suppressed altogether. The organization's total national membership is said to be only 30,000, and officially it is a strictly non-political organization. Otherwise, it would not be permitted to exist.

The unofficial Catholic opposition is badly fragmented and divided. The three most important segments of the underground movement can roughly be described as the Christian Democrats of the right, the Christian Democrats of the left, and the Social Democrats. Since they are all illegal and cannot publish any official records or hold any public meetings, it is almost impossible to estimate their real strength. Probably the most important segment is the Christian Democratic grouping of the right, led for the time being by the famous leader of CEDA (Confederacion Espanola de Derechas Autonomas) under the Second Republic, Gil Robles.

Gil Robles is considered too old for logical succession to Franco, but if there should be a conservative Catholic revolution with a mildly modified constitutional monarchy he might be the most logical temporary chief of state. His attitudes are probably to the right of the Christian Democratic statesmen who have risen to power in other parts of Europe, such as De Gasperi in Italy and Adenauer in West Germany. De Gasperi and Adenauer depended largely on Catholic support in their rise to power, and Gil Robles is hopeful of the same support.[17] But the very fact that the Vatican has in the past smiled on him makes him anathema to many followers of the left. He is still a much-hated man, although he has made friends among the liberals in recent years by serving as a defense counsel for opposition leaders who have been imprisoned by Franco's police. His rise to power would not guarantee any great increase in religious liberty to Spain's non-Catholic minorities. When, in behalf of his group, he applied for admission to the Paris headquarters of the Catholic political international in 1961, his statement of Fundamental Principles supported the present Concordat with the Vatican and authorized the cultivation of non-Catholic confessions only in private.

More hopeful from the democratic point of view is the small underground segment of left Christian Democrats who might collaborate with the Socialists, although they would almost certainly reject any collaboration with the Communists. The name mentioned most often as a hope of this Democratic Catholic left is Manuel Gimenez Fernandez, Professor of Canon Law at the University of Seville, who was once Minister of Agriculture in the Second Republic. In a possible Social-Democratic grouping to the left of the left Catholics, the leader most often mentioned is Dionisio Ridruejo, independent poet and intellectual who has one of the strangest backgrounds in left-wing history. He was once a leader of the Falange, even fought in the Blue Division of Spain side by side with the Nazis against the Soviets in World War II. (I found that he was the only mildly leftist leader in Spain willing to talk for quotation, even though his words might result in a prison sentence.) After many periods of imprisonment under Franco he was acquitted in an open trial in March 1961, a fact that many observers took to mean that Franco was afraid of him. Although Gimenez, as a left Christian Democrat, is considered a possibility for power under a Christian Democratic government; and Ridruejo is considered a possibility for a regime with slightly more of a socialist tinge, many observers believe that the two most likely successors to Franco in a Spanish revolution are now in Franco's prisons.

On one item all the anti-Franco forces, except the Communist agree: Franco should be succeeded by a constitutional monarchy. The two unanswered questions about that monarchy concern timing and the nature of the monarchy itself. No one close to Franco ever publicly expresses any eagerness to hasten the transition. The Caudillo continues to be hailed as Spain's god-given leader for as long as he wishes to stay in power. The Church and the Army and the Falange all declare that they want a monarchy—all for different reasons. The Church wants to hang on to its privileges; the Army wants to continue to be the power behind the throne; and the Falange hopes to use a restoration of the monarchy to restore its fallen prestige. By officially favoring a monarchy himself, Franco has, to a certain extent, drawn the teeth of the opposition.

The reason why the opposition wants a monarchy is entirely negative. There is no love for kings as such in the opposition camp, but there is a great fear of complete chaos if another Republic is launched and there is no national symbol of power to hold the people together emotionally. Also, a constitutional monarchy with a reasonably powerful Cortes represents in Spanish history the most successful of its democratic traditions. Accordingly, the opposition believes that a constitutional monarchy is the safest and surest way to effect a transition from Franco without involving the nation in another bloody and costly civil war.

It is probably safe to say that any future monarchy will be, at least in name, a Catholic monarchy. The Church is too deeply imbedded in the traditional life of the Spanish people to be cast off, and there is no present disposition among the great majority of the anti-Francoists to go back to the drastic anti-clericalism of the Second Republic. However, there is so much feeling against the bishops that almost any growth in democracy is bound to bring with it a reduction in the power of the Church.

Whether the king who succeeds Franco, or ascends the throne during his lifetime, is Don Juan Carlos, born in 1937 and now receiving his education in Spain, or his father, Don Juan de Bourbon, third son of Alfonso XIII, who has been living for many years in Portugal, seems to be relatively unimportant. Time is in favor of the son, but if the father is in good health when Franco goes, he is the more logical successor. As king, either one would probably be a conventional Catholic monarch for the same reason that Alfonso XIII was a conventional Catholic monarch. The alliance with Catholicism is one of the devices of the Spanish upper class for maintaining its position in power.

Left and Right Within the Church

One thing that surprises the American visitor about the members of the Catholic opposition is that they are eager to cooperate with socialists and sometimes even with Communists. (The Communists are very small in number but they are so well organized that most opposition groups envy them.) The hatred against Franco is so intense that in a crisis the Marxist and anti-Marxist animosities tend to be forgotten. I talked with leaders of the abortive general strike against the Franco regime in Barcelona in June

1959 both before the strike and after it had failed, and I found a surprising willingness on the part of all factions to fight together regardless of religious or political labels.

Of course, when Catholics show any readiness to cooperate with Communists, Franco uses such collaboration to the limit. He fills his jails with "Communists" who never had any sympathy with Communism except to share the Communist hatred of Franco. He treats all with the same savagery. When university students who sided with the socialists in the 1959 strike in Barcelona were captured, some of them were beaten almost to death by the Franco police in the presence of their parents. (Some of their friends told me of the beatings in vivid detail.) To the credit of the Church, some young priests risked their whole clerical futures by going again and again to local police headquarters to protest against that brutality.

In the Barcelona area the priests are more outspoken against Franco than in some other areas because Catalonia wants independence for its own reasons, and the priests have some regional backing in their mildly anti-Franco position. The most eminent leader of this Catalan opposition within the Church, Abbot Escarre of Montserrat, once had the courage to send a telegram to Franco protesting against the "repression and tortures" inflicted on young Catholic Catalans by Franco's police. He is sometimes called—or miscalled—the Catalonian Makarios in the mistaken belief that he might some day successfully imitate the Greek Orthodox leader of Cyprus. A personal friend of Pope John XXIII, he has enough influence at the Vatican to cause Franco some concern. The Vatican conspicuously recognized him in 1959 by sending Cardinal Tisserant to dedicate a new altar at the famous mountaintop monastery on Montserrat, outside Barcelona. But when it was seen that the Abbot and his mountaintop might be used for promoting a move for political freedom through a so-called "Retreat for Studies," the Holy Office issued a solemn warning prohibiting the retreat on the ground that the sessions called for the mixing of "religious, lay and even heterodox elements from abroad." The Abbot himself was soon afterwards sent out of Spain for his "health," but later was allowed to return.

The Abbot's assistant told me quite frankly that most of the younger priests in Spain were anti-Franco in spite of their bishops and that at least half of the people of Barcelona were anti-clerical. He thought that there should be more freedom in Spain, but he was equally insistent that in a Catholic nation like Spain there should be some state protection for the ideas of the Church. "It would be bad," he said, "to allow too many ideas to come into Spain too fast from the other nations of Europe."

This equivocal endorsement of freedom by the Abbot of Monserrat's assistant is quite typical of even the best of the anti-Franco Catholic clerics of Spain. Their words about freedom do not carry the meaning that those same words would convey if expressed by a priest in the United States. What they usually mean by the expression "more freedom" is (1) some relaxation in Spanish censorship; (2) less physical cruelty by Franco's police in dealing with the opposition; and (3) more freedom for the Church itself in its institutional activities. They do not want a completely democratic nation with guaranties for civil liberties and religious equality in the American manner.

This fact was brought home to me forcibly in one of the most interesting interviews I had in Spain in 1959 with two of the nation's leading Jesuit writers, Pedro Meseguer and Eustaquio Guerrero, at the Jesuit headquarters in Madrid where the order's leading magazine, *Razon y Fe*, is edited. Father Meseguer is the Madrid representative of the Jesuit magazine *America*, and Father Guerrero is no less distinguished as a writer. Here are extracts from the notes I wrote immediately after that interview.

These are kindly, scholarly men in appearance. They have the faces of devotees committed to a holy cause. They do not seem to be aware that, from the point of view of democracy and liberty their philosophy is hair-raising. It is a total denial of freedom of the mind in the name of holy truth, the truth of their Church, all expressed with firm and amiable mien as if this were the most ordinary and acceptable moral doctrine that civilized men could embrace. They seem to be quite frank.

Q. Is it your view that no non-Catholic professor should be given employment at a Spanish university?

A. Yes. One should consider the whole historical perspective of Spain. It is a Catholic country and Spain has a right to preserve the faith of the people. A professor who disbelieves in the moral law might endanger the minds of young students who are not mature enough to encounter such concepts.

Q. How about professors who do not teach religious subjects, professors of mathematics, for example?

A. I am ready to concede that the argument for non-Catholic professors is stronger in such cases, but even in mathematics non-

Catholic attitudes may be contrary to natural law and the welfare of the students.

Q. How about freedom for Protestants in your country?

A. Foreign Protestants are undisturbed in our country. It is recognized that they have a right to worship in their own way. With Spanish Protestants it is somewhat different. They can worship, but they cannot conduct activities in such a way as to proselyte.

Q. Do you personally believe that it is fair to deny Spanish Protestant churches the right to put crosses on their exteriors, for example?

A. You must understand how Spanish Protestants act in this country. It isn't as if they were converting anyone to Christianity who is not a Christian. They are divisive. They are aggressive and even at times noisy. They distract the people from moral unity. They insist on public propaganda and they try to make converts from the Church. And the Vatican took care of all that in the Concordat.

Q. Wasn't the Franco government responsible for establishing the rules against Protestants in that Concordat?

A. Emphatically not. It was the Church. The Holy See and the Spanish Church exacted from the present Spanish government two things in the Concordat for the protection of our Catholic faith: the ruling that every baptized Catholic should be treated as a Catholic under our marriage laws, and a rule against open proselytism.

Q. Isn't this type of suppression contrary to the teaching of leading members of your order in the United States, such as Father John Courtney Murray? I believe he has argued that freedom for non-Catholics *might* be granted in a perfect Catholic state without destroying Catholic principles.

A. We have respect for Father Murray, but he did not correctly state Catholic doctrine and policy. That was stated by Cardinal Ottaviani of the Holy Office, who completely supported our position against Father Murray. Truth must be protected, particularly in a Catholic country. There may be some exceptions in practical policy in non-Catholic countries. But that is not the Catholic thesis.

Q. When do you think tolerance for non-Catholic minorities should begin? At 20 per cent? At 10 per cent?

A. (*Laughing.*) It is not a matter of mathematics. We must deal in terms of Spanish history and the outlook of the Spanish people. This is a Catholic country, and truth is entitled to protection in a Catholic country.

There was nothing essentially new in what these two distinguished Jesuits told me so frankly. In fact, the pages of *Razon y Fe* contain many more extreme things. Father John Courtney

Murray has cited several of them.[18] Father Guerrero himself has said in print that freedom of religious propaganda in Spain would open the door to "international Jewry and Masonry" and reduce Spain to the cultural level of the "materialist and pagan Anglo-Saxon spirit." He added: "Persecution inflicted on heretics preserved the faith in France when she was in danger from the Albigensians; preserved it too in Spain, when she was attacked by Lutheranism and other heresies. And we shall continue to believe that, if France and all Europe are not Protestant, it is proportionately owing to the armed defense of the true faith by the Catholic nation. . . ."

Father Pablo Lopez, S.J., declared in a 1946 article in *Razon y Fe*:

Moreover, Spaniards discontented *for religious reasons* have no right to enjoy more ample religious freedom than they do enjoy. For one reason they are non-Catholics, and therefore in error; and error even when in good faith, has strictly speaking no right to show itself or be professed. For another reason, the religious ideal of a tiny erring minority ought not to be respected in its public manifestations, when these gravely injure the Catholicism of the immense majority of the nation, and can be prevented without danger to peace.[19]

We shall see in the next three chapters what it means to be "non-Catholics, and therefore in error" in Spain today.

4. THE PROTESTANTS

In terms of numbers Protestantism is not a very important factor in Spain. There are so few Protestants in the country that several Catholic writers, in discussing the Catholic-versus-Protestant situation, have asked scornfully: Would you be interested in religious freedom for Eskimos in Panama?

For most Americans this quantitative standard for measuring the importance of religious freedom for minorities is not very convincing. Religious freedom either exists or it does not exist. If it is denied to the tiniest minority in the most Catholic nation in the world under a system of discrimination sanctioned by Rome itself, the Roman Catholic Church cannot escape responsibility by resorting to mathematics. For most Americans the treatment of Protestants in Spain is probably more important than any other religious phenomenon in Spain. It is the touchstone of the whole issue that lies between Catholic power and Western democracy. It seems to provide an ominous answer to the question: How much does the Catholic Church believe in liberty when it has the power to destroy liberty? That question seems to provide a far better yardstick for measuring Catholic policy than the Church's pronouncements on freedom in the United States, where Catholicism is a minority faith and must therefore depend upon the maintenance of freedom by a non-Catholic majority.

I was able to see for myself the physical proof of the constant discrimination practiced against Protestants by the Franco regime with the systematic and open collaboration of the Catholic hierarchy. One of my first exposures to the practice of discrimination came on July 8, 1959 in a Madrid criminal court where I saw the Reverend Gregorio Jose Nunez Moreno, pastor of the Second Baptist Church, tried for the "crime" of opening the doors of his own church after those doors had been sealed by the Spanish police.[1] He was convicted of subversion on October 3, fined one thousand pesetas and sentenced to two months' imprisonment.

He escaped the prison sentence because of a technicality. The address of his church, which had been closed by the police without any trial of the issues five years before, is Calle Madre de Dios, 4, Barrio de Usera, Madrid.

The Non-Existent Church

It should be said here that, so far as the government of Spain is concerned, there is no such thing as the Second Baptist Church of Madrid. No Spanish Protestant church for Spaniards has what lawyers call "juridical existence." It cannot be listed in the telephone directory as a church; it cannot own property as a church; it cannot look like a church or bear on its exterior a cross or any sign whatever of its religious function. The Second Baptist Church of Madrid, after being closed by the Spanish police in 1954, existed for the five years thereafter simply as an extralegal and informal group of Spaniards meeting in a small private room.

There were many things about this trial of Pastor Nunez worthy of note. I recorded some of my impressions at the time.[2]

The Franco government does not recognize this event as particularly important. No Spanish reporters are present, and if they had been present their accounts of the trial would never have survived the censor's pencil. No newspapers within Spain have told the people of the event in advance, nor will any Spanish newspaper ever mention the fact that the trial has occurred. Nevertheless, the foreign newspapers recognize its significance, and the front bench in the court room is crowded with correspondents from some of the most important newspapers in the United States and Europe.

The three black-robed judges with their elegant lace cuffs gaze austerely down from their lofty bench. The face of the chief judge is partly obscured by a tall brass crucifix which stands on the bench on his right hand. The ornate glass chandeliers spread a dim light over the heavy carved trappings and the weathered faces of the spectators. The word LEX is written in gold on the wall above the bench.

The trial proceedings are quite unlike those in an American court. The prosecutor and the defense counsel cannot directly challenge improper questions. It is the chief judge who, acting on his own initiative, rings a little bell when he believes that either lawyer has strayed beyond the limits of admissible evidence. There is no jury trial in Spain even for murder, and no public written transcript of testimony is automatically made available to the defendant or his counsel. As a matter of fact, this public trial of Pastor Nunez is an act of grace by the government, since he could "legally" be handled as a "subversive" under summary proceedings in the manner of a drum-head court martial.

The criminal court room is crowded. Every seat is taken and every inch of standing room along the walls is occupied by Protestant workers in their Sunday clothes. At great sacrifice, they have left their jobs for the day to support their pastor in his hour of trial.

A stir goes through the crowd as the charge against Pastor Nunez is presented: Grave disobedience of the authorities in that in October 1957 the said defendant did take from the doors of a certain building, located at Calle Madre de Dios 4, certain seals which had been placed there by the police, thus violating the criminal law of Spain, for which offense a penalty of imprisonment or fine is demanded according to the discretion of this court.

Q. Guilty or not guilty?

A. Not guilty.

Q. (The prosecutor goes directly to the point.) Did you or did you not break the seals on this building?

A. No, the seals were already broken. I only cleared them off after they had rotted and partially washed away in the years since 1954 when the police closed the church.

Q. But did you not enter the chapel and celebrate private worship there?

A. Yes.

Q. And did you not know when you entered this chapel that it had been closed by the authorities?

A. Yes.

Q. How did you know it?

A. Only because it had become a matter of common knowledge.

Q. Did you communicate with the government about the sealing of this building?

A. Yes, four times I wrote for an explanation and a lifting of the seals, to the Chief of Police, to the Minister of the Interior, to the Civil Governor and to the President of the Cabinet. I received no answer to any communication.

(The defense counsel examines. Ernesto Vellve Bueno is the only Protestant lawyer in Spain who acts openly as a Protestant lawyer. He is a successful businessman who draws an income from other sources. He is now counsel to the newly organized Evangelical Defense Commission of Spain.)

Q. When you entered the chapel did you find it in much disorder from disuse and the weather?

A. Yes, and I also found a place consecrated to God's worship which had been profaned——

Q. Stop right there (booms the presiding judge, and he rings the little bell on his desk). Answer the questions but do not bring in anything religious. (No one dares to smile at this proscription of religion in a religious trial.)

A. I allowed the seals to fall off because I was led to do so by my conscience.

Q. Did you also enter because you understood that official silence could be interpreted as permission?

A. Yes.

Q. What was the main reason you wanted to reopen this chapel?

A. I was led by my conscience and my duty to my church members and my duty to God——

(Again the judicial bell rings furiously, and an angry chief judge breaks in to say that the answer is irrelevant.)

At this particular trial the brilliant defense counsel secured a delay because one of the government's essential documents was missing, but the Protestant triumph was short-lived. Three months later, when the excitement had died down, Pastor Nunez was convicted.

Historic Discrimination

Pastor Nunez was only one victim of a legal system of religious discrimination which is unexampled in Western countries. In no other so-called Christian nation do Christians discriminate against other Christians with such continuing severity. Protestants of Spain have lived in a ghetto of Catholic construction for more than four hundred years, and their treatment is no better today than it was in 1950, when the *Christian Century* observed that: "Not even Russia presents a similar spectacle of systematic cradle-to-the-grave discrimination against a religious minority."

It is true that there are only about 11,000 official members of Protestant churches in Spain in a population of almost 30 million, and this represents less than one-tenth of 1 per cent of the population.[3] But how small does a minority need to be to make its suppression justifiable? It should be remembered that less than 1 per cent of the American people were Roman Catholic at the time of the American Revolution. If Protestants had practiced suppression of all minute religious blocs in America from colonial days to the present time, the Roman Catholic Church in the United

States might still occupy a position comparable to that of Protestantism in Spain today. In the United States the 1 per cent Catholic minority has grown to about 40 million, or 23 per cent of the American population.[4] Catholicism has attained this position of power and influence partly because the overwhelming Protestant majority in America gave to the Catholic Church the right to enter, to proselyte freely and to multiply.

From the very beginning of the birth of Protestantism down to the present day, with a few brief interruptions, the Roman Catholic Church of Spain, with the full backing of the Vatican, has practiced a contrary policy. The Spanish Church has united with the state in blocking and suppressing Protestant development with both ecclesiastical and physical weapons.

Spain had no Reformation. This is the classic explanation commonly given for the failure of Protestantism to take hold in Spain in the sixteenth century, when Luther's opposition to the hierarchy was capturing the imagination of the people in the British Isles and the northern Continent. But the primary reason why the Protestant opposition did not take hold in Spain was that the hierarchy and the government united in suppressing it. The real beginning of a great religious revolt took place in the sixteenth century; it was snuffed out by violence and tyranny.

As we have pointed out, those Catholic sovereigns, Ferdinand and Isabella, brought the Inquisition to Spain as early as 1480, with the consent of the Vatican, and made it into a political crusade as well as a religious instrument. It was not designed especially for a war on Protestantism, but as soon as Protestantism began, its full power was turned against the "heretics."[5] A few Protestant groups, chiefly in Seville and Valladolid, operated for a time in spite of persecution, and they attained perhaps a maximum membership of 3,000. The first Lutheran to be burned at a Spanish stake died in 1545. Spanish Protestantism was almost completely wiped out in four great *auto de fe's* in Valladolid and Seville in 1559 and 1560. After that, those Protestants who chose to remain in Spain publicly professed the Catholic faith.

This suppression of the Protestant heresy is glossed over by current Spanish textbooks and hailed by the pro-Franco leaders in Spain today as a triumph of truth and national unity. Franco himself, in a 1950 address, boasted of the "noble and holy intransigence" of Spain in religious matters, and said: "You have wished to come to the place from which your ancestors went to carry the

gospel to America, and you find the same Spain . . . of the fifteenth and sixteenth centuries, the same noble and intransigent
Spain—intransigent, yes, for in the things of the spirit and of the
true faith there must be a noble and holy intransigence. When nations have received the divine blessing of a single faith and are living under the true religion, concessions cannot be made to error." [6]

It would be difficult to find a more orthodox statement of the
position of the Vatican itself in regard to Protestantism. Many
Popes and many official Roman journals have expressed the same
thought in regard to Protestant heresy. It is "error," and error does
not have the same rights as truth. Under Canon 1399 no Catholic
may read a book advocating Protestant doctrine; under Canon
1258 he may not participate in any way in a Protestant service;
under Canon 1063 he may not marry a Protestant; and under
Canon 1374 he may not attend a Protestant school. Under Canon
684 and a special Holy Office ruling of November 5, 1920, Catholics are forbidden to join the YMCA and YWCA because of their
Protestant traditions. [7] Under Canons 1203-1242, Catholics are
told that they must not be buried in the same cemeteries with
Protestants. Any Catholic who leaves the one true Church to join
a Protestant body is subject to immediate excommunication and
branding as a *vitandus,* which means in practice that Catholics are
instructed to shun him personally and boycott him professionally.
Because of these rules it is clear that the Spanish attitude toward
Protestantism is not merely a national phenomenon. It is a Catholic phenomenon, more fully realized in Spain than in any other
country.

Protestantism was almost non-existent in Spain for some
three hundred years, from the sixteenth through the nineteenth
centuries, although, as we have seen, Catholic anti-clericalism was
very strong at times. Then a few Protestant missionaries began to
trickle into the country. The most famous of them was the Englishman George Borrow, whose work, *The Bible in Spain,* has become a literary classic. Borrow distributed Bibles and talked to
thousands of "beknighted" Catholics in both Spain and Portugal.
He even went to jail for a time in Spain in 1838, and received much
foreign publicity.

There were very few permanent results from Borrow's work
or the work of other Protestant missionaries who cultivated the
Spanish field before the 1860s. Protestantism in Spain labored under special emotional as well as legal handicaps. It was considered

a distinctly foreign product. The British and Foreign Bible Society was the chief Protestant instrument for many years, and this very label was an index of its weakness. Even in the nineteenth century almost all of the Protestants in Spain were foreign visitors and residents. They were permitted to worship in their own small foreign churches so long as they left the Spanish people alone—and this relative freedom for foreign Protestants, not for Spanish Protestants, still continues.

When the British and Foreign Bible Society had 10,000 Bibles printed in Spain in the 1860s, the government simply stopped their circulation, and they were finally shipped out of the country. Such direct action against this society has been repeated so often in its history that its survival in Spain is quite remarkable. It still has a small office in Madrid with limited operations, and it still works with determination for the right to distribute non-Catholic Bibles.

All the early nineteenth-century measures to suppress Protestantism were sanctified by the 1851 Concordat between the government and the Vatican which made Catholicism the state religion "with the exclusion of all other cults." Pius IX in his Syllabus of Errors in 1864 gave the Spanish arrangement additional sanction by denouncing as one of the "principal errors" of modern times the proposition that "it is no longer expedient that the Catholic religion shall be held as the only religion of the State, to the exclusion of all other modes of worship." He did not even speak out for the rights of non-Catholics in private, nor did the Spanish laws before 1868 guarantee Protestant rights in private.

The Double Standard

The double standard for dealing with Catholic truth and Protestant error was used all through the nineteenth century. One of its dramatic manifestations came in 1869 in Spain, after a short-lived revolution. A new Constitution had been proposed, giving non-Catholics more rights. Liberals hoped to see genuine religious liberty established. Canon Manterola appeared in behalf of the Church before a committee of the Cortes which was considering religious laws and opposed any concession to non-Catholics. According to Professor Hughey's narrative about the events of this period, the good canon argued as follows: The truth has the right to be received by man but man has duties and not rights with respect to truth. When the true religion, which is Catholicism, has been preached to a people and accepted by a minority, the civil power has the obligation to protect that religion. When it has become the religion of the majority, the civil power has the obligation to establish it as the privileged religion of the state. It must not be argued that toleration should be granted to others so that they will grant it to Catholics. The Church has always insisted on the exclusive rights of truth. It does not follow that since religious freedom is defended by Catholic prelates in France and England, it should be established in Spain. Conditions are different.[8]

So ran the classic argument in 1869—and there are only slight variations in that argument today. As we have already seen, this is precisely the one-sided view that is being used today by the Spanish Jesuits to justify suppressing Protestantism in Spain, although this same religious order argues for the opposite policy in dealing with the Catholic minority in the United States. Religious liberty is accepted by Catholicism in non-Catholic societies as a means to power without recognizing any obligation to practice reciprocity for Protestants in Catholic societies.

A writer in *Ecclesia* declared in the issue of May 10, 1952:

We do not deny that a world situation might arise in which it would be advisable for Spain to sacrifice its Catholic unity in order to obtain religious liberty for Catholics in the majority of other countries; this is not the case today, nor is it likely to be in the future, as in Protestant countries religious liberty is granted to all confessions.

Until the days of the Second Republic the treatment of Protestants depended not so much on their own strength as on the strength of anti-clericalism. The Protestants never had enough strength to challenge either the Church or the state directly. Their congregations were given sufferance rather than liberty. They were not free from discrimination in matters of marriage, censorship, burial or education. Except during brief periods of anti-clerical power, every public manifestation of Protestantism could always be punished under the Spanish penal code. The Church, as late as the 1890s, excommunicated Catholics who ate a meal with Protestants.

A gigantic petition for Protestant freedom was addressed to the government in 1910 and signed by 150,000 people. It produced a little new tolerance, but when Pius X countered in 1911 with an appeal for more strict intolerance, the liberals as well as the Protestants were put on the defensive. Pius, in his letter to the Archbishop of Toledo said:

> It must be maintained as a certain principle that in Spain it is possible to support, as many do in fact most ably support, the Catholic thesis, and with it the re-establishment of religious unity. It is, furthermore, the duty of every Catholic to combat all the errors condemned by the Holy See, especially those included in the *Syllabus* and the *liberties of perdition* proclaimed by the new law, or liberalism, whose application to the government of Spain is the cause of so many evils.[9]

It is well to note the significance of this letter on intolerance by Pius X. It was a directive from Rome to Spanish Catholicism to maintain nineteenth-century standards of suppression even in the twentieth century. The argument is often made by American Catholic apologists that the famous strictures on human liberty in the *Syllabus of Errors* of 1864 were meant to apply only to nineteenth-century European conditions. They were actually imposed on Protestants in Spain shortly before World War I by this letter of Pius X, and the authority of this directive has never been revoked.

The Spanish government and the hierarchy immediately used the directive of Pius X as a new justification for further suppressions of Protestant activities. One Spanish statesman, Jose Canalejas, forced a modicum of tolerance for Protestants upon the Church in 1910 in spite of bitter Vatican protest; but when he was assassinated in 1912, Spain moved backward toward the spirit of the Inquisition. Primo de Rivera, during the seven years of his dictatorship (1923 to 1930), gave the Protestants no additional guarantees of liberty. He suspended the Spanish Constitution and installed censorship. Although his central government permitted many Protestant activities, it allowed local government officials and local courts to block Protestant meetings and close Protestant schools. In one case in 1926 a woman was sentenced to prison for saying publicly that the Virgin Mary had other children after the birth of Jesus. This standard Protestant teaching about the Virgin Mary, based upon the New Testament references to the brothers of Jesus, is universally treated as blasphemy in Spain today. Primo de Rivera, toward the end of his regime, summed up his and the

Church's policy on Protestantism quite adequately when he said: "If in a country of twenty million inhabitants, nineteen and a half million are well protected in their rights, it is not of great importance that the remaining half million want fuller rights."

The Second Republic temporarily changed the whole legal atmosphere for Protestants. Open activity for Protestant sects was promptly authorized. Some Protestant publications went so far as to recommend voting for the left coalition in 1936 because they felt that victory for the left was necessary to guarantee the freedom to proselyte.

For Protestantism those five years of the peacetime Republic, from 1931 to 1936, were delightfully free years. Spaniards could worship freely, or refuse to worship. All the clerical laws making the Protestants into second-class citizens were repealed. A few Protestants even gained honorable places in the army and in public office.

But when Spanish Protestants struck a balance at the end of the Republic's five years, they found that they had not actually gained much in numbers. Released from the compulsions and pressures that characterized the Catholic monarchy, the liberal-minded Spaniard tended to turn against all organized religion. For every new Protestant there were a dozen professed skeptics. None of the great leaders of the Republic was a Protestant. The Socialists, the Communists, the anarchists and the liberals all tended to honor the new religious liberty not by joining a Protestant chapel, but by thumbing their noses at the priests.

Naturally, when the Civil War came, the Protestants were almost unanimously on the side of the Loyalists. The Republican government had given them liberty and they tended to repay the debt with interest. Also, the Protestants were nearly all proletarians and the proletarians tended to favor the Republic. In Barcelona the pro-Republican mobs burned nearly every Catholic church in the city, but when they unintentionally included a Protestant church in their vandalism, they quickly put the fire out and apologized.

The Old Order Is Restored

The triumph of the Church in the Civil War restored all the old legal and social disabilities of Protestants, and added a few new ones by way of punishment for their association with "atheistic Communism." At first, immediately after the Civil War, Franco proceeded with some caution against the Protestants. He was not quite sure what the outcome of World War II would be. It had begun within a few months of his triumph. He was evidently surprised when that war ended in a victory for the anti-Axis forces, and for a while he was cautious. He was faced with a hostile United Nations which denounced him as a tool of fascism. Since he felt the need of creating religious liberty on paper, even for heretics, he promulgated the so-called Spanish Charter of 1945, the *Fuero de los Espanoles*. For Protestantism it allowed rights so ambiguous that they might just as well never have been granted.

This 1945 Charter, going back to some of the religious distinctions and limitations of the nineteenth century, draws a line between permissible freedom of worship for non-Catholics in private and "outward demonstrations" of any non-Catholic faith. In Article 6 it says:

> The profession and practice of the Catholic religion, which is that of the Spanish State, shall enjoy official protection. No one shall be disturbed because of his religious beliefs or the private practice of his worship. No other outward ceremonies or demonstrations than those of the Catholic religion shall be permitted.[10]

This famous article, still in force, establishes two grades of religion in Spain: the state religion which enjoys official protection, and the other religions which do not enjoy official protection. Protestants as well as Jews belong outside privileged territory. The law also establishes two kinds of religious practice: the permissible "private" practice, and the non-permissible "outward" practice. Both the word "private" and the word "outward" are ambiguous, since the distinctions are not defined.

The most reactionary of the leaders of the Catholic hierarchy tend to interpret the law as limiting Protestant manifestations to private homes. Some Protestants counter this misinterpretation with an extreme view of their own, that the law permitting Protestantism actually allows every privilege except that of official street processions. For about two years after the Charter was promulgated, Protestant chapels showed some growth and Protestant missionaries operated more openly than they had before. But the Franco government had never intended to permit such growth.

When it realized that growth was taking place, the police clamped down with harsh measures.

Incidentally, the period of comparative charity toward Protestantism in the early 1940s is often emphasized in Catholic propaganda in the United States concerning Spain. When a writer in the American Catholic press attempts to prove that Spain grants "religious liberty" to Protestants, he is likely to cite a ruling or practice from the period of 1945 to 1948, omitting all mention of the fact that the most serious suppressions of Protestantism by Franco developed after these dates.

If the Franco regime in the law of 1945 had actually intended to give to Protestants the liberties granted to non-state cults in such countries as the United States, the law could have provided for the right to build churches, to assemble in such churches, to employ clergymen, to conduct funerals, to hold religious processions in public, and to publish religious literature. It could even have allowed the operation of religious schools. All of these basic rights, which the Catholic Church successfully claims in such countries as the United States, are left hanging in the air in Spain, and most of them are denied outright.

The Spanish Protestants did not have long to wait to discover how empty were the promises about the "private" practice of worship in the Charter. Old Protestant churches, etablished before the Civil War, frequently were left unmolested so long as they observed the rule that they must not look like churches architecturally. New churches were, almost everywhere, obstructed, prohibited or actually torn down by mobs or the police. The whole process of suppression and persecution—except the physical violence involved —was instigated and applauded by the Catholic Church.

As soon as Spanish Protestants began to exericse some of the alleged liberties granted them by the Charter, Church authorities countered with their own pressure in behalf of a narrow interpretation of the phraseology. As a result of this Church pressure, Franco's Ministry of Interior in 1948 issued a secret decree, which was finally made public in 1950, interpreting the Charter in such a way that most Protestant activities were outlawed. The decree declared that by "private worship," the law meant "strictly personal worship, or services inside the building consecrated to the denomination in question." And the decree added:

In consequence, all propaganda or proselytizing for non-Catholic religions is illicit, whatever the methods used, as for instance the founding of schools for teaching, the distribution of gifts, supposedly with charitable intent; the operation of recreational centers, summer camps, etc.; for these would obviously be outward ceremonies or demonstrations, which are not allowed.[11]

This decree accurately represented the policy of the Vatican itself. In a famous article on "The Condition of Protestants in Spain," in *Civilta Catolica* (April 1948), the Jesuit priest Father F. Cavalli said:

The Catholic Church being convinced by reason of her Divine prerogatives, that she is the one true Church, claims for herself alone the right to freedom, for this right may only be possessed by truth and never by error. Where the other religions are concerned, she will not take up the sword against them, but she will ask that, by lawful means worthy of the human creature, they shall not be allowed to propagate false doctrine. Consequently in a State where the majority of the people are Catholic, the Church asks that error shall not be accorded a legal existence, and that if religious minorities exist they shall have a *de facto* existence only, not the opportunity of spreading their beliefs.

Where material circumstances—whether the hostility of a Government or the numerical strength of dissenting factions—do not allow of this principle being applied in all its entirety, the Church requires that she shall have all possible concessions, confining herself to accepting as the least of all evils the *de jure* toleration of other forms of worship. The Catholic Church would be betraying her mission if she were to proclaim either in theory or in practice that error can have the same rights as truth, especially when the highest duties and interests of man are at stake. The Church can feel no shame at her intransigence as she asserts it in principle and carries it out in practice, though the Areopagus of the nations today may smile pityingly or rage against it as tyrannical.

While this famous statement in the highest Jesuit magazine in the world produced a considerable shock in non-Catholic circles in many countries, it produced no shock whatever in Spain. Father Cavalli was simply expressing the traditional outlook of the Vatican toward the problem of religious liberty for non-Catholics in an overwhelmingly Catholic country.

The chief editor of *Civilta Catolica* is appointed by the Pope himself. Two months after publication of Father Cavalli's analysis, his theories were justified in a joint pastoral letter by the Spanish bishops as a "magnificent defense of our position on Catholic unity." The bishops saw nothing in their policies or in the Cavalli statement "incompatible with serenity, understanding, gentleness and the true charity that Christ teaches us to practice even with respect to our enemies."

As the Church's representatives began their long negotiations with Franco for the new 1953 Concordat, there was no inclination whatever in Rome or Madrid to recognize the rights of Spanish Protestants even in the abstract. The Primate of Spain, Cardinal Pla y Deniel, a political creature of Franco who had won his post by his pro-Franco activities during the Civil War, told Homer Bigart of the New York *Herald-Tribune* in January 1949 that the guarantee to worship privately for *foreign* Protestants was a "sort of friendly action toward foreigners living in Spain." [12] The friendliness did not extend to Spanish Protestants. The cardinal deplored any guarantee of the right of public worship for Spanish non-Catholics because of "the danger that some political minorities would take advantage of these ceremonies to disseminate their propaganda." Bigart declared: "The Protestant in Spain remains a second-class citizen under the Falangist government. He may practice his religion in a semi-clandestine atmosphere. Proselytizing is strictly forbidden. . . . The Protestant clergyman in Spain suffers much the same type of persecution as the Roman Catholic clergy endure in Communist Hungary."

If there was any inclination on Franco's part to relax the restrictions on Protestant activity it was soon snuffed out by pronouncements from the hierarchy. "It would be an error," said *Ecclesia,* "for anyone to believe that the charter of Spanish rights is legal justification for the opening of chapels, the publications of reviews and pamphlets, the distribution of Bibles which are not Catholic, or propaganda of any kind."

Cardinal Segura was more violent in opposing Protestantism than most other Catholic leaders. In 1955 he berated the Spanish government from his pulpit in the Seville Cathedral for its "softness" in permitting any Protestant churches to proselytize at all.[13] However, other Spanish prelates were almost as extreme. The Archbishop of Saragossa pinned the labels "ignorant" and "decadent" on those "bad Spaniards" who became "internal enemies" of the nation by embracing Protestantism. "The law in Spain," he insisted, "does not permit either the public worship of other religions nor the diffusion of their doctrines, and they can engage in acts of proselytism only fraudulently and by flouting the vigilance of the authorities." [14]

The Franco government put its seal of approval on this prohibition of all Protestant proselyting when the Minister of Foreign Affairs in a letter to Rev. Paul E. Freed in 1952 said: "It must be taken into account that neither the *Fuero de los Espanoles,* the fundamental constitutional mandate of the Spanish people, nor our Concordat with the Holy See, gives power to the government to authorize Protestant proselytism, by which is understood the winning over of new proselytes. The Government may not go beyond that which the legal text authorizes." [15]

When the 1953 Concordat with the Vatican was made public, it became apparent that Franco had granted the Church virtually everything that it could desire in the way of repressive power over Protestantism. The Concordat guaranteed only "the free and public worship of the Catholic religion," and no other. In explaining what Article I of the Concordat meant when it established Catholicism as "the sole religion of the Spanish nation," the Protocol of the Concordat referred citizens to Article 6 of the Spanish Charter which gives Protestants rights of private worship, but no "outward" rights. The Concordat, although it did not once use the words "Protestant" or "Evangelical" or "Jew," established and confirmed a whole system of discrimination against Protestants and Jews.

I shall discuss later the practical application of these policies to marriage and burial. Let it be said here that the wording of the Concordat justifies both the Church and Franco in their joint policy of suppressing all non-Catholic cults. There is not a word in the instrument establishing religious liberty for non-Catholics. The details of the Concordat are important in themselves but not half so important as the underlying fact that in the second half of the twentieth century the Roman Catholic Church, with full power to revise its policy concerning church and state, chose to suppress religious liberty for non-Catholics in that nation where it possessed the greatest power. The Church felt no obligation to practice reciprocity in religious freedom in return for the freedom which Catholicism had been granted in Protestant countries.

The Present Position

In May 1959, Benjamin Welles of the *New York Times* declared in a dispatch to his paper: "In the last few years, at least thirty Protestant chapels or other places of worship have been ordered closed. . . . within the last year all provincial governors have received confidential instructions prejudicial to Protestant interests . . . reliably understood to direct civil governors to start gradually closing all Protestant places of worship that do not have express written authorization from the Government." [16]

Two months later I was able to verify many particulars regarding Mr. Welles' summary in almost every corner of Spain by visiting and photographing various closed Protestant churches. Some of them had been wrecked by Franco's police. Several bore the brown-paper seals used by the Spanish police in closing churches, such as Pastor Nunez' Baptist Church in Madrid.

Nominally there are about 230 Spanish Protestant congregations in Spain, of which 70 to 80 have paid pastors. (The number cannot be determined exactly because there are no official Protestant statistics in Spain and there is a considerable disagreement as to what a "congregation" is. Small congregations are being formed and disbanded quite frequently.) Spanish Protestants are not united either in theological outlook or in corporate life, although nearly all of them have recently united in mutual defense of religious liberty under a newly organized Spanish Protestant Defense Commission with offices in Madrid. This Defense Commission is an agent of the Protestant churches themselves, not an independent unit.

The largest groupings of Spanish Protestants are in the Spanish Evangelical Church (*Iglesia Evangelica Espanola*) which brings together Methodists, Presbyterians and Lutherans; the Baptist organizations, which may be somewhat larger than the Spanish Evangelical Church but which are divided into several entities; the Plymouth Brethren denomination which at one time was the largest single evangelical grouping in Spain; and the independent Episcopal Reformed Church of Spain which has only a small membership, but is particularly important because it has as its head the chairman of the Spanish Protestant Defense Commission, Bishop Molina. The Seventh Day Adventists have a small sector of the

Protestant total but they do not cooperate actively with other denominations.

Nearly all the Protestant congregations in Spain get some financial support from abroad, a very substantial portion of which comes from Baptist organizations in the United States. Some American missionaries participate in Spanish church work as advisers and cooperators, and help in the operation of two small underground seminaries, but, under a new policy, all the official direction of Spanish Protestant churches is now put in the hands of native Spaniards.

If an American visitor sets out to locate a Spanish Protestant Church or a Spanish Protestant pastor, he will immediately find himself in difficulties. The Spanish newspapers never mention such institutions or individuals, or list their names or services. A pastor's name cannot be found in any telephone book or city directory, as a pastor. Even Protestant real estate is not listed in the names of Protestant organizations in the public records, since there is no such thing in Spanish law as a Protestant corporation.

The Franco tourist authorities have recently taken to printing the addresses of a few non-Catholic institutions for Spaniards on a small blue card inserted in Madrid tourist guides for foreign visitors. The facts are printed in English and this creates a favorable impression on visiting tourists, but the Spanish-speaking natives do not receive such information.

Protestant clergymen are forbidden to carry professional cards as clergymen, and this is a very serious handicap in Spain since all Spanish citizens are required to carry identification cards with fingerprints, giving a statement of their occupation. The Protestant clergyman must be considered a clerk, or a student, or a teacher, or librarian, but never a clergyman. I located one Protestant clergyman in a northern Spanish city who was allowed to carry a certificate as a Protestant clergyman, issued in 1957, but he declared that the government had not issued such a certificate to any other Protestant minister since that date.

I also located a small illegal "Directory" of Protestant churches and pastors in Spain in pamphlet form, circulated underground and containing nine pages of Protestant names. There was pathos in the small inscription printed on the first page of this illegal "Directory," a quotation from Article 6 of the Spanish Charter of 1945: "No one shall be disturbed because of his religious beliefs or the private practice of his worship."

The architectural plans for a Protestant church for Spaniards must not contain any distinctive ecclesiastical features facing the street.[17] These features must be strictly secular. I attended Spanish Protestant services in Madrid with as many as four hundred in the congregation, but a passerby on the street would not know that the church was located in that spot except for the sound of congregational singing.

In such matters there is no general rule that can be applied to Spain, since local governors and city architects vary in their amiability according to the severity of the pressures exerted by local Catholic bishops. Any feature of any Protestant church building may be declared contrary to the Spanish Charter and the 1953 Concordat as a "public manifestation" of a non-Catholic faith if a local official is inclined to condemn it. The general practice is to refuse any Protestant church the right to build any entirely new structure. One of the leading Protestant churches of Madrid was held up for many months in the construction of an inner auditorium, entirely invisible from the street, simply because the wall behind the pulpit was curved and the official architect would not approve a curved wall. He said it looked too much like the apse of a Catholic Church. A compromise was finally effected when the Protestant pastor agreed to reshape the curve in the form of a hexagon. Usually the Protestant churches in the cities are housed in underprivileged residential areas, often in narrow alleys in slum districts.

The Record Speaks

Generally this systematic suppression of Protestantism in Spain is represented in the American Catholic press as merely a denial of the right to hold street meetings or processions. Such evasions do not deceive the independent American newspaper correspondents in Spain. With a few exceptions they are reasonably candid about telling the American public the truth—although the American public rarely listens. Benjamin Welles of the *New York Times* has summarized in a number of articles many of the disabilities described in this chapter. Richard Scott Mowrer, correspondent of the *Christian Science Monitor* and other American newspapers, published on November 2, 1959, a list of eight disabilities of Spanish Protestants. They included ample evidence to justify his title, "Discrimination in Spain."

Since the American Catholic press has so frequently denied

the basic facts of the situation, there is justification here for printing the names and locations of twenty-eight churches of Spanish Protestants which have been closed in recent years, or denied permission to open. I am also printing the names of five which have now reopened. The list was supplied and verified by the Protestant Defense Commission of Madrid in 1959, and revised and verified in 1961. I visited many of these churches in 1959, photographed them and, in some cases, examined the structural ruins after police raids.

List of Churches Closed and Reopened

1. *Baptist*

Altea (Alicante)	Denied permit for worship.
Lorca (Murcia)	Permit denied. Worship celebrated without license.
Cartagena	Permit denied. Worship celebrated without license.
Valencia. Grao	Permission denied to open. Permanently locked.
Valencia. 2nd Church	Permit denied. Worship celebrated clandestinely.
Denia (Alicante)	Permit denied. Worship celebrated without license.
Elche	Church closed since 1959.
Elda	Permit denied. Worship celebrated without license.
Murcia	Permit denied. Worship celebrated without license.
Santa Cruz (Tenerife)	Permit denied. Worship celebrated without license.
Malaga	Permit denied. Worship celebrated without license.
Madrid. Usera	Church closed since 1954.
Jaen	Permit denied. Worship celebrated without license.

2. *Methodist and Episcopal*

Saragossa	Permit denied. Worship celebrated without license.
Badajoz	Permit denied. Worship celebrated without license.

Salamanca	Permit denied. Worship celebrated without license.
Jaca	Permit denied. Worship celebrated without license.
Alicante	Permit denied. Worship celebrated without license.

3. *Assemblies of God*

Infesta (Orense)	Permit denied. Worship celebrated without license.
San Clodio (Lugo)	Permit denied. Worship celebrated without license.
Archena (Murcia)	Permit denied. Worship celebrated without license.

4. *Spanish Evangelical Churches*

Alde Hermosa (Jaen)	Permit denied, and church closed.
Chiclana (Jaen)	Permit denied, and church closed.
Palencia	Ordered to suspend worship in March 1961.
Medina Del Campo	Ordered to suspend worship in 1961.
Tarrasa (Bethel)	Closed for illegal worship, but continuing.
Carcagente	Ordered suspended in March 1961.
Puerto Sagunto	Permit denied. Worship celebrated without license.

Reopenings

Figueras (U.E.B.)	Reopened for worship July 19, 1960.
Vigo (A.H.)	Reopened for worship September 9, 1960.
Seville (U.E.B.)	Reopened for worship December 30, 1960.
Pueblo Nuevo (I.E.E.)	Reopened by verbal order in 1960.
Barcelona. Verdi (F.I.E.)	Reopened by verbal order in 1960.

The Spanish authorities are shrewd enough not to execute or imprison Protestant pastors or leading laymen simply for operating their churches without the required permits. No long prison terms are imposed, and Protestant prisoners are usually treated with reasonable courtesy by the police—unless they are also charged with being Masons.

Usually the suppression of a Protestant congregation is accomplished more by harassment than by physical demolition. The favorite device for harassment is the denial by local authorities of all the necessary permits for operation, or prolonged delay in their issuance. If this is not enough to discourage the congregation, raids, arrests and short detentions may be resorted to. Under Franco's law a Protestant arrested for opening his church or holding an unauthorized meeting in his house is not entitled to any formal trial—he can be summarily handled by the police without publicity or delay.

The accepted pattern is to arrest a few Protestant leaders of any congregation which insists on trying to meet without a permit, after complaint by the local priest. They are then taken to a police station, penalized by a small fine, and warned not to do it again. If the offense is repeated, the fine is increased. Perhaps police seals are put upon the doors—long strips of brown paper containing announcement that the place is closed by legal order. If these seals are broken and the building is used for a church service, the walls and furniture may be demolished. The extreme remedy of demolition is rarely resorted to.

If any parallel persecution of a minority religion took place in the United States, the student could go to written transcripts of testimony, detailed briefs, lengthy court decisons and the files of the great newspapers. The student of Catholic persecution of Protestantism in Spain has none of these resources. At least 99 per cent of all cases involving Protestantism are summarily decided without briefs, written testimony, or detailed decisions. Only the Protestant organizations themselves keep any lists of the victims of this process, and only in recent months has the tabulation been centralized.

Here are my notes on a few sample cases listed by the newly organized Protestant Defense Commission, mostly from eastern Spain where I was able to visit several of the defendants and see for myself the devastation wrought by Franco's police. The verifying documents, which I examined in Jativa, Valencia, are in the files of the Reverend Jose Cardona Gregori, Secretary of the Protestant Defense Commission, Madrid.[18]

1. *The case of the Christmas pageant.* Document 58,

January 11, 1957, Navarres, Valencia. Some passages from the Bible were dramatized indoors, with a manger, in the presence of about sixty Baptists in a meeting place whose use had been approved for ordinary worship services. Denounced by local priest and the archbishop of Valencia. Fine of 500 pesetas on owner of building, Joaquin Calatayud Garcia, because "you have celebrated a theatrical evening without permission of proper authority."

2. *The case of the disdainful Protestant.* Case 1361, Elda, Alicante, fine imposed August 2, 1957. Vicente Belda Miralles of Francisco Alonso 20, Elda, in conversation with friends about religion on town promenade, was overheard. Charged with making "in public a disdainful comment against the ecclesiastical authority involving disparagement of religious principles." No disorder; no specifications; no discussion of Catholicism, but defendant mentioned Protestantism. Fine: 1,000 pesetas.

3. *The case of the unmarried defiant.* Twenty-three Spanish Baptists of Jativa, Valencia, arrested for attending a baptism by their church in Rio Albaida, a regular event up to that time. (File numbers at civil government headquarters dated December 10, 1954.) No violence; no resistance; no trial. Total fines: 6,010 pesetas. The pastor, Jose Cardona Gregori, was not compelled to pay his fine because his name was Jose and the day of the offense was St. Joseph's saint's day. Five single young men and young ladies refused to pay their fines and spent eight to fifteen days in jail. Their names are Carlos Duet, Jose Garcia Arnau, Manolita Duet, Lidia Garcia Arnau and Carmen Baldres.

4. *The case of the pastor and the landlady.* In Navarres, Valencia, a Protestant pastor, Aurelio del Campo Santamaria, arrived in town December 14, 1953. Told by provincial governor, Diego Sala Pombo, on December 17 to leave town. Pastor demanded order in writing; was served same day with three documents fining him (1) 1,000 pesetas in document 2534 "because you have committed public scandal"; (2) 1,000 pesetas in document 2535 for "diffusing an unauthorized publication"; (3) 1,000 pesetas in document 2536 "because you have been apprehended in blasphemy." Refused to pay fines and served one month in jail. His landlady was fined 1,000 pesetas in order 2532 "for refusing to grant your house to a teacher," although no teacher wished to rent it at that time.

5. *The case of American food for Catholics only.* In Jativa,

Valencia, the Baptist pastor, Jose Cardona Gregori, asked the local Catholic diocesan office in a letter dated May 27, 1958, for the right of his members to share in the food supplied largely by the United States government and distributed exclusively in Spain by the Catholic agency, *Caritas*. He specified aid for Protestant persons suffering from tuberculosis, nursing mothers and small children. Abbot Juan Vaya Bonet replied on his stationery: "The articles given by *Caritas Diocesan* are distributed among the poor whose names I have in my parish files. . . . The parish is not likely to get and give food to those who spend large sums in spreading error. Let God enlighten you!" (The ICA reports the Catholic Relief Services as the only American agency distributing surplus agricultural goods financed by the United States in Spain.)

ʼ   6. *The case of the wrecked church in Elche.* In Elche, Alicante, Reverend Jose Bonifacio, after six petitions to the governor in two years for a permit for a meetinghouse for his small congregation, was refused authority to remodel the interior of a dwelling for worship services, and the refusal in this case was finally confirmed by the Spanish Supreme Court on May 20, 1957. The interior of the building at Benito Perez Galdos 29, was demolished by the police in December 1958 after it had been remodeled, and police seals were attached saying: "Closed by order of the governor of this province." (I photographed the seals and examined the wreckage on August 5, 1959.)

These things are still going on. From time to time the Franco press allows reports to go out that the regime is liberalizing its policy in respect to Protestants, but there have been no basic or general changes in that policy in recent years. Tolerance is spasmodic and irregular. The Protestants never know when a fanatical local official, goaded by a local bishop, will deprive them of their limited privileges.

In May and June 1961, after I had left Spain, an old and established Protestant church in Saragossa was abruptly closed, and a pastor in Jaen was arbitrarily fined. According to the Protestant Defense Commission, the Brethren Chapel of Saragossa was closed by the Spanish police on June 9, 1961, at 11 A.M., and the doors sealed on the ground that "it did not have permission to function." Actually, it did have official permission to hold worship services under a permit, No. 708 of the Superior Headquarters of the Saragossa police, issued December 7, 1949, and it had been in existence for more than thirty years. In the province of Jaen on May

5, 1961, Document 210 of Jodar shows that on that date Pastor Narciso Nunez and Andres Perez Leon, a neighbor, were each fined 5,000 pesetas on the charge that an evangelical worship service was held in the house of Senor Perez Leon because seven people had gathered to see some colored slides of Bible stories.

The facts about these policies of the repression of Protestants in Spain, as we shall see, are systematically understated and misstated in the American Catholic press, and treated with elaborate inattention by the State Department of the United States. Independent scholars, however, have frequently spoken out against these policies in no uncertain language. Professor Arthur Whitaker of the University of Pennsylvania, in his summary of the Spanish situation, *Spain and Defense of the West* (1961), says flatly: "There is less religious freedom in Spain today for non-Catholics than in any European country."

5. THE MASONS AND THE JEWS

There are three classes of persons in Spanish society today
who are at least as low as the Protestants, in status. They are the
Communists, the Masons and the Jews. In Spanish Catholic propaganda the Masons are more often associated with the Communists than are the Jews, but the propaganda against both is severe.
The present—not the past—opposition to Jews is more moderate than to Masons, partly because the tiny communities of professing Jews in Spain have assumed a relatively passive role for
several centuries. They never attempt to proselyte, and proselytism is the unforgivable sin in the eyes of the Spanish hierarchy.

Occasionally in European Catholic propaganda Masons, Jews
and Communists are accused of participating jointly and consciously
in a general world conspiracy to destroy the Catholic Church.
This view was promoted in the highest Catholic publication in
the Irish Republic during the Spanish Civil War—and of course it
was vigorously promoted within Spain itself. Said Father James A.
Cleary, writing on "Smoke Screen Over Spain" in the September
1938 *Irish Ecclesiastical Record,* the official organ of the Irish
Catholic hierarchy: "It is natural enough that men who lack
Christian training, and who are urged by a craze for notoriety,
should fall easy victims to the subtle Communist propaganda which,
supported by the great Jewish news agencies, the Masonic societies
and by Communist finance, has, for the past two years, been engaged in spreading a dense smoke screen of falsehood and prejudice over unhappy Spain."

A strong movement developed in Ireland for intervention on
Franco's side during the Spanish Civil War, and it was quite definitely anti-masonic as well as anti-Semitic. It was led by Father
Dennis Fahey, leader of the Republic's right-wing Catholic organization, Maria Duce. Father Fahey frequently coupled Masonry, Judaism and Communism in his writings as the three-headed
devils who were bent on destroying the Catholic Church. His best-

selling book, *The Mystical Body of Christ in the Modern World,* printed under official Church imprimatur, ascribed the republican movement in Spain to "Judeo-Communist agents," denounced the "Masonic League of Nations," and suggested that "Marxism is simply one of the weapons of Jewish nationalism." [1]

In Spain the coupling of Judaism, Masonry and Communism in both government and Church propaganda is still quite common, although it is not as prevalent as it was immediately after the Civil War. In 1939 a widely used syllabus for Spanish high schools contained the characteristic outline: "Freemasonry and international Jewish finance cause the fall of the Monarchy. The Second Republic. Its international and anti-Catholic propaganda." [2]

The Masonic Criminals

The opposition to Masons is so extreme that a special joint court, composed originally of three generals, has been created for trying Communists and Masons. It is a court for "subversives," operated with ruthless cruelty. "Criminals" who are arraigned in this court do not have even the meager protection of the ordinary criminal courts of Spain. They are handled as traitors against Spanish society until they have proved their innocence of Masonic taint, and in attempting to submit such proof they are denied due process of law. At least two thousand Masons have been imprisoned under this special system of persecution, and many have been executed. Masonic membership is a crime per se and persons charged with the offense do not have the protection of a civil trial.

Children in Spanish schools are taught opposition to Masonry in very tender years. Masons, they are told, are virtually devils. Here are typical sentences in the elementary instruction book, *Nuevo ripalda,*[3] which describe Masonry:

Q. What is Masonry?

A. A perverse association which, with apparent humanitarian purposes, is plotting in its mysterious way to ruin society and the Church.

Q. What means does it use for accomplishing such perverse purposes?

A. Crime, hypocrisy and mystery.

Q. What sin do those commit who belong to a Masonic organization?

A. A most grave sin which causes them to incur excommunication by the Church.

In *Yo soy espanol,* a standard textbook for children, by Augustin Serrano de Haro, chief inspector of primary schools in Granada, the description of the Spanish Civil War includes the following sentences:

There were many Socialists and many Masons in Spain, and very little fear of God.

The Socialists urged on the poor against the rich.

The Masons wanted a revolution to take place.

And since there was very little fear of God, there was very little charity, and the Commandments were not observed.

That is why the Republic came. And with the Republic the peace was lost. Churches and convents were burned and once again Spaniards were fighting against each other.

This Spanish Catholic attitude toward Masonry is not wholly distinctive. It is based upon the highest official teaching of Rome. Nine popes, beginning with Clement XII in 1738, have issued bulls or encyclicals against Masonry. To this day even in the United States, where Masonry is by no means united in opposing Catholicism, no Catholic may knowingly, under Catholic law, become a Mason.

Nominally, there are no exceptions; for the worldwide Catholic rule, expressed in Canon 2335, reads: "Those who join a Masonic sect or other societies of the same sort, which plot against the Church or against legitimate civil authority, incur *ipso facto* an excommunication reserved to the Holy See." The skillful coupling of Masonry with hostile religious sects and subversion is characteristic of both Spanish Catholicism and the Vatican itself.[4]

A dark image of subversive conspiracy is conjured up. Emphasis is placed upon the element of secrecy, particularly if the secrecy is alleged to contain any religious ritual. Socialism and Communism are usually dragged in. Alleged socialist and Communist connections are mentioned in the highest official attacks on Masonry, even the United States, where it would be difficult to find a body of citizens less friendly to socialism and Communism.

In Spain the Catholic people are never told about those mild and constructive forms of Masonry which have developed in North

America. The Catholic press in Spain constantly features the most severe attacks on the organization which it can secure in the foreign press. In its issue of March 21, 1959, *Ecclesia* featured the attack on Masonry made that year by the Argentine bishops under the heading: "Communism and Masonry Among the Roots of Modern Apostasy." The attack began by quoting Leo XIII in his encyclical *Humanum Genus*: "The first thing you must do is to try to take the mask from the Masons so that you may know them for what they are." Then Pius XII is quoted as supporting the same severe gospel in 1958 when he scored "the roots of modern apostasy, scientific atheism, dialectical materialism, rationalism, laicism and Masonry, common mother of all these." It would seem that Masonry rather than the love of money is the root of all evil!

The Argentine bishops are quoted as ending their attack on Communism and Masonry with a flourish: "To those who feel in their innermost hearts love for the Fatherland, we point to Communism and Masonry as enemies of our traditions and our future greatness. They long for the destruction of everything which is noble and sacred in our land." [5]

In the completely controlled Spanish press it is not necessary to prove charges of subversion against Masons. Any revolt against the authority of the Church or the authority of a Catholic chief of state is likely to be traced to "international Freemasonry." When the Portuguese cruise liner *Santa Maria* was seized in the Caribbean in 1961 by an anti-Salazar "pirate," Henrique Galvao, Madrid's Catholic Action daily *Ya* blamed the cautious and non-punitive treatment accorded Galvao by the United States on the machinations of international Masonry in the British and American governments. [6] In *Ya*'s vocabulary, liberalism, Masonry and subversion are all tainted with anti-clericalism, and the whole mixture is somehow connected with Moscow.

In mitigation of *Ya*'s attack on Galvao, it should be said that the comic opera seizure of the *Santa Maria* was actually the beginning of an attempted revolution in Portugal, as well as in Spain, which undoubtedly would have destroyed a large part of the power of the Catholic Church in both countries if it had succeeded. It would be quite surprising if the body of revolutionists involved in this enterprise did not include some Communists as well as some Masons.

The Historic Conflict

The Catholic battle against Masonic organizations has a long history, and the enmity has been mutual. European Masonry, particularly Continental Masonry, has been much more partisan and political than corresponding Masonic organizations in the United States. Certain European lodges have been not only anti-clerical but also openly anti-Catholic from the beginning. At one time the Grand Orient of France eliminated from its rituals all statements indicating a belief in God. Spanish Masonry has not tended toward atheism, but it has tended toward republican as well as anti-clerical ideas. Its leaders were conspicuous opponents of Franco before, during and after the Civil War. (In Italy the corresponding Masonic leaders were sufficiently anti-Fascist to earn the abolition of their lodges by Mussolini in 1925).

Manuel Azana, the most important prime minister during the Republic's life, was both a Mason and a vigorous anti-clerical, and at least six of his cabinet members were said to be members of Masonic lodges. Throughout Spanish history the Masons and the Jesuits have been implacable enemies, working at opposite extremes of the religious spectrum. Masonic pressure was given credit for the dissolution of the Jesuit organizations under the Republic, and for the earlier expulsion of the Jesuits.

It was natural that the most effective opposition to Church power in Spain should come from a secret society, since open opposition has been banned ever since the days of the Inquisition. When anti-clericalism went underground as Franco rose to power, the very secrecy of the Masonic orders proved a source of strength. Lovers of liberty met by night during the Inquisition, and they still meet by night in Franco's Spain.

Freemasonry came to Spain in the first place from England, well after the Reformation, and it was doubly suspect as coming from an alien land and a Protestant nation which was Spain's strongest military enemy. The Grand Lodge of England first gave a license to establish a branch at Gibraltar in 1726, and by 1734 there were four lodges in Madrid. Their members were drawn largely from the free-thinking aristocracy of the time who were politically and religiously anti-clerical. Professor Madariaga has suggested a certain connection between early Spanish Masonry and Judaism, since there was a resemblance between some of the symbols used by each group.[7] Today there is no connection between the two in Spain, unless it is that natural sympathy which tends to spring up between persecuted minorities.

After the Vatican had condemned Masonry in a papal bull in 1738, the Spanish government dutifully banned the secret society in its colonies fourteen years later. In colonial Mexico, Masons were hunted out and punished by the Mexican Inquisition. In spite of such persecution, Spanish Masonry survived through the eighteenth and nineteenth centuries, and many strong lodges existed at the time of the Spanish Civil War.

During the Republic, the lodges came out in the open. This was exceedingly unfortunate for those members who were publicly identified, since they were later victimized even before the end of the Republic. To be on a Masonic list was as serious as being on a Red list. Members of the armed forces in nationalist territory were prohibited from joining most Masonic lodges and in 1939, on assuming power, Franco outlawed Masonry altogether in a decree which was really an ex post facto law. It not only punished Masons for current membership but also ordered them to divulge old secrets and surrender the names of their former lodge associates to the secret police.

In nationalist territory—and ultimately in the larger Spanish territory—some twelve thousand Spaniards were accused of the crime of being Masons. If specific "rebellious" conduct could be added to this charge, they often died before a firing squad. Their sentences were likely to be graded according to their rank within the Masonic lodges. Anyone possessing the eighteenth or higher degree received a more severe sentence. In one anti-Masonic orgy of the Civil War in Malaga in 1937, eighty Spanish Masons were executed by that ancient instrument of savagery, the garrote, a collapsible iron collar which is squeezed about the throat until death comes. In 1938, Franco issued a special order directing that all Masonic symbols should be removed from the gravestones of any Masons buried within nationalist territory.[8]

This savage anti-Masonic policy was partly the fruit of the bitter Civil War. Many conservative politicians and generals had been Masons before 1931 without losing their social and military standing. Franco reasoned that a Mason who continued to be a Mason after 1931, and particularly after 1936, was likely to be a militant republican—and there was some truth in this assumption.

Today there is virtually nothing left of Masonry in Spain. The Supreme Council of the Spanish organization established itself in exile in Mexico City in 1943, but its affiliated members do not dare to resume any open activity on Spanish soil. Those Masonic leaders I met in Spain on my latest visit seemed profoundly discouraged about the future. They recognized that their primary enemy was not the Franco regime itself but the Church, and that the Church was likely to stay in partial power for a long time. They believed that nothing short of an anti-clerical revolution could restore their right to exist and to develop.

At the present time any evidence of past membership, in a Masonic lodge, even of membership in the distant past, is still used as an excuse for extra punishment for any victim. I was told of one eminent republican prisoner in one of Franco's jails who had been granted amnesty and release. Suddenly it was discovered that he had once, many years before, written a magazine article in which he had said something favorable about Masonry. His amnesty was immediately cancelled and he was sent back to prison for a long term. Herbert Matthews in his *The Yoke and the Arrows* tells of the severity of the Spanish police in excluding all Masons for "security reasons" from employment in the construction of the oil pipeline used by American bases in Spain. The police would clear even former Communists and Anarchists for employment, but not Masons.

Probably Franco himself would not resort to such vengeful policies if it were not for the vindictive attitude of the higher clergy. The bishops, and particularly the Jesuits, continue to see in Masonry their chief political enemy, and this attitude apparently has the support of the Vatican.

Franco's extreme cruelty to Masons has produced some reaction in the United States Congress. Since nearly half the members of Congress are Masons, and since they have voted Franco many millions in aid in recent years, it is not surprising that they have been disturbed by his anti-Masonic policies. In the summer of 1959 a group of American congressmen, during the course of a visit to Spain, insisted on bringing to the personal attention of Franco the fact that many Masonic members were still languishing in Spanish prisons for the sole offense of previous Masonic membership. Why, they asked, should American Masonic Congressmen continue to pour millions of dollars worth of American aid into Franco's coffers when he did not even grant elementary justice to their fellow lodge members? Franco took the suggestion graciously—or sagaciously—and quietly released a considerable number of Spanish Masons. There was no publicity about the matter either in the United States or in Spain.

Meanwhile in the Catholic press of the United States, Masonry, Protestantism and "Marxism" are being coupled in a rather astonishing manner. The leading diocesan chain newspaper of American Catholicism, the *Register* of Denver, in a 1956 editorial on comparative freedom in Ireland and Spain, justified the suppression of Protestants in the latter country partly because they were so small in number and partly because they were infiltrated by foreigners, Masons and "Marxists" who were "strongly imbued with foreign and revolutionary ideas." This official American Catholic paper quoted the charge of the Bishop of Vizcarra that among the alleged 477 Protestant preachers in Spain were "13 Masons, 6 who were gravely suspected of being Masons, 68 Marxists, and 63 foreigners. Moreover, it is known and admitted that one of the groups working in Spain, Jehovah's Witnesses, has Masonic encouragement." The *Register* noted that "adherence to Catholicity in Spain has been a test of patriotism." [9]

Anti-Semitism in Education

Although the Vatican has been moving away from official anti-Semitism in recent years, the Spanish Church and state still promulgate and promote a certain amount of anti-Semitic doctrine in the schools and in general literature. Jewry and Masonry are frequently connected in political speeches in much the same way as Communism and atheism. The Jew is a convenient whipping boy, and Spanish literature which summarizes his shortcomings is not always very much more accurate than the notorious Protocols of the Elders of Zion.

Franco was especially zealous in denouncing Jews in the period when it seemed possible that Hitler would be the victor in World War II. At a Falange meeting in 1941 he lumped together plutocrats, liberals and Jews as enemies of the people in a way worthy of Hitler at his eloquent worst. Then he added: "The Allies made a mistake when they declared the war, and they have lost it." [10]

Before the war started, the Spanish Falange echoed much of

the anti-Semitic philosophy of Hitler in its general propaganda, and coupled it with hostility to the United States. *Arriba,* the Madrid Falange daily, in an article in May 1939, declared: "Since in the United States there has come to be recognized the profound bonds which unite the interests of international Judaism with the Yankee world, there begins to be seen clearly the object against which the colossal armament plans of President Roosevelt are directed, the Third Reich." [11]

Franco's actual policies in dealing with Spanish Jews have been much more humane than such quotations would imply. He never accepted all of Hitler's racial fanaticism, and after it seemed likely that Hitler would be defeated in World War II he adopted a military policy that could almost be described as pro-Semitic. He permitted a great many Jews to escape from Hitler's persecutions into Spain during the war, especially if they could prove that they were Sephardic Jews who might claim some vestige of Spanish nationality.

Perhaps there was behind this policy a trace of personal feeling for his mother's people. Franco is partly Jewish himself, although he never discusses the matter publicly. His mother's family name, Bahamonde, is that of a family of Jewish origin which remained in Spain and became Catholic when the great purge of Spanish Jews occurred in the fifteenth century. Sometimes these converted Jews, or Marranos—partly in self-defense—became the most fanatical doctrinal protagonists for Catholicism, but many retained some filial feeling for the people of their family's faith.

Whatever may be Franco's real feelings toward Jews, he has not stopped the traditional flood of anti-Semitic literature, nor has he favored social equality or complete religious freedom for Jews. The textbooks in the national schools still carry openly anti-Semitic diatribes.

I have already cited a typical extract from a syllabus for Spanish high schools coupling Freemasonry and international Jewish finance. More specific and detailed in its anti-Semitism is the textbook previously quoted, *Yo soy espanol,* by Augustin Serrano de Haro, which was brought to my attention by an American writer, Philip Karant. It is the most popular of all primary school histories in Spain, and has gone into twenty-two editions. Its seventeenth edition, bearing official Church approval, tells the little Spanish children that Spain won the desperate struggle against the

Moors in the fifteenth century in spite of the treachery of the Jews
who attempted to betray the nation. In describing the Spanish victory over the Moors, the text says:

> There were then in Spain many Jews, and since the Jews didn't
> like the Spaniards either they told the Moors where they could enter
> in order to overpower Spain. . . . Some treacherous soldiers sided
> with the Moors and the Moors won the Battle of Guadalete, and the
> Moors ran all over Spain. They burned churches and murdered
> Christians. . . .
>
> *Study Suggestions.* . . . Dwell on the treason of the Jews and
> the negligence of the governing Christians—both dangers remain al-
> ways in the life of the fatherland. Provoke repugnance in the heart of
> the children toward the vileness of the traitors and have the children
> write and learn the following phrase: *The Moors overpowered Spain
> because they were helped by the Jews and traitors.*

Chapter 18 of *Yo soy espanol* is called "The Jews Kill a
Child." It is illustrated with three striking pictures in which a Jew
is made to look somewhat repulsive while the young Christian
hero, Santo Domingo de Val, is appropriately angelic in appearance. Here is the substantive text of that chapter:

> Once upon a time Spain had many Jews.
> And the Jews hated Christians and they loathed children who
> loved the Virgin and the Lord.
> Because of this hatred they killed Santo Domingo de Val.
> Dominguito lived in Saragossa and wanted to be a leader.
> One silent afternoon, as he passed by the door of a Jew, the Jew
> set upon him quickly, threw a cloth over his head and dragged him
> into his house and locked him up.
> In the middle of the night the leading Jews got together. They
> tried to take Dominguito's crucifix away from him. They said they
> wanted to trample it. But he replied valiantly, even though he was
> only seven years old.
> "This never, it is my God."
> "Then you will die as your God died," said the Jews.
> And they put a crown of thorns on him and crucified him and
> pierced his breast with a spear.
> And Dominguito died crucified like Our Lord.

The Political Roots of Anti-Semitism

Anti-Semitism in Spain has a much more political flavor than it has in the United States; it is not a matter of exclusive golf clubs or hotels "for Christians only." It has been part of the national political tradition since the fourteenth century, and long before that it was part of the commercial tradition in various parts of the territory which is now Spain. Professor Livermore points out that anti-Semitic legislation goes back as far as Visigothic Spain and the year 613 when it was decreed that Jews had to accept conversion or leave the territory. In 693 unconverted Jews were denied access to the market places and forbidden to trade with Christians. Cecil Roth in *The Spanish Inquisition* describes the great wave of massacres of Spanish Jews in 1391 and says that, although the Inquisition was not supposed to include Jews as such, its first actual task was to search out and punish those Jews whose conversion to Christianity was suspected as fraudulent.[12]

One reason for traditional Spanish anti-Semitism was that Catholicism, with its exclusive claim to state privilege, had become part of the state apparatus. Any faith opposed to Catholicism was inevitably treated as an enemy of the state. Also, the official expulsion of the Jews from Spain in 1492, although it preceded the expulsion of the Moors, was associated with the national drive against those Moors. Because of Spanish anti-Semitism, the Spanish Jews rallied to the side of the Moslem invaders in self-defense, and Christian Spain regarded them as tools of the invaders. A great deal of the political animosity directed against the Moors rubbed off on the Jews. Now Moors and Jews are the bad men of the Spanish past, while Communists, Masons and Protestants are the bad men of the Spanish present.

Some Catholic anti-Semitism also entered Spain from countries like Belgium, England, Germany and the Papal States. Facing continent-wide hostility, the Jews never knew when a "Christian" sovereign might expel them from his country in the name of Christ and that vague value known as national security. England had expelled her Jewish residents two hundred years before the expulsion by Ferdinand and Isabella.

When Ferdinand and Isabella signed the decree expelling

Jews from Spain in 1492, it was fully approved by the Vatican, and these sovereigns were later honored by the Pope for the performance. The expulsion was accomplished in the spirit of the Crusades, and ten years later a parallel order of permanent exile, the Edict of Expulsion of 1502, was issued against the Moslems, with the proviso that Moslem children should be kept in Spain and baptized as Christians. Those Moslem parents who refused to part with their children were virtually forced to accept conversion. They were permitted to stay in Spain only if they completely renounced their religion. Perhaps two hundred thousand of them refused conversion and left the country to become permanent wanderers or to settle in some country in the Mediterranean basin.

The Sephardic Jews, as they came to be called, expelled from the territory now belonging to Portugal as well as from Spain, preserved among themselves the ancient Spanish language of the fifteenth century. They became the aristocrats of European Jewry, more cultured and wealthy than their confreres from northern Europe and Asia. As a matter of community pride they tended to preserve a kind of biological separatism through the centuries.

Professor Madariaga describes the relationship of these exiled Sephardic Jews to Spain as a kind of love-hate relationship. They had loved Spain passionately when they lived there, partly because Spain had given them unusual opportunities for success. Then, when they were unceremoniously driven out, their love was turned to hate. They became the bitterest enemies of the Spanish Empire. Everywhere throughout the world they helped to disrupt and destroy it. They even cooperated with Protestantism because of their hatred for the Church that had been partly instrumental in expelling them.

Probably the story of the Spanish Jews who remained in Spain at the time of the great fifteenth-century purge can never be adequately told. The estimate of their numbers runs all the way from 50,000 to 800,000. Many of them went to Portugal for a time, and then came back quietly. All officially Jewish institutions were destroyed. Although they tended at first to remain segregated, the Jews were gradually absorbed biologically by the Spanish community. That may be one reason why purely racial anti-Semitism has never been popular in Spain. The "best" Spanish families have more than a little Jewish blood. Professor G. G. Coulton says that King Ferdinand himself and even Torquemada came from families with Jewish blood.[13] The biological mixture long antedated the Inquisition.

The Jewish "conversions" to Christianity were naturally suspect, and the converted Jews, Marranos, were watched for signs of heresy. It was Torquemada who urged Isabella to rid her kingdom of all Jews because he thought so many were faking conversion. If they were caught in the performance of any Jewish ritual even "changing into clean personal linen on Saturdays," the Church and state might dispose of them by strangulation or fire. Soon there were none so hardy as to profess Judaism officially in all of Spain.

For about four hundred years Judaism remained absolutely silent. After the revolution of 1868, the Sephardic Jews who lived abroad were assured that the fifteenth-century edict expelling them had been cancelled, and they could return to Spain with guarantees of religious liberty. But the assurance was never made good. Rome, under Pius IX, struck back at the forces of tolerance, and the ancient policy of suppression was resumed. Spanish religious Jews did not dare to come out in the open until the twentieth century. Although they were given complete nominal freedom under the Second Republic, they were not in a good position to take advantage of the brief era of liberty.

Spanish Judaism Today

Today the Jews of Spain who profess the Jewish faith still constitute only a tiny remnant in an officially Catholic nation. They do not choose to be as militant as the Protestants, although as individuals they are higher in the social scale than the Protestants. On the whole, they are subdued and subservient. This is partly because there are so few religious Jews in Spain, perhaps 3,000 in a population of 30 million. There are only two Jewish congregations as against 230 Protestant congregations. Madrid has fifty or sixty families attached to its apartment-house synagogue; Barcelona has perhaps three times as many, meeting in an older and larger synagogue. There are almost no Jewish members in Spain outside of these two centers.

Until 1959, Barcelona had the only real synagogue building in all of Spain, although it was never permitted to look like a synagogue or to carry any external signs of Judaism. Inside its

gray masonry exterior it has quite substantial and handsome
meeting rooms where the orthodox ritual is faithfully observed
and where congregational meetings are undisturbed as long as
there is no "public manifestation" of Judaism. During the summer
of 1959 the Jews of Spain, so far as I could discover, had only one
functioning rabbi in the whole country, the leader of this congregation in Barcelona.

Judaism, of course, is subjected to the same disabilities as Protestantism under the Spanish Charter of 1945 and the Vatican
Concordat of 1953. It is outside the pale of the one true—and privileged—faith. Under this law and treaty the Jewish sect is entitled only to private freedom of worship; any outward manifestation may be quickly suppressed by the police without trial. No
Jewish day schools are permitted or Jewish magazines for general circulation. Jewish burial rites are allowed in Barcelona and
Madrid because of the existence of ancient Jewish cemeteries.
But all the Spanish media of information are closed to anything
that might remotely resemble Jewish religious propaganda.

The Madrid congregation, after being confined for many
years to a dingy basement in an apartment building, was finally
allowed late in 1959 to move to a new and much handsomer building, well equipped internally with a 132-seat auditorium but still
disguised as a non-religious structure. The plans for the new building were maneuvered through the appropriate building bureaus
in Franco's government by strategy and deception. Ownership
papers were filed under private names, and the plans were described as plans for a secular structure. Otherwise, no permit for
construction would ever have been granted.

The government, of course, knew exactly what the new building was designed for, and the appropriate officials looked the other
way at the appropriate moment. This was considered good political strategy so long as the faith of Spain was not disturbed in any
way. The new Spanish "synagogue" could be described in the foreign press as a symbol of Franco's tolerance, while the people of
Spain knew nothing about it. Sure enough, *Time* magazine described it as a full-blown synagogue without mentioning the fact
that it was not permitted to look like a synagogue. One Jewish
leader of Madrid was quoted as expressing gratitude that Madrid
Jews had been permitted their first regular synagogue since 1492.

To some of the synagogue members the dates—1492 to

1960—must have seemed sardonic. It had taken the Jews of the city as long to achieve one disguised synagogue as it had taken two American continents to develop their so-called civilization since their discovery by Columbus. The president of the congregation led the members in a grateful prayer calling upon God to look with kindness upon Franco.

Unlike the Protestants, the Jews of Spain do not operate any illegal and underground printing plants. They buy most of their religious literature in England and New York, and Franco does not interfere with this importation, partly because the amount of the importation is so small and partly because it is never used for proselytism. Jews marry Catholics in Spain so rarely that the problem of mixed marriage is not particularly critical. When a marriage does take place between a Spanish Jew and a Spanish Catholic, special permission must come all the way from Rome, since Catholic Canon Law places Catholic-Jewish marriage one step lower than Catholic-Protestant marriage. The Jews accept this humiliating procedure because there is no alternative. The children of a Jewish-Catholic mixed marriage must be absorbed, of course, into the all-powerful Church, since that is the law of Catholicism in mixed marriage. "I am sending my daughters to Israel to prevent that," said a northern Jewish leader to me in Madrid. "At least they can find Jewish husbands there." And he added wistfully, "It is possible that my grandchildren may be Jews and not Catholics."

An added complication has arisen in recent years to increase the anxiety of the Spanish Jews. Franco has been conspicuously pro-Arab and the new government of Israel has been courageously anti-Franco. Neither has ever recognized the other diplomatically. In 1959 when the Franco government, through Foreign Minister Castiella, publicly renewed its determination not to recognize the Ben Gurion regime, it also gave assurance to the Arabs that Spain would be willing to help them against Israeli "aggression."

So a new and special political animosity has been added to the ancient hostility of the Spaniard against the Jew. It is partly derived from the Vatican's consistent opposition to Israel's territorial ambitions; and in part it is based on Israel's firm stand against Franco in the United Nations in 1950. Before it went down to defeat on the issue of admitting Franco into UN company, Israel was the only one of four nations outside the Soviet bloc to vote against a resolution modifying the UN's condemnation of Franco. The government of Spain, said Israel's delegate to the UN, had been blessed by Hitler and Mussolini.[14] Although it did not directly participate in the fascist extermination of Jews, the Jewish people remembered that Franco had "bound up his fate with those two regimes." If the Jews within Spain are subservient through necessity, the Jews outside of Spain have not forgotten.

6. SEX, MARRIAGE AND BURIAL

It is difficult for Americans to appreciate the far-reaching effect of the Catholic sexual and family code upon a nation when it is enforced by the power of a Catholic state. We have been accustomed to thinking of marriage, divorce, separation and birth control, as well as maternal medicine and burial practices, as matters of free choice by individuals and families. We make our own laws on all these subjects by democratic process and we resent any attempt to deny citizens their rights. No church is above the state in our domestic relations law, and courts never incorporate ecclesiastical rules into civil law.

In Spain the laws of the country must take into account the Canon Laws of the Church in all matters of domestic life. Since those Canon Laws have a very wide range of application, it means that a great area of personal conduct comes under ecclesiastical rather than civil rule.

Under Canon 1060 no Catholic may marry a non-Catholic without episcopal permission. Under Canon 1118 no Catholic may get a divorce after a valid marriage is consummated. Under Pius XI's 1930 encyclical "Christian Marriage," no Catholic may practice contraception. Under Canon 132, no priest may marry or have sexual intercourse. Under Canon 2350 no Catholic woman may have a therapeutic abortion even when it is deemed necessary to save her life and the fetus is bound to die anyway. Under Canon 1203 no Catholic may be cremated. Under Canons 1205 and 1206 every Catholic must be buried when possible in Catholic consecrated soil.

In Spain this entire sexual and family code is embodied in one way or another in civil law. This embodiment, of course, was implied in Article I of the 1953 Concordat when it recognized "the Catholic Apostolic Roman religion" as "the sole religion of the Spanish nation." After such a commitment, it was natural that the moral law of the state religion should become the civil law of

94

the nation. That is what the union of church and state means today in the field of domestic relations in Spain.

Some Catholic family concepts are so firmly embedded in the mores of the country that they are not even mentioned in the Concordat, or in statutes. It is simply assumed that they will be observed because Spain is a Catholic country and the Catholic Church has spoken upon them officially. An unwritten assumption, for example, applies in the case of birth control and therapeutic abortion. Virtually all hospitals in Spain are Catholic in operation even when they are not denominationally Catholic in ownership. They must nominally observe every item in the Catholic medical code or go out of business.

Discrimination against non-Catholics is also implicit in Catholic hospital ownership. "All hospitals in Spain," says Jacques Delpech in his *The Suppression of Protestants in Spain,* "are under Catholic control. A Protestant mother giving birth in a hospital must generally fight to prevent the baptism of her child as a Catholic. Women who remain firm are sometimes sent home early."

Although no contraceptives may lawfully be sold or prescribed anywhere in Spain, the enforcement of the law is farcical. Contraceptives are sold under the counters in Madrid and Barcelona almost as briskly as they are sold in Massachusetts and Connecticut. The Spanish people, at least in the large cities, have discarded the medical-sexual code of their celibate priests in many particulars, but the Spanish state, so long as it is Catholic, may not openly acknowledge the abandonment. This leads to continuing tension and continuing hypocrisy as the nation practices one sexual code on paper and another in reality.

The Control of Marriage

Article XXIII of the 1953 Concordat says: "The Spanish state recognizes the full civil validity of marriages performed according to the norms of Canon Law." This recognition in itself is relatively harmless. Most governments in the world, including state governments in the United States, recognize some rights of participation in marriage ceremonies by religious spokesmen or officials. American states license priests, preachers and rabbis to marry members of their faith, and others, and they impose no special conditions on the type of ceremony used if clergymen obey the prohibitions against child marriage, venereal disease and consanguinity. What makes the marriage law of Spain so different from that of the United States is that there is an exclusive and discriminatory favoritism extended to the Catholic Church.

The favoritism is consecrated by the 1953 Concordat with the Vatican in special marriage clauses. In effect the Catholic marriage courts are made into courts of the nation for all Spanish Catholics and so incorporated by reference into the judicial system. The judges in these courts are priests chosen by the Church, not by the people of Spain or the government of Spain. Yet their judgments have the force of law for all baptized Catholics. This interpolation of Catholic power into the governmental system of the nation represents, for the Catholic Church, the ideal marital arrangement.[1] It gives to the Church government sanction, for its marriage rules, without the danger of reversal by any democratic Cortes, since a Cortes may not repudiate the Concordat without Vatican consent.

Throughout most of the history of Spain the favoritism to the Church in marriage has been even more pronounced than it is today. Before 1870 there was no civil marriage at all in the sense in which Americans use those words. The priests even controlled the registry of births, marriages and deaths. In the nineteenth century the Vatican fought very bitterly against those Spanish anticlerical leaders who attempted to take away this exclusive control and give it to the government; and for a time the anti-clericals were successful. Today the Church's control of baptism, marriage and death is secure in every respect, except in the retention of records. The state now controls the registry, but the priest is the most influential adviser in determining how that registry shall be used.

In Spain the priest is the only religious personage who has the power to marry. No Protestant minister or Jewish rabbi has that power. The Protestant and Jewish marriage ceremonies, therefore, are simply extralegal surplus added to the legal civil ceremony. The marriage certificate issued by the priest is automatically accepted for recording by the Civil Registry, under the Final Protocol of Article XXIII of the Concordat. There is no corresponding certificate of marriage for Protestant or Jewish clergymen, since their power is extralegal. The Spaniard who is married only by a Protestant minister or Jewish rabbi is not legally married. The protocol of the Concordat even requires that the Spanish state shall not impose on Catholics any impediments "contrary to natural law." That means that the state, as long as the Concordat exists, cannot go beyond Catholic law in imposing its own type of impediment. Although civil marriage is nominally permitted non-Catholics in Spain, in practice it is extraordinarily difficult for any baptized Catholic—and nearly all the people of Spain are baptized Catholics. For them so many obstacles are put in the way of civil marriage that the impediments amount to a denial of the right. So few people resort to civil ceremonies that the statistical annuals do not even carry the official figures on the subject. As we have already seen, Franco abolished all divorce in March 1938, even while the Republic was still in existence. He even gave some retroactive effect to his no-divorce decree by allowing either party to a divorce which had been obtained under the Republic to reopen the proceedings and ask for cancellation of the divorce. Today the Church refuses to recognize the validity of any past or present divorce unless the parties involved in such an unrecognized divorce can reprocess the proceeding in a Catholic marriage court and so transform it technically into the phenomenon known as "annulment." This sleight-of-hand transformation is rare. When it is accomplished, it creates the fiction that a marriage once terminated by divorce never existed in the first place.

Of course, under Catholic law, the power to annul a marriage of Catholics rests wholly in the Catholic marriage courts, and the priest-judges in those courts may adopt definitions to suit their purposes. Article XXIV of the 1953 Concordat places Catholic law on marriage annulment above Spanish civil law by saying: "The Spanish state recognizes the exclusive competence of the ecclesiastical courts in cases involving the nullity of ecclesiastical marriage. . . ."

As in most countries, the process of formal Catholic annulment is difficult and expensive, and the poorer people of Spain rarely resort to it. Only forty-nine decrees of annulment were recorded in the diocesan courts of Spain in 1957. These annulment figures do not include any "attempted" marriages of baptized Catholics before civil registrars, Protestant ministers or Jewish rabbis. Such so-called marriages are, in the Catholic lexicons, non-existent and their termination does not need to be formally recorded.

Sex Morals, Priestly and Otherwise

When a whole nation is subjected to such artificial sex regulations, the question naturally arises: How do the people evade the regulations? In Italy the corresponding no-divorce rule produces millions of extralegal households which have been organized —or reorganized—without benefit of clergy. In Spain, because the women are less free, the unsuccessful marriage is more likely to continue formally while the husband has a mistress on the side. Few countries in the world give the "outside" mistress more unofficial recognition. The wives of Spain have no recourse except to accept the institution. The double standard in family morals has existed for centuries.

The married women of Spain, particularly rural Spain, are guarded and hearthbound; the men are not. Nominally, the double standard applies to women with equal strictness both before and after marriage. A "nice" girl before marriage even in Madrid usually is required by convention to return to her home by 9 P.M. After marriage her extra-family life is almost equally restricted.

Recently, for the first time in history, a law was passed allowing a wife to use the adultery of her husband as a ground for separation—not divorce.[2] Even today a husband may desert his home for from one to three years without losing his family rights, whereas a wife may lose those rights by one day's absence. One reason for the perpetuation of this double standard is that relatively few Spanish women can attain self-support in the professions. Marriage is almost their only respectable career.

Until recently this predominantly male code permitted an extensive national system of licensed houses of prostitution. Prostitution had been nominally outlawed by the Republic, although the prohibition was not strictly enforced. When Franco won the Civil War, he re-established licensed houses with required medical check-ups and a minimum age of twenty-three for the approximately 13,000 card-carrying prostitutes. In 1955, *Time* magazine estimated the number of prostitutes at 100,000, many of them under twenty-three and it said that "Spain has a frightening venereal disease rate: some 200,000 cases annually in public dispensaries, an unknown number treated privately or not at all."[3] The

Church fought this system of legalized prostitution as "the major shame of the nation," and in March 1956 prostitution was again legally "abolished" by decree. I could find no one in Spain who believed that it had actually been abolished.

As to the sexual standards of the celibate priests, almost everybody talks about the subject in private and almost everybody deplores the laxity in those standards. Perhaps some Spanish Kinsey report could prove that the morals of priests in Spain are not different from the morals of priests in the United States. I can only record my impressions from many conversations in both places that (1) the moral standards of priests in the United States are high; and (2) the moral standards of priests in Spain are low. The constant talk about the "niece" and the semirecognized illegitimate child of the priest is so open in many Spanish parishes that it cannot be dismissed as groundless. A foreign observer can only comment that if the Spanish people have this opinion of the moral standards of their own priests, he is in no position to contradict them.

The late Negro novelist, Richard Wright, when he went to Spain in 1954, made a special attempt to observe the sex morals of the Spanish people. He reached the conclusion that prostitution and actual white slavery were then as appalling as in any nation in the world. He made this very frank statement about the sex morality of the priests. (I cannot vouch for its accuracy, but the reaction of those Spaniards who spoke to me about the standards of their priests was essentially the same as that of the Spaniards who spoke to Mr. Wright.)

Still another buttressing aspect of this sexual atmosphere must be mentioned. I, for one, feel it naive in our Freudian, twentieth-century world even to allude to the bruited sexual lives of priests and nuns. I do not know nor am I interested in whether they have sexual lives or not. I hope that they do, for their own sake: and I'm sure that God does not mind. But while in Spain I found an amazing degree of preoccupation on the part of the ordinary men and women with the legend of the supposed torrid sexual lives of the men of the Church. It was a kind of sexual projection of the common populace upon the priesthood. I heard whispers of priests keeping mistresses; in clubs and bars I was shown many little wooden carvings of priests, carvings that displayed, under the religious habit, the genitals, indicating that there existed a tremendous sexual jealousy and tension on the part of the laymen for the rumored sexual prerogatives of the men of the Church. It does not matter whether these allegations about the priesthood are true or not; what does matter is that the laymen are preoccupied with them. Their reasoning seems to be: if they can do it and get away with it, so can I.[4]

This popular belief about the alleged looseness of priestly morals goes back a long way in Spanish history. For centuries the celibacy of the Spanish priests existed only on paper. In the Middle Ages they were permitted by their bishops to have concubines quite openly, and these church concubines even wore a special costume. When celibacy was nominally imposed on the entire Church in 1139 by the Roman hierarchy, the Spanish priests fought against it vigorously. They have never actually accepted the rule. In fact, it is doubtful that the Spanish people want them to accept the rule. Gerald Brenan, one of the most acute of modern analysts of Spanish life, says of the laymen's attitude toward the morals of the priests: "Their parishioners, far from being shocked, prefer them to live in concubinage, as otherwise they would not always care to let their womenfolk confess to them." [5]

Perhaps this double standard of sexual morals for priests should be described as Iberian rather than Spanish. It prevails in Portugal as obviously as it prevails in Spain, and it prevails in those Latin American countries which have been evangelized by Spanish and Portuguese priests. Writing on "Catholics in Latin America" in Commonweal for March 23, 1961, the well-known Catholic author, Erik von Kuehnelt-Leddihn, said: "In the Andean region, concubinage is such a regular phenomenon that priests who maintain celibacy (unless they are 'crazy foreigners') invite diverse suspicions."

Meanwhile, the Spanish bishops, who undoubtedly take their oaths of chastity very seriously, have become something of a laughing stock in Spain because of futile attempts to enforce puritanical standards in matters of dress and courtship. Even American priests who come to Spain join in subdued laughter. Monsignor Arthur H. Ryan in Spain and the World of Today tells how he was compelled to refrain from wearing trunks on a San Sebastian bathing beach and ordered to tie on over his full length suit "loose calico pantaloons that reached to our knees."

This was in the 1940s. Today the great influx of tourists, especially from France, is changing the trend. France favors bikini bathing suits, and the French lassies who wear them seem to excite more admiration than anger among the members of the civil guard who are supposed to "capture" them. On a certain very warm afternoon in Valencia in July 1959, the City Hall carried on its door the notice that ten requirements were in force for "the defense of Christian morals," among which were: "It is prohibited for persons of different sexes to use the same cabana." Also: "Indecorous suits, such as two-piece suits, are prohibited." *"El desnudismo"* would be penalized by a maximum fine, according to the notice, of two thousand pesetas and thirty days in jail. Meanwhile, pulchritudinous young ladies, even some Spanish young ladies, were ignoring the stern reminder quite openly. I could find no records of any arrests.

The eighty-two-year-old Primate of Spain, Cardinal Pla y Deniel, during that month, reminded engaged Spanish couples that it might be a mortal sin to participate in any kind of mixed bathing, and he added: "Among diversions, probably none constitutes a graver and more frequent danger than dancing. Modern dances, among which we can classify all those involving an embrace, are a serious danger to Christian morals because they are very close to a state of sin." [6]

When the storm of adverse comment had even reached the controlled Franco press, the Catholic Action daily of Madrid, *Ya,* was somewhat embarrassed. It could only protest: "We think that he [the Cardinal] deserves Catholic obedience and deep respect on our part and on the part of the strangers within our gates, a respect for a Prince of the Church who is doing his duty." [7]

Ya's obedient Puritanism reflects the opposition of the Spanish hierarchy to the whole pattern of modern and relaxed French Catholicism. In fact, the Spanish hierarchy never did like French Catholicism. The Spanish bishops have always felt that nakedness, anti-clericalism and suggestive vaudeville have entered Spain from France, and they even suspect that all of these French evils have something to do with Communism.

Mixed Marriage and Clerical Red Tape

The Final Protocol of Article XXIII of the 1953 Concordat says: "In the matter of acknowledgement of a mixed marriage between Catholic and non-Catholic persons, the State shall formulate its legislation so as to harmonize with Canon Law." And Catholic

Canon Law absolutely forbids the marriage of a baptized Catholic to a non-Catholic except under conditions which discriminate against the non-Catholic party. Accordingly, Spanish marriage law is so written that discrimination is built into every mixed marriage situation. At worst this means criminal prosecution for any Spaniard who evades the Church's rules on mixed marriage. At best it means that non-Catholics who have once been baptized as Catholics in their youth may be compelled to negotiate with hostile local authorities before being allowed to marry outside their Church.

In chapter 4, I described the trial and conviction of a Spanish Baptist pastor in a criminal court in Madrid in the summer of 1959 for breaking and entering his own church. In that same criminal court in that same month, I saw a baptized Catholic layman, who had ceased to be a Catholic many years before, prosecuted for recording himself as "married" in the Madrid census after he had been married to a Protestant bride by a Protestant pastor.[8] He had tried unsuccessfully for years to get the civil authorities to marry him according to Spanish law; he had been refused even this favor because of his "heretical" status.

This particular defendant was put on trial because local priests wanted to punish him for past defiance of Catholic marriage laws. He had left his Church and continued to renounce it for many years; before his trial began he had even persuaded a Madrid civil registrar to marry him. So the case against him was morally dead, and he was lawfully married to his wife at the time of the trial. But the government insisted on trying him anyway for the *past* sin of recording himself as married when he had been married only by a Protestant clergyman. He was finally acquitted —in the presence of curious and critical foreign journalists— only because of the technicality that the written census which he had "falsified" was not the recognized document for the proof of marriage in Spain.

In 1941, a stringent decree was issued saying: "The municipal judges shall authorize no civil marriages but those for which the parties have proved by documented evidence that they do not belong to the Catholic religion. If it is not possible for them to produce such documents, they must declare under oath that they have not been baptized as Catholics. The validity of the marriage shall depend upon the veracity of these declarations." [9]

This new demand for "documents" was a crushing blow to

all Spaniards who had been baptized as Catholics and wished to marry outside the Church. In effect it prevented them from making a change in faith. Both parties to the marriage had to prove to the satisfaction of Catholic officials and priests that they were non-Catholics in order to secure non-Catholic marriage, and the burden of proof was placed upon the bride and the groom.

What did this Franco decree of 1941 mean when it called for "documented evidence" that neither party belonged to the Catholic religion? Non-Catholics soon found out. The 1953 Concordat had established the general principle that every marriage of a baptized Catholic had to be celebrated by a priest. Then, in November 1956, the government dutifully stiffened the regulations against civil marriage by making the bishop in each diocese a party to the decision of the local judge concerning a baptized Catholic's right to have a civil ceremony.

When a Catholic applied to a local judge for a civil instead of a Catholic marriage, the local judge was instructed to notify the local bishop within eight days and, in any case, to wait for a month before any civil marriage was permitted for such a baptized Catholic. During that month, the bishop and the local priest were free to bring clerical pressure to bear upon the beleaguered young couple and their families, using the ancient argument that non-Catholic marriage for a Catholic is simply a foyer to adultery. Often the priests acted as clerical FBI agents in searching out any fact in the victims' past which might be used to prove that they did not have the right to marry.

If they failed to stop the marriage with this manipulation and pressure, the whole problem could be passed on to higher ecclesiastical and civil authorities for review before any civil marriage was permitted. In practice the month of delay became a month of cruel espionage for couples planning mixed marriage. The practice became almost universal among local officials to call in the local priest and accept his judgment if any question arose concerning the right to marry. Since the prestige of the local priest is at stake in a community when young people desert the Church, it can be imagined how impartial his factual findings would be.

Volumes could be devoted to tales of agony and frustration among young Spanish couples who have been denied the right of non-Catholic marriage under present law. Usually the tactics of obstruction employed by Catholic officials are inspired and guided by priests and bishops. Here is one typical tale from eastern Spain, given to me by a participant, with all the identifying labels removed.

Young Mr. X was a Protestant in North City; Miss Y was a baptized Catholic who had moved to North City from the South. She met Mr. X, attended his church, and finally became a Protestant. They asked their Protestant pastor to marry them. He advised them to go first to a local judge for a civil ceremony in conformity with the law, but the local judge denied them a civil ceremony because Miss Y had been baptized a Catholic. Her change of religion was perfectly obvious and documented, but the local priest refused to recognize it. The civil authorities followed the ruling of the priest and refused to move without his sanction.

Then the Protestant pastor pressed the case with the local bishop in frequent visits stretching over two years, always being treated with the utmost rudeness and contempt. Finally the pastor persuaded the couple to go to a priest and ask for a priestly marriage, although such a marriage was against his principles and theirs. The priest refused when he learned that Mr. X was a Protestant.

Then the Protestant minister appealed to the Catholic bishop and asked for a written statement saying that the Church *refused* to marry the couple. He reasoned that if he could present a legal case to the courts showing that such a couple could not marry at all in Spain, the court might make the marriage possible as a matter of public policy.

Meanwhile, serving as clerical detectives, the priests of the region had been sent out to dig up and scrutinize every particular of Mr. X's past history in order to prove that he might have been baptized a Catholic in his infancy without his knowledge. In their eyes, this would have nullified his claim that he was born a Protestant. The whole proceeding became very much like a "Red" witch hunt during the height of our McCarthy era, with the priests playing the role of investigators for Church and state, and greatly embarrassing the families of both young people.

Finally the Protestant pastor, through an artifice, secured in writing from the local bishop a *refusal* to marry the beleaguered couple. He considered this a great triumph. Then, and only then, was a civil judge persuaded to marry them. Meanwhile, having become impatient, and being very much in love, the couple had persuaded a Protestant pastor to go through the forms of a Protestant marriage with them. They accepted his ceremony as bind-

ing them in the eyes of God. They had a baby girl one week
after the final achievement of a civil ceremony. Little Miss XY is
now retroactively legitimate under Spanish law, but illegitimate
under Church law!

If the reader wonders why Spanish Protestants do not go
ahead and live together anyway after Protestant ceremonies without benefit of the civil register, he should know that the social and
economic penalties for such independence are very severe. "Illegitimate" children are denied many legal as well as social rights
in Spain. The word "harlots" may often be applied to good Spanish women who have left the Catholic Church to marry Protestants
extralegally. They are frequently denounced from the pulpits by
the priests. Their life in the ordinary Spanish community is rendered utterly miserable. Also, in the syndicalist system in industry, a man's wage is automatically increased when he marries lawfully and so becomes the head of a family. Without priest-approved
certificates of marriage his family must exist on a bachelor's income. Irregular Protestant marriage may be the equivalent of a
perpetual wage cut.

Mixed Marriage and Americans

The clerical manipulation resorted to in the fight against
mixed marriage is applied even to the thousands of members of
the American armed forces at our bases in Spain. If an American
GI is a Catholic and wishes to marry a Spanish Catholic girl before
a priest, the Church is quite ready to sanction the marriage. If he
is a Protestant or a Jew—and at least 65 per cent of our armed
forces in Spain are Protestants or Jews—and he wishes to marry a
Spanish girl who has been baptized a Catholic, he will be refused
the right to marry inside of Spain unless he is converted to the
Catholic faith or unless he takes the Catholic pledges to bring
up all children as Catholics. A few amorous "converts" among
American GI's have married a few Spanish girls under these rules,
but the common remedy for those who hanker after mixed marriage is flight to Gibraltar. There civil marriage under British
auspices is possible, with subsequent recognition by Spanish law.

Americans were startled in 1954 to read a front-page headline
in the *New York Times*: "United States Would Give Church in
Spain Veto on Marriages of Americans." The late Camille Cian-

farra, one of the ablest of European correspondents, a Catholic himself and a former *Times* correspondent at the Vatican, told how an American and a Spanish general acting as representatives of their countries had entered into an agreement about the marriage of members of the American armed forces in Spain, under which the United States accepted Catholic restrictions on the mixed marriage of Americans.[10]

A storm of protests came from non-Catholics in the United States. Bishop James Pike of the Episcopal church in San Francisco called it "an attempt to sell down the river our most precious heritage, our religious freedom," and he pointed out that American GIs in England who wished to marry English girls were not subjected to Anglican law, although the Church of England is still technically an established church in that country.[11] The large American organization known as the National Association of Evangelicals declared that the alleged agreement was "an affront to all Protestants."

The affront was underscored by the fact that the discriminatory mixed-marriage agreement had been worked out by a Reno Catholic priest who had been serving as chief chaplain of American armed forces in Spain at the time. Officials in the Pentagon and the State Department, who had been about to sanction the surrender of marital liberty for several thousand American GIs, retreated in some confusion and announced that the reported agreement had not actually been signed.

It is true that the agreement was never formally signed, but the Franco regime is quietly *enforcing* it today against mixed marriages of Americans in Spain. Our military authorities in that country have in practice, quietly surrendered. The Jesuit magazine *America* expressed annoyance in 1955 that "Protestant pressures" had swayed Washington so effectively that the projected marriage pact was never signed. But it added: "This does not mean, as hasty readers might imagine, that our GIs will not now be bound by the civil laws of Spain, which, in marriage matters, are coordinated with Church laws." [12] In this case, "coordinated with" should read "subordinated to."

Burying Baptists at Night

Among Spanish Baptists the name of Harry Truman is quite popular. One reason for the popularity is that Truman in an off-the-cuff attack on the Spanish dictator in 1959 said: "Franco's no good. If you are a Baptist in Spain you cannot be buried in daylight." [13]

The Spanish ambassador to the United States, José Maria de Areilza, immediately challenged Truman's statement in an ambiguous pronouncement: "The Spanish legislation on the matter, inspired by Catholic doctrine, places no condition on the burial of Protestants, including those of the Baptist Church to which Mr. Truman alludes."

To the uninitiated the ambassador's denial seemed adequate. He did not explain what he meant by burial legislation "inspired by Catholic doctrine" or the phrase "places no condition." It is true that there is no statute in Spain which singles out Baptists or other Protestants by name and says that they must be discriminated against in death. But the Catholic doctrine on burial is cruelly exclusive and the administrative practice of Spain imposes many unfair conditions on the burial of Protestants.

In most localities in Spain there is only one good cemetery, and Protestants are excluded from that cemetery because of the Catholic rule of separatism for all heretics in death. As a result of that rule Protestants are consigned for burial to small, weed-infested, separate plots, surrounded by a wall which divides their miserable resting place from the large and well-kept "public" cemetery reserved exclusively for Catholics. I have visited at least a dozen burial grounds for non-Catholics in various parts of Spain, and I found them worse than pauper burial grounds in the United States. In many instances Protestants have no place for burial except side by side with murderers who have been hanged. The Church and the Catholic state will not permit their burial in regular cemeteries.

The Spanish policy of discrimination against non-Catholics in death is an indirect product of the Catholic theory of consecrated and non-consecrated soil. The Catholic rules on this subject are strict and detailed, occupying a whole chapter in Canon

Law, beginning with Canon 1203. Catholics in death must be treated as a distinct class, and if they are not so treated the actual progress of their souls through purgatory may be impeded. Their dust must never be commingled with that of Protestants or Jews except in abnormal conditions such as war or plague. The priestly control of burial goes so far that relatives are instructed in some cases to defy the burial instructions of the deceased himself if they are contrary to Catholic policy. This is the rule on cremation under Canon 1203, which says: "If a person has in any way ordered that his body be cremated, it is illicit to obey such instructions; and if such a provision occurs in a contract, last testament, or in any document whatsoever, it is to be disregarded." (It is not necessary to appeal to this general Catholic rule in Spain since the Catholic government prohibits all cremation.)

Under Canons 1205, 1239 and 1240, the soil in which Catholics are buried must be consecrated exclusively for Catholics. Under Canons 1212 and 1240, "another place" must be provided for all heretics. Under Canon 1242, if any excommunicated former Catholic is buried in Catholic soil by mistake, his remains must be dug up and removed. Otherwise, the whole cemetery is polluted.

In Spain, burial discrimination works almost wholly against Protestants in small towns and country districts. Protestants in Madrid and Barcelona are not seriously affected so long as they do not attempt any funeral processions in the streets or any too-audible services at the grave. However, this deprivation is considered a hardship because a street procession to mourn for the dead is a traditional ritual, and Protestants in small towns feel deeply grieved when their Catholic neighbors are allowed small processions and they themselves are denied this privilege.

This denial is based upon the charge that even a small funeral procession is an illegal "public manifestation" of a non-Catholic faith under the 1953 Concordat and the 1945 Spanish Charter. Such denials are often accompanied by quixotic rulings of local officials requiring any non-Catholic funeral or burial rites to be conducted very early in the morning or after dark at night in order to save local Catholics from "contamination."

The Republic, in its Constitution of 1931, joyously threw out all of these separatist rules and decreed democracy in death by taking over the cemeteries and by ordering, in Article 27 of the Constitution, that: "Cemeteries will be subject exclusively to civil jurisdiction. There may not be a separation of parts within them for religious reasons." The constitutional provision was made effective in a law of January 30, 1932.

This did not mean that Catholic priests could not consecrate a lot in a public cemetery under their own ritual—there was no interference with Catholic burials as such if the deceased had requested a Catholic burial. The new constitutional rule meant only that priests could not divide public burial areas on sectarian lines and force non-Catholics out of municipal cemeteries. The Republic started to tear down the traditional walls between the elegant and well-groomed sections of Spanish cemeteries which are reserved for Catholics and the dreary and unkempt plots reserved for suicides, Protestants and murderers. But the anticlericals ruled the nation for so short a time under the 1931 Constitution that many of the walls were never torn down.

Franco rescinded the order to break down division walls in 1938, restored the ownership of parish cemeteries to the Church, and ordered all city authorities to restore the sectarian separations. Under the new law all administrators of cemeteries were ordered to remove from gravestones all non-Catholic symbols or anything "offensive or hostile" to Catholic religion or morality. Then, in 1953, the Catholic burial code was incorporated by reference into the Vatican Concordat.

Article XXII of the Concordat guarantees the "inviolability" of all Catholic cemeteries. Article XXIV adds:

> In general all services, decrees and decisions of an administrative nature issued by ecclesiastical authorities regarding any of the matters subject to their jurisdiction will have validity also in the civil order. Once they have been notified, the state authorities and civil officials will render the necessary assistance in carrying out these sentences, decisions and decrees.

In practice this means that Catholic authorities write their own program for discrimination in death. If a local priest in a Spanish village is vehement enough, he insists that every baptized Catholic even after many years of apostasy, must still be buried as a Catholic. I heard of many instances of bodies of ex-Catholics, who had become devout Protestants, being spirited away by joint action of priest and police for burial as Catholics, even in defiance of family wishes. Usually the priests do not go that far because it is not necessary. If they tell the local police not to grant a permit for an evangelical funeral, the police usually manage to obey clerical orders, directly or indirectly.

Here are two descriptions of typical acts of police suppression, written by a Protestant evangelist in 1952 for an English gospel mission. They are quite typical of the personal narratives given to me in Alicante and Valencia by many Spanish Protestants.

DONA G. C., a baptized member of the Evangelical Church since 1928 and married in the Evangelical Church in 1931, died on April 21st, 1952. In her will she stated that she was an Evangelical and wished to be buried in accordance with the rites of her Church. Her family obtained from the police verbal permission to celebrate an evangelical funeral, but, thanks to the intervention of the parish priest, the permission was withdrawn, and she was given a Roman Catholic funeral although she had never confessed nor taken Communion in that church.

DONA F. A., a member of the Evangelical Church since 1925, died on 22nd May, 1952. She had also expressed in her will her wish to be buried with evangelical rites and the family again obtained verbal permission from the police. The following day a funeral service was begun in the house of the deceased but was interrupted by two policemen who informed the evangelist that the permission was withdrawn and the burial must take place with Roman Catholic rites. Immediately four more policemen presented themselves, accompanied by the priest, and took charge of the body which was interred according to Roman Catholic rites against the wishes of the family.[14]

If a local public official is too tolerant in permitting Protestant burial services in the daytime, he is likely to be removed by Franco authorities at the request of the Church. I was able to document in part a case in Alicantara, Valencia, a town of about five thousand, as follows. A girl of eight died in 1952. Her father, a watchmaker, was a Baptist. He asked the local civil authorities for permission for civil burial and the authorities gave verbal permission. This would have meant burial in the respectable part of an ordinary cemetery.

In order to prevent any trouble the father went to see the local priest to ask his permission also. He was told that he could not see the priest. Then he was called to the office of the mayor and informed in the presence of several witnesses that full non-

Catholic rites had been prohibited, but the girl's body could be interred in the civil cemetery if only one person accompanied it to the grave. The father pleaded his case effectively and the mayor finally yielded and allowed friends and family to go into the cemetery. About two hundred people watched the burial at the cemetery. There was no ceremony there and the proceeding was entirely quiet. Civil guards were present as witnesses and policemen.

Then someone, possibly the priest, denounced the family members for participating in an illegal gathering. The father, Vicente Argente Frances and another member of the family, Miguel Argente Frances, were fined 5,000 pesetas each as recorded in Document 292 of April 2, 1952, "for provoking an act or affair in Alicantara which could give rise to a destruction of public order and which was previously prohibited by this civil government." The mayor was dismissed from office and the civil guard leader was transferred.

The greatest hardship for non-Catholics in burial is economic. Only the Catholic cemeteries are large enough and well equipped enough to have those wall crypts for the burial of the common people which are so prevalent in Europe. The wall crypts, very much like the sliding drawers of a file cabinet, are masonry squares in a great wall. They are leased to the bereaved family for a number of years, usually for five years. At the end of this period the remains are removed and destroyed, and the crypts are leased over again to a new customer. The little people of Spain are usually buried in this way; they cannot afford the expensive permanent graves of the American style of burial.

7. EDUCATION IN THE SHADOW OF THE CHURCH

Under the Franco regime it is quite natural that the Caudillo's particular brand of fascism and the doctrines of Catholicism should be completely dovetailed in school textbooks.[1] If there is doubt in anyone's mind that the Catholic hierarchy itself opposes freedom, the doubts are instantly resolved when one reads the catechisms used by the children in Spanish national schools. They are naked and unashamed in their scorn of freedom of the mind. They are equally outspoken in condemning the institutions of Western democracy.

In different parts of Spain I purchased several of the standard school textbooks which outline the moral basis of clerical fascism for young children. Their official character is indicated by a bishop's imprimatur or the *Obra aprobada por la Autoridad Eclesiastica*. Although it is possible for a book bearing the imprimatur to contain incidental errors not connected with Catholic doctrine, the official stamp is a guarantee that it is "free of doctrinal or moral error" when it considers religion.

The Gospel in the Schools

Some of the Church textbooks used in Spain's national schools have already become quite famous through quotation. This is particularly true of *Nuevo ripalda,* already cited, which has been used in the elementary schools of Spain without serious substantive change for at least seventeen years. It teaches the Spanish children the identical, reactionary ideas of Pius XI's Syllabus of Errors. I found a number of young Spaniards who told me that they had been compelled by their teachers to memorize virtually all of this work from cover to cover when they attended the national

112

schools. It is the political and moral Bible of Spanish elementary education.

The book begins its "Summary of Modern Errors" by listing thirteen errors by name: materialism, Darwinism, atheism, pantheism, deism, rationalism, Protestantism, socialism, communism, syndicalism, liberalism, modernism and Masonry. Of Darwinism the author says:

What does Darwinism teach?

That perfect animals come from those which are imperfect and especially that men come from monkeys.

What would you say about Darwinism?

That it is a ridiculous and absurd system.

Why?

Because it is ridiculous and absurd to establish any kinship between an intelligent and free man and a stupid animal.

The work rather skillfully combines Protestantism and socialism in one general condemnation, with a picture of Luther, looking very much like an inquisitor, burning a papal bull. Luther is described in the caption as "haughty and corrupt," and the following questions and answers are inserted concerning him and Protestantism:

What does Protestantism deny?

It denies the authority and infallibility of the Church, and admits only the authority of Scripture, interpreted by individual caprice.

Who was the founder of this heresy?

An apostate friar of the name of Luther, arrogant and corrupt. . . .

Nuevo ripalda combines an attack on the lay state with an attack on all non-sectarian public schools, giving the impression to Spanish children that a predominantly public school system implies the denial to Catholics of the right to have their own schools. Of the lay state, *Nuevo ripalda* says:

"Must the state be lay?"

"By no means; on the contrary, it must have the Catholic religion, which is the only true one."

Concerning the free public school which is supported by general taxation and exempt from sectarian control, *Nuevo ripalda* is quite pugnacious:

What do we mean by lay school?
Any teaching institution where God and religion are ignored and attention is given only to scientific and profane education.
Why are these schools pernicious?
Because they ignore religious duties in the education they give, leave scientific education incomplete and moral education without a foundation.
What is the main reason for this?
The main reason is that it is a lay school in theory but an antireligious school in practice.
What does "unique school" mean?
A single organization of teaching institutions directed by the state, free, coeducational and above all, lay and compulsory for all the citizens.
What do you think of the "unique" school?
That it has one good point, many bad ones and some which are ridiculous and absurd.
Let us see how.
One good point is that it is free and compulsory; but religion and Christian morals do not allow it to be lay and coeducational.
What is the ridiculous and absurd aspect?
It is to offer to all the families free schooling paid for by themselves whether or not they have enough economic means.

The chief target of *Nuevo ripalda* is "liberalism." The word as used in European dialectics is not quite a synonym for the word as used in the United States. It tends to be identified with those European political parties that have striven for freedom of belief and the separation of church and state. Hence, when *Nuevo ripalda* exposes liberalism for the children of Spain, it is attacking both independent educated Catholics and the professional enemies of the priests. Here is *Nuevo ripalda*'s extensive analysis of the opposition:

What does liberalism teach?
That the state is independent from the Church.
How many degrees can be distinguished in liberalism?
Three principal ones.
What does the first degree teach?

That the Church must be subject to the State.

What do the liberals deduce from this doctrine?

That Church laws are not to be complied with (the same holds for Protestant councils) when they conflict with the State.

What does the second degree teach?

That the power of the Church and that of the State are equal and independent.

What can be deduced from this?

That all civil laws are just and compulsory, even when they oppose Church precepts.

What does the third degree teach?

That the Church is above the State, but that in the present times the independence of the Church must be permitted along with the other freedoms that Liberalism teaches.

Has the Church condemned all these errors?

Yes, Father, especially in the Encyclical *Quanta Cura* and in *The Syllabus of Errors*.

What does the Catholic Church teach on this point?

That the State must be subject to the Church, as the body to the soul and the temporal to the eternal.

On what is the Church superiority over the State founded?

On its most noble purpose, which is man's eternal salvation, far superior to all the temporary purposes which appertain to the State.

Are there cases in which the State is independent from the Church?

Yes, when temporal matters are concerned which have no connection with spiritual and eternal affairs.

Is it certain that the Church should not "interfere" in politics?

Most certainly, as long as politics, keeping within its own limits, does not "interfere" with religion.

The Case Against Freedom

Then the editors plunge into the heart of the Catholic case against liberalism, democracy and the separation of church and state.

What other freedoms does liberalism defend?

Freedom of conscience, freedom of worship, and freedom of the press.

What does "freedom of conscience" mean?

That everyone can profess the religion dictated by his conscience, and none if his conscience does not dictate any.

Is it true that man may choose the religion which pleases him best?

No, because he must profess the Catholic apostolic Roman religion, which is the only true one.

What does "freedom of worship" mean?

That the Government must protect the free practice of all faiths, even if they are false.

What then is the Government's duty in this respect?

The Government itself must profess and then protect the only true religion, which is Catholicism.

Must not the Government protect all the opinions of its subjects?

Yes, sir, but always provided that these opinions are not condemned by the Church.

What does "freedom of the press" mean?

The right to print and publish without censorship all kinds of opinions, no matter how absurd and corrupt they may be.

Should the Government repress this freedom by means of previous censorship?

Evidently yes.

Why?

Because it must prevent the deception, calumny and corruption of its subjects, which are harmful to the common good.

Are there other pernicious freedoms?

Yes, sir; freedom to teach, freedom to make propaganda and to hold meetings.

Why are these freedoms pernicious?

Because they are used for teaching error, spreading vice and plotting against the Church.

Does the Church tolerate these freedoms?

No, sir; it has repeatedly condemned them.

These general denunciations of freedom of speech and the press are not considered quite specific enough to protect the children, even in a country where there have been no free newspapers for a generation. So *Nueva ripalda* inserts a special set of questions on "The Reading of Periodicals," being careful to allow the Church's wealthy members to follow stock exchange reports even in liberal newspapers so long as they do not read the rest of the paper.

Does he who subscribes to liberal papers sin gravely?

Yes, sir.

Why?

Because he contributes to evil with his money, endangers his faith and gives to others a bad example.

Is it sometimes a minor sin to read the liberal press?

Yes, sir, if one occasionally reads news or articles that are only slightly dangerous.

Can there be serious reasons which might justify reading liberal papers?

That is possible but it would seldom happen.

What would be best to do then, in order not to sin?

To ask in advance for the advice of a prudent and learned director. (Bear in mind that there might be reason for reading part of a paper, for instance, the stock exchange ratings, but not a reason for reading the rest.)

What rules can you give for recognizing liberal papers?

The following:

1. If they call themselves liberal.
2. If they stand for freedom of conscience, freedom of worship, freedom of the press, or any one of the other liberal errors.
3. If they attack the Roman Pontiff, the clergy, or the religious orders.
4. If they belong to liberal parties.
5. If they comment on the news or judge people with a liberal criterion.
6. If they praise without reserve the good intellectual and moral qualities of liberal people or parties.
7. If they, on referring to the facts concerning the battle that Our Lord Jesus Christ and His Church are waging against their enemies, remain neutral.

(One safe rule for knowing whether a newspaper is liberal or not is to see whether it is published with ecclesiastical censorship. Censorship must be stamped on a conspicuous place and with perfectly visible letters in order to avoid any kind of deceit.)

What is the best rule for not erring in these cases?

Not to read any paper at all without having previously consulted and received permission from the confessor.

Nuevo ripalda strikes at civil marriage as follows:

What is so-called civil marriage?

The kind celebrated in front of a civil authority without the intervention of Church authority.

Is civil marriage a real marriage?

No, only obscene concubinage.

Why?

Because true marriage must be celebrated in front of the ecclesiastical authority, carrying out all that was ordered by Jesus Christ
and our Holy Mother Church.

The authors do not fail to indoctrinate all Spanish children
with the gospel that the state owes the Church a living.

Must the State support worship and the clergy?
Yes, sir.
Why?
Because the Catholic religion contributes to the national, scien-
tific, and moral progress of the people, and governments should be
grateful to God, supporting and encouraging His worship.

Educational Philosophy

Spain has virtually no non-sectarian schools in the American
sense of that term. Its entire educational system, from the nur-
sery through the national universities, is committed to Catholic
doctrine, and it is impossible for an ordinary Spanish child to get
full education without submitting to a process of indoctrination.
Spain has no real tradition of any other kind of education—except
during the brief ascendancy of the Second Republic. Thus the
Spanish people have been taught that schools which omit sectarian
religion from the curriculum are definitely anti-religious, and the
only religion they know anything about is Catholicism.

The philosophy behind such sectarian ascendancy in the
schools has been enthusiastically accepted by Franco. The Church
according to Franco is "a guardian of essential values in education." One of the most popular and oft-quoted papal encyclicals in
Spain is Pius XI's *Christian Education of Youth* which not only
asserts the Church's rights over the school system but theoretically
relegates the government to a secondary role in that system. "And
first of all," said Pius XI (italics added), "education belongs *pre-
eminently* to the Church by reason of a double title in the super-
natural order, conferred *exclusively* upon her by God himself; absolutely *superior* therefore to any other title in the natural order." [2]
Later in that same encyclical Pius went on to say: "Again it is the
inalienable right as well as the indispensable duty of the Church,

to watch over the *entire* education of her children, *in all institutions, public or private,* not merely in regard to the religious instruction there given, but in regard to *every other branch of learning* and every regulation in so far as religion and morality are concerned." The Pope conceded that the state has an independent right to operate schools for military service and for "certain civic duties," if it is careful not to injure the Church in the process.

Pius's claim to rule over "the entire education of her children, in all institutions, public or private" means in practice in Spain that no teachers are allowed to teach Protestantism or Judaism to any children in *any* school. "Professors of religion at non-state schools," says Article XXVII of the 1953 Concordat, "must have a certificate of aptitude issued by the Ordinary [the Catholic Bishop]. Revocation of this certificate will instantly deprive the teacher of his function." No Spanish bishop is ready to admit that any Protestant or Jew has any "aptitude" to teach religion.

In practice, the application of this monopolistic philosophy of education means that no teacher in Spain's national schools can climb to a position of leadership and authority unless he is prepared to accept and promote Catholic teaching. The present statute law does not directly exclude all Protestant and Jewish teachers by calling them "Protestant" or "Jewish," but the regulations and administrative requirements make such service impossible for conscientious Protestants and Jews. As Father Neil G. McCluskey, formerly education editor of *America,* has conceded: "Open profession of Protestantism makes it practically impossible for a Spaniard to hold a commission in the Army or a government position or to become a teacher." [3] Even in the national universities, where the great majority of the students scorn clerical concepts, no professor would have any reasonable chance of appointment or promotion unless he, nominally at least, accepted the Church as a necessary partner in the educational system.

Every teacher in the national schools must be prepared to teach Catholicism as part of the curriculum if he is called upon to do so. In Madrid I asked a high educational official what would happen if a public school teacher refused to take such an assignment—he had already told me that religious teaching in most of the national schools is performed by ordinary lay teachers rather than priests.

"That is part of his job," the official replied. "This is a Cath-

olic country, you know. You Americans must remember that."
"But what if he were an atheist or a Protestant?"
"It would be best for him to keep quiet about that."

Depressed Standards

By American standards, Spain is about a century behind in the development of free schools for all children.[4] There are too few schools, they operate for too short a time, and they fail to reach an astonishing proportion of the children of school age. Some of the reasons for this educational backwardness are economic; others are purely ecclesiastical. It is impossible to avoid the conclusion that the Church has been quite willing to keep the people in partial ignorance in order to prevent a loss of faith.

The Spanish Minister of Education estimated in 1954 that 1.4 million Spanish children of school age were unable to attend elementary school. If an American school-age test were applied to the Spanish situation, the attendance figures would indicate that, with all due allowance for normal absences, about 2.5 million Spanish children were out of school who, under American requirements, would be attending. By every relative, comparative test, the Spanish school system seems to be inferior to that of every Protestant country in the world. I am fully aware that this comparison with Protestant countries, taken in isolation, is invidious and unjust, because religion is only one of the many factors in society which have a bearing on education, and comparative judgments should be based on total situations. I insert this comparison here simply as a defense against those proponents of sectarian education who are constantly emphasizing the primary right of the Church, and claiming that it has carried out its mission with due competence. The experience of Spain, the most Catholic country in the world, does not support that claim.

Nominally all children between the ages of six and twelve are obliged to attend school under a compulsory education act. Actually, not more than 71 per cent of the Spanish children whose names are on the school rolls are in school at any one time, as against a comparative figure of 88 per cent for enrolled children in the United States. And no one knows how many children there are in Spain of school age who are never enrolled. Some of them are too hungry to attend, and there is no national school lunch pro-gram to fill their stomachs. Some powdered milk and other sup-plies are distributed as charity gifts by Catholic agencies, most of it consisting of surplus goods from the United States, but it is quite inadequate to meet the need. Many children of school age in the country districts continue working in the fields when they should be in school, attempting to eke out a living for peasant families when the parents desperately need their labor. Some of them live too far from any school to walk, and Spain provides no bus trans-portation for these.

As late as 1923 the Church and the state were educating about an equal number of Spanish children, but *about half the juvenile population of the country was not getting any education at all.* The state was raising only about half enough money in taxes to support the schools.

Spain progressed toward an adequate school system only as it curbed exclusive clerical control. Even in Madrid in 1931[5] there were more primary schoolchildren with no schools to go to than there were children in the schools—46,000 against 35,000—and the children who did attend the schools had average classes of fifty-seven pupils in each class. The Republic, of course, tried desper-ately to remedy these conditions.

Although there has been a striking improvement in the school situation in recent years, the nation has a great distance to go. The school attendance laws are not rigorously enforced in those rural districts where the illiteracy is worst. I heard from an authentic source about one rural schoolteacher who was hired to teach eleven children in a small country school, but discovered when she reached the region that only one of the eleven attended classes. The other ten were "needed at home," meaning that they were needed in the fields.

The government almost never punishes rural parents for this kind of truancy in spite of the sweeping penalties on the statute books. Although the law is enforced in some cities, the task of en-forcing it in the country is too onerous for the government to as-sume. In any case, the compulsory attendance law reaches only the first six years of school, and at the end of those six years the overwhelming majority of Spanish children drop out with barely enough knowledge of reading to say that they can read. Officially they are permitted to go to work at fourteen; the hotels of Barcelona and Madrid are full of soprano-voiced bellboys who appear to be about twelve years old, who claim they have completed their "education."

When "Public" Schools Are Catholic

Since Spain is so overwhelmingly a Catholic nation, most American visitors expect to find a great parochial school system operated under exclusively Catholic auspices. In the United States, where the Catholic parochial school system is the largest system of its type in the world, non-Catholics tend to identify this system with the Catholic ideal. They do not realize that the separate parochial school system is at best a second choice in Catholic educational policy. The first choice is a "public" educational system which is wholly Catholic, that is to say, a Catholic system paid for by the state. That is what the union of Church and state in Spain has attained. In operation, the Spanish system is even more Catholic than the system in Italy, although the two systems are very much alike.

In Spain the spirit of Catholicism is so militant in the national schools that even the Communists prefer not to advertise their dissidence by asking that their children be excused from catechism classes. As we have already seen, most of the Protestants are in the same situation.

The entrance requirements into the schools also present a stumbling block for any Spaniards who do not accept Catholicism. The children must have a baptismal certificate to get into a school. A baptismal certificate signed by a priest is universally acceptable; one signed by a Protestant pastor immediately raises doubts, particularly when it is handled by a devout school official. From that point forward the non-Catholic child in a national school is a marked child. Some Protestant parents are so reluctant to subject a child to such treatment that they have their children baptized as Catholics in order to gain equality of treatment in the schools, even though such a Catholic baptism may later deprive the child, as an adult, of the privilege of marrying outside the Church.

Under Article XXVII of the 1953 Concordat it is provided that: "The Spanish state guarantees the teaching of the Catholic religion as a regular and compulsory subject in all educational institutions, whether state controlled or not, and whatever their level or purpose." Even a private engineering school would not be exempt from Catholic indoctrination under such a law.

It is interesting to compare this Spanish provision with Article XXI of the Hitler-Vatican Concordat of 1933, made by the same Catholic representative, Pacelli, who was later Pius XII, one week after Hitler had abolished all political parties except the Nazi Party. Article XXI of this Hitler-Vatican Concordat reads: "The teaching of the Catholic religion in the elementary, continuation, secondary, and higher schools shall be a regular subject and shall be given in conformity with the principles of the Catholic Church." [6] Hitler, in this Concordat, secured much more liberty for non-Catholics than Franco demanded or secured in Spain.

The Vatican was not content in the 1953 Concordat to secure a parallel to the German guarantee. It went much farther and secured protection against *any* anti-Catholic teaching in *any* classroom in Spain, no matter what the subject. Article XXVI of the 1953 Concordat reads: "In all institutions of learning—whatever their level and purpose and whether belonging to the State or not —education will be imparted in accordance with the dogmatic and moral principles of the Catholic Church. . . . Ordinaries [bishops] may demand the banning and suppression of textbooks, publications and other teaching material which are contrary to Catholic dogma and morals."

This gives the bishops and their subordinates the power to enter any classroom in Spain, to examine any textbook, or to probe into the moral outlook of any teacher who might be suspected of imparting any ideas inconsistent with "the dogmatic and moral principles" of the Church. In practice it is almost never necessary for any bishop to exercise this right. The writers, the printers, the teachers and the political officials are all so regimented into the Catholic system of thought that heresy in textbooks and teaching is quite unthinkable.

Nominally the state provides "freedom of education." Article V of the Spanish Charter of 1945 says: "All Spaniards have the right to receive education and instruction and the obligation to acquire it, either within the family circle or in private or public centers, at their free choice." The "free choice" is meaningless in terms of religion, since the freedom to operate non-Catholic schools is denied. The Law of Primary Education, which was promulgated on the same day as the Spanish Charter, said: "It is recognized that the Church has the right to watch over and inspect all teaching in both public and private institutions. . . . Primary education—taking its inspiration from Catholic thought, which is in harmony with Spanish scholastic traditions—shall conform to principles of Catholic dogma and ethics and to the provisions of Canon Law in force." [7]

Under such laws, the artistic and decorative paraphernalia of the national schools are in keeping with the Catholic monopoly. Religious pictures and statues are omnipresent. There is a crucifix on the wall of nearly all classrooms, commonly flanked by a picture or statue of the Virgin Mary and of Franco. Sometimes Jose Antonio de Rivera, the great Falange leader, is honored in similar fashion. The pupils begin the day with a salute to the Virgin Mary.

Under these circumstances the Church does not need to operate the majority of the elementary schools—it has sufficient control of the national schools to make this unnecessary. Nuns almost never teach in these national schools but are used in certain private Catholic schools. More than three-fourths of all Spanish children attend the national schools, which are nominally owned by the Spanish state but operate in cooperation with the Church.

The great concentration of Church educational effort is at the secondary level, covering the grades from the sixth to the university. It has been estimated that 80 to 90 per cent of these secondary schools are conducted under Catholic auspices. Although they are in many instances the best schools in Spain, they reach a very small proportion of the young people, partly because they are not free. In fact, no high schools in Spain are completely free for the people.

It is in this segment of the educational system that the Church places its ablest men, members of the Society of Jesus and other orders who are safely loyal both to the Pope and to Franco. And it is from these secondary schools that the Church secures its nuns, priests and missionaries. They pass on from the heavily indoctrinated courses to seminaries and convents, carefully guarded against heresy and modern thought, and trained to class Protestantism, Western democracy and Communism in the group of forbidden concepts. Under the Law of Secondary Education which was promulgated in April 1952, it is provided that "secondary education shall conform to the standards of Catholic dogma and ethics. . . . The number of teachers of religion shall be established in proportion to the number of students."

Since coeducation has been officially condemned by many popes as contrary to Catholic policy,[8] all the schools of Spain are divided according to sex wherever possible. When a village or town is large enough, there are separate buildings for boys and girls. In the smallest villages and towns the schools usually have a wing for girls and a wing for boys, with separate entrances and, if possible, entirely separate classes. Girls and boys are likely to be dismissed at separate recess periods to use the playground separately. If there is a master in the school, he is usually assigned to the boys, while a woman teacher is assigned to the girls. The extra expense involved in this division of small children is traceable to the Catholic bishops whose coeducational policy is dictated by Rome's traditional rule.

The control of the secondary schools by the religious orders is particularly important for the Church's dominance over Spanish women because very few women ever go beyond secondary school. In 1957–1958 there were 50,000 males in Spanish universities and only 11,000 females.

These sex divisions in Spanish culture run through the whole scheme of things. About twice as many women are illiterate as men, and the women are at least twice as faithful to the Church. It is difficult to avoid the inference that there is some connection between these two facts. The priests who impose coeducation on the country have used their power also to impose upon women a docility which is anti-intellectual. "I cannot find anything intelligent to talk about with a Spanish girl," said one young Spanish engineer to me. (He had studied in England and made contacts with educated women.) "They rarely read serious books, and they haven't gone far enough in school to understand much about the outside world. They swallow what the priests and nuns tell them because they know nothing better. I've never known a Spanish young lady of my own age who could engage in adult conversation with men unless she had studied abroad."

A Starved Educational System

The small number of women in Spanish universities indicates not only the lowly status of women within Spanish culture but also the lowly status of general education in Spain. Informed Spanish writers are the first to recognize this fact. One responsible Spanish journalist, Victor Alba, writing in *Iberica,* said: "Public education in Spain today is among the worst in the world." [9] Earlier Mr. Alba had pointed out that Franco had allocated less than 1 per cent of the national income to education, whereas no other European country spent less than 2.5 per cent. However, many new schools have been built by Franco in recent years and he has made a great show of an extensive expansion program which impresses foreign tourists. Nevertheless, the attendance figures show that the proportion of pupils in the schools has actually dropped since the Civil War. The government admitted in 1956 that Spain needed 25,000 new schools for the age group from six to twelve alone.

Alba attributes the slump in attendance to both intellectual and physical starvation among the teachers. Professional morale is at a low ebb. If a teacher seeks to improve his capacity and standing, he must accept training that is largely theological. "In the normal schools," says Alba, "there are many more classes in theology than methodology." Clerical conservatism tends to dominate the whole curriculum. No stimulating books from the outside world are permitted if they challenge Catholic ideas.

Spanish school teachers average less than $500 a year in income. Sometimes their annual income is far below this amount—in 1954 the average pay of teachers in state elementary schools was estimated at $230 a year.[10] In 1959 the Madrid newspaper *Pueblo* was even allowed by the censorship to say: "Only rarely does a grade-school teacher today earn over 3,000 pesetas a month [less than $60]. Teachers exist who have worked 22 years who earn no more than 1,600 pesetas a month [less than $32]." [11]

Almost the whole financial burden of education falls on the national government, and the control of education likewise is national. This centralized control of Spanish education makes the task of the Church somewhat easier, and the Church is heartily in favor of it. In Spain all the American Catholic slogans about the dangers of centralized state control of education are reversed. There the priests contend that an all-powerful centralized government contributes to the "unity of the nation" and the glory of the Church. It does—when the government is obediently Catholic. It also makes censorship more efficient. One disapproval of a doubtful textbook by a Cardinal Primate or his agent means that the questionable book is outlawed in every village in the nation.

Comparisons between a rich country like the United States and a relatively poor country like Spain are bound to be unfair, since historical accident plays so large a part in shaping national institutions. But the comparison should be recorded here in order to counter Catholic misrepresentations. The "godless" public educational system of the United States is under almost constant attack in the Catholic press throughout the world, and this same press quite frequently refrains from any corresponding exposure of the weaknesses in a "godly" educational system such as that in Spain.

The United States Census in 1960 showed that 88 per cent of all American children between fourteen and seventeen were enrolled in schools.[12] Although equally exact statistics on the parallel situation in Spain are not available, it is certain that in Spain at least 88 per cent of the children from fourteen to seventeen were *not* in school. In respect to the proportion of children of fourteen to seventeen in school, Spain seems to be in about the same situation as the United States was in 1890.

The differences in illiteracy are just as striking. After more than one thousand years of clerical control of culture, the Spanish nation came to the period of Republican control in the 1930s with almost one-third of the people illiterate.[13] At the turn of the century more than two-thirds of the people had been illiterate. In 1937 the estimate was about 30 per cent. Today illiteracy may be no more than 15 per cent, but there has not been an accurate accounting on a national scale in recent years. The 1957 "Report on the World Situation" by the United Nations gave Spain's illiteracy as 17.3 per cent and that of the United States as 2.5 per cent. The figure for France in the 1957 report was 3.7 per cent; for England 1.2 per cent; for Switzerland 1.2 per cent. The American figure is now about 2 per cent.

Some leaders of the Church, and apparently Franco himself, feel the humiliation of Spain's backward educational position quite keenly. Jose Maria de Areilza, Spanish ambassador to the United States, boasted in 1958 that his government through a five-year plan of construction was making a "massive fight against illiteracy, one of Spain's traditional plagues. Twenty-five thousand schools are being built at a rate of five thousand a year, so that by 1962 there will be practically no child without a basic culture and education." [14] A less optimistic critic has estimated that at the actual rate of progress now being made in Spain the process will take until 1991.[15]

One leader of the Church is taking a very active role in combating illiteracy,[16] the famous Bishop of Malaga, Don Angel Herrera y Oria, former editor of the Madrid daily, *El Debate,* who became a priest late in life and rapidly climbed to a position of great influence in the Spanish Church. His mountainous and barren diocese is one of the most illiterate in Europe, with only 3 per cent of the people having any education above elementary level, and more than half of the people without any schooling at all. Unfortunately, Bishop Herrera does not seem to be typical of the Spanish hierarchy.

The Universities and Opus Dei

The universities in Spain are somewhat freer of clerical control than are the elementary and secondary schools, although every student in every university in Spain is obliged to pass a course in Catholic doctrine in order to receive a degree. If a university student wishes to receive a passing mark in that course, he must not reveal a too determined attitude of opposition.

The course is not an objective course in comparative religion; it is a course of carefully weighted Church propaganda, usually taught by a priest, in which the non-Catholic world is treated as alien. If a university student wishes to become a lawyer, he must take at least five courses in Catholic Canon law taught by a lawyer-priest. In these courses the Church courts are treated with as much respect as the civil courts, divorce is considered as non-existent, and the legal outlook of Western secular states is treated as heretical liberalism.

An increasing number of Spanish university students resent the compulsion involved in these Catholic religion courses, and as a result the priest-professors are very unpopular figures. "Our course in religion," a student at the University of Madrid told me, "is the one course on the university's calendar in which everybody cheats. We resent the fact that it is imposed on us from above. Cheating is the device we use to show our resentment." Even in the Falange student organization (SEU) which has a political monopoly in Spanish universities, a large minority of the students angrily challenge the compulsory teaching of Catholicism and accept it only because they must.

Even in this Catholic kingdom, the national government rather than the Church retains official control of Spain's twelve universities. There are Church faculties, and partial Church universities, but all the non-theological degrees in the university world are granted after examinations controlled by state authorities. Spanish university professors still get appointment and promotion after competitive examinations and, although both political and clerical influences sometimes twist the results, intellectual merit remains the primary criterion. Hence, the university scholar is still the most respected man in Spain.

As for the students, it is possible to get completely conflicting versions of their attitudes toward religion and the dictatorship. There is a powerful opposition minority with confused loyalties to socialism, Communism, anti-clericalism, and republicanism; and this minority tends to be bitterly anti-American as well as bitterly anti-Franco. Occasionally their leaders engage in extreme acts of heroism and are promptly put in prison. But after more than twenty years of non-participation in democratic processes, the present younger generation of Spain is severely handicapped. The young people lack both political experience and trained democratic leadership. They are specialists in disorder and demonstrations, but even in this department their opportunities are foreshortened by quick arrest.

A vigorous minority bloc is especially active at Madrid University with its 25,000 students, and at the University of Barcelona, the center of Catalonia dissent. Madrid University was closed for a time early in 1956 because of riotous opposition to the government, directed chiefly against Falange student leaders on the campus. Students, said the university's rector, objected to "the prohibition of ideas," and they should be heeded because they are "the first to express the state of latent opinion in the societies to which they belong."

Franco was unmoved. The limit of his accommodation was to allow the unusual privilege of an open trial for some of the student rebels. To make sure that this was only a temporary concession he suspended for three months the operation of the two key articles in the Spanish Charter, the right to choose a place of residence within Spain, and the right after arrest to be turned over to judicial authorities for due process within seventy-two hours. These rights had already become non-existent for "subversives."

The one new, clerical shadow on cultural freedom in the universities is an organization known as Opus Dei whose full name is The Sacerdotal Society of the Holy Cross and Opus Dei. Although it is now a worldwide organization with members in fifty countries, it is usually regarded as a Spanish instrument, since it was founded in Spain and has grown to its greatest power in that country. It is considered by many Spanish university professors to be the most ominous threat to intellectual freedom that has been manufactured under the Franco regime.[17]

"Membership in Opus Dei," said one distinguished professor to me, "is absolutely necessary for promotion in this university. I know, for example, that in the philosophy department every one of the professors, with one exception, is Opus Dei. The members cooperate in promoting their own interests, and they combine those interests with those of the regime. Opus Dei has been formally written up in American Catholic magazines as a holy force opposed to political corruption. I am willing to grant that it has done good things in eliminating bureaucratic corruption in some of our government departments. But in university life I can testify that it stands for a deeper intellectual corruption, the denial of cultural independence."

This was one of Spain's most distinguished scholars speaking, and his opinion seems to be shared by all Spanish liberals. They regard the new Opus Dei as an intellectual agent of the Spanish police, dressed up in the garments of clerical service. They especially deplore its growing influence in university life. Although they concede that an actual majority of Spain's university professors may not belong to the organization, they believe that the well-organized and carefully controlled Catholic cells in the center of university life dominate virtually all appointments and promotions. Most of the professors, not because of any special friendliness to Opus Dei, cooperate with it because they want survival in a Catholic kingdom.

Opus Dei may not be as powerful or as evil as its reputation. It is a Catholic religious order which operates partly in secret, but it does not seem to be any more secret than many ordinary fraternal lodges. It was founded in 1928 by a wealthy Spanish priest now living in Rome, Jose Maria Escriva de Balaguer, an accomplished intellectual who has been both a lawyer and a professor of journalism. His special interest has been the organizing of Spanish laymen to serve the Church with the same devotion as priests, but without their costume or professional routine. In 1939, Father Escriva wrote a book that is considered the Bible of the new order, *Camino* (*The Way*), which neatly combines maxims, proverbs and missionary suasion. It is said to have sold more than a million copies.

Escriva, who now functions under the direct control of the Vatican, secured official approval for his organization in 1947, thus making it the first secular institute in the Catholic Church to win papal sanction. Now the idea has spread and a number of other secular institutes have been founded.

The thing that makes a secular institute different from an ordinary Catholic religious order is that the members participate in ordinary professional life and do not wear the identifying costumes of priests or monks. Nor do they live in community life as so many religious-order members do. They take the recognized vows of poverty, chastity and obedience but they cannot be identified. It is easy to see why this lack of identification has been the cause of special fear in a police state like Spain. Anti-clerical and anti-Franco citizens cannot be sure whether, when they are talking to a public official who is known for his piety and faithfulness, he is a member of Opus Dei or not. Most of the organization's members are laymen, although some priests are admitted, and there is also an auxiliary membership class for those who married before they decided to join. The order also has so-called "cooperators" who, it is alleged, may even be Protestants or Jews.[18] In practice, I have never heard of a Protestant or Jewish auxiliary member.

The Spanish membership of Opus Dei may be 5,000 or 10,000 or 50,000. No one knows the exact figures, but it is common knowledge that membership rolls contain the names of some of Spain's most powerful and wealthiest citizens. Their financial power is tremendous because their members contribute all their surplus income above living expenses to the order. They own a private university at Pamplona, several schools in other parts of Spain, a chain of daily newspapers in Madrid and the provinces, and they are said to control several banks. But their most active area is in the world of the universities where they are said to control the whole system of appointment and promotion in key departments in many institutions. The liberals regard them as a kind of Uncatholic Affairs Committee searching out in the university world all those intellectuals who show signs of rebellion against Rome or Franco.

Franco himself is not a member of Opus Dei but he has been

exceedingly cooperative in appointing Opus Dei leaders to key positions in his administration, particularly since 1957. In his cabinet the Secretary of the Presidency and the Minister of Tourism and Information have both been Opus Dei members. The organization's leaders effectively control the national system of censorship.

Like the Falange, the Opus Dei began in a burst of social idealism, using the slogans of clean and efficient government and devotion to the public service. The organization's particular target was corruption in public life, and it undoubtedly had a healthful effect on Spanish administration in its early years. However, as it grew in power it became more and more a clandestine weapon of espionage and self-promotion. Its lofty social idealism became routine paternalism, emphasizing the personal aspects of Christian conduct and avoiding any responsibility for changing the social structure or bringing in more democratic freedom. The organization has often been described as "the white Masons," but the analogy is farfetched. It demands complete fanaticism and complete dedication in its members, and willingness to be subject to dictation from Rome. Its president is appointed for life by the Pope himself.

Opus Dei strenuously denies that it is either political or class conscious. Its chief lay spokesman in Spain, Rafael Calvo Serer, has declared that: "Opus Dei is not a social caste, nor a group of aristocrats or monarchists, nor a coterie of intellectuals. . . . Each member is absolutely free to think and act on the political level according to his personal convictions." I could not find any liberal in Spain who believed this, since the organization has not only taken all the traditional oaths of allegiance to the Pope but it operates essentially as an upper-class adjunct of the most conservative wing of the Spanish Church.

Ironically enough, the most important anti-Opus Dei force in Spain today is the Society of Jesus, whose fanatical devotion to a central authority in Catholicism has been notorious for centuries. In this case the opposition of the Jesuits is based upon plain institutional jealousy. For centuries they have cultivated the same intellectual fields which are now being invaded by Opus Dei. They see the control of education slipping from their hands into the hands of non-costumed upstarts, and they deeply resent it. Although the two organizations are ostensibly friendly, the Jesuits

EDUCATION IN THE SHADOW OF THE CHURCH

have begun to manipulate against Opus Dei behind the scenes and the future of the organization is therefore in doubt.

This is the kind of manipulation in which Franco especially delights. He retains his power largely by balancing one faction against another, and nothing could make him happier than a protracted struggle for power between the Jesuits and Opus Dei.

The Opus Dei classic, Father Escriva's *The Way,* which was published in an English translation in the United States in 1954 with the blessing of Cardinal Stritch of Chicago, contains 999 aphorisms or pronouncements which stress complete obedience to religious superiors in much the same way as do Jesuit manuals. "In apostolic work," it says, "there is no such thing as a trifling disobedience." As to poverty, it says: "Detach yourself from the goods of the world," but it does not prescribe the limits of detachment.

Its prescriptions for chastity have naturally led to extensive rumors that it has been infiltrated by men with homosexual tendencies. Father Escriva's book is certainly quite anti-sexual, even emphasizing mortification to overcome the sexual appetites. "Where there is no mortification," he says, "there is no virtue." Members are reminded: "To defend his purity, St. Francis of Assisi rolled in the snow, St. Benedict threw himself into a thornbush, St. Bernard plunged into an icy pond. . . . You . . . what have you done?"

8. HOW THE CENSORSHIP WORKS

The life of a newspaper or magazine editor under the Spanish dictatorship is not a happy one. Every editor and every writer in Spain must edit and write with at least one censor looking over his shoulder. That censor is a political official but he is guided by Catholic principles. In terms of the criteria used, there is no division of censorial functions in Spain between Church and state. With the exception of the theater, the state's censors virtually always accept the standards of the Church in judging any material which encroaches upon moral territory. Every government censor, of course, is a Catholic, and usually he is a fanatical Catholic committed to the Church's primary thesis that error has no rights against truth.[1] Since approximately one-third of all the daily newspapers in Spain are Church journals, and no anti-Catholic journals are permitted, the Church's point of view is assured of an audience.

Although Spain's censorship system is more complete than that of Ireland, the Church's participation in the scheme is less direct. In the Irish Republic, a priest served for many years as the chairman of the government's censorship board. No self-respecting Protestant or independent scholar would serve as a member of such a body. The board is still completely dominated by the Catholic point of view. It has banned more than four thousand books, including many of the most popular British and American novels, chiefly on the ground of "obscenity." Every Irishman knows that the criteria used in the banning have come from the priests.

Ireland, however, has a relatively free press headed by the Republic's most important paper, the non-Catholic *Irish Times*. The lists of banned books are made public each year, and are often ridiculed by the *Irish Times*. As a result of this exposure of the workings of government censorship, Irish intellectuals rush to buy the censored books abroad, usually in England or Ulster, and they are allowed to bring single copies back into the country without being molested. The result is that the censorship board of Eire has become the most discredited and futile feature of clerical power in the Irish Republic.

In Spain the censorship is so complete that it destroys the people's knowledge of censorship. Even the intellectuals never hear of most of the important works that are suppressed. The control of thought extends to every branch of the national life, blacking out not only all objectionable stories in newspapers but also all books, plays, motion pictures, and radio and television programs that church and state wish to ban.

This successful system of suppression is based upon the fact that the government has one central supervisory agency for all censorship, the Ministry of Information and Tourism, headed for many years by a clerical-minded reactionary, Gabriel Arias Salgado. He has such complete censorship powers that even when a group of Spain's most distinguished intellectuals unite to risk their own careers by protesting against the censorship system, the protest never reaches a single outlet in Spain. In fact, this is what happened in December 1960 when 227 authors and artists "publicly" protested the censorship system.[2] Their public was located in Paris, London and New York; it never included the Spanish people, except by underground rumor.

The censorship includes in its ban all advertising in all media of information. Discussion of the works that have been banned and the machinery used in the banning are also taboo—except in coffeehouse conversations.

The suppression of freedom of the press is, I suppose, the most distinctive difference between the Spanish Republic of 1931-1936 and the dictatorship of Franco. In the days of the Republic, the Spanish newspapers blazed with vital controversy. Books, newspapers and magazines representing capitalist, Communist, republican, socialist, Catholic and atheist points of view were freely circulated. The winds of world opinion were sweeping through Spain after generations of curtailed freedom. Universities were alive with serious discussion. The Cortes was a great intellectual battleground, and its proceedings and debates were followed carefully in every part of Spain.

By contrast the Spain of today seems intellectually asleep. The newspapers are so dull and uniform that millions of people have stopped reading them. Their circulation has fallen to a pitiable level—in all of Madrid, with its 2 million people, it is doubtful if more than 200,000 copies of newspapers are sold on the average day. However, these newspapers do carry a considerable amount of substantially accurate foreign news. Franco is much more receptive to honest journalism coming from abroad than to honest journalism at home. And he allows the magazines slightly more freedom than the newspapers.

The Machinery of Press Surveillance

The Spanish press law of April 23, 1938, although it has been modified in many details, is still the basic law of Spain.[3] Franco and his aides wrote the law long before the end of the Civil War for application and enforcement in nationalist territory. It was in part a war measure designed to prevent the enemy—meaning the duly elected government of Spain—from publishing in Franco territory anything that might discourage or defeat the rebellion. Its standards of suppression were severe, since even the most democratic nations traditionally control newspapers in war time.

But ultimately Franco's censorship system went far beyond standard wartime practice. In the introduction to the 1938 law it was argued that the notion is obsolete that democratic freedoms should be preserved in publishing information. The press, it was claimed, is an instrument to inform the people about truth. Error does not have commensurate rights. Naturally, therefore, the press must be closely associated with the state since it is a kind of fourth power, assisting the other basic powers in Spanish society, the Army, the Church and the government.

Franco has preserved the iron control of that 1938 law through more than twenty-three years of "peace," and the machinery of suppression has greatly expanded. In spite of recent statements to the contrary, there has been no substantial increase in literary liberty. Columns of publicity were published in the Spanish newspapers in the summer of 1959 about a new Law of the Bases of Information which was alleged to grant slightly increased liberty to the press. Out of the mountain of publicity there emerged a molehill of minor changes, chiefly in the nature of codification and clarity. The basic policy of repression was reaffirmed on September 26, 1960, when a new decree included in the crime of military rebellion any dissemination of "false or tendentious news" that might "attack the prestige of the State."

Under the 1938 law, the state is entitled to complete surveillance over the periodical press, including the power to determine the number and nature of periodicals. It may intervene to appoint directors and editors, to regulate the journalistic profession, and censor all material published. The minister in charge of the press service may appoint the chief of the press service in each province, and the director of every paper must be approved by the agent of this Ministry. If a local censor is bought off—and this frequently occurs—a provincial governor can censor material on his own authority. This allows a little leeway, but the independent writer or editor can never be certain of how much mercy will be meted out to him.

An editor or writer must be registered as a journalist, and if he wishes to become a director of a newspaper or a magazine, his application must be sent in to the ministry and approved. Even when his application has been approved, the minister may dismiss any director without making any public statement concerning the reason for dismissal. (The director of a Spanish newspaper exercises the functions of an American managing editor.)

A director ordinarily may dismiss any journalist for saying anything in opposition to the regime. The entrance to the journalistic profession is itself completely controlled by the censoring agency, since schools of journalism must be approved and journalists must come up from those schools to be registered for their profession. If a journalist cannot show his professional registration card, he cannot work for any Spanish periodical. These rules for the control of journalists are almost exactly the same rules promulgated by Mussolini for the control of Italian journalists in July, 1924.[4]

With one exception, all the magazines in Spain which have the right of publication and general circulation must submit their material to the central or regional censorship office before publication. (We have already seen that no Jewish or Protestant magazines are allowed.) Most of the newspapers of Spain fall in this pre-censored category in spite of their press deadlines; a few are subjected only to post-publication control, but the result is essentially the same. Their directors are held responsible for anything printed, and they face immediate discharge if they permit the publication of any article that displeases the government.

Knowing the general policy of the government, the Church and the censorship office, Spanish editors usually reject out of hand at least 90 per cent of any borderline stories or articles which might possibly offend either church or state. If an editor becomes too bold and submits an article which seems to reflect upon the system of authoritarian rule, the article is returned to him with a single sheet of paper stamped with the words "No hay lugar," which means in effect: Not suitable now. No further explanation needs to be offered.

The head of a newspaper is in a sense an appointee of the Franco regime, inferentially approved by the Church; his career and his very freedom from arrest depend on conformity. In effect, he must act as an internal agent of the Franco police in judging his own columns, and his standards of judgment must be essentially the same as those of the secret police.

These are negative features of press control in Franco's Catholic Kingdom. Franco himself is shrewd enough to permit the various groups supporting his government to publish their own papers and to indulge in some disagreement. *Ya,* the Madrid daily which represents Catholic Action, prints more ecclesiastical material than *Arriba,* the organ of the Falange, but both support the regime on all fundamental matters. He uses them both at will as personal publicity organs for the regime. Whenever the government wants some Franco speech or some government edict featured in a favorable way, the front pages of both organs are available. The most tedious conglomeration of cliches affirming the importance of unimportant reforms is spread across the front pages of all Spanish newspapers. Any criticism which the government wishes to suppress is never mentioned.

Although there are a few privately owned newspapers, such as *ABC* in Madrid and *La Vanguardia* in Barcelona, which have a slight tinge of independent critical judgment, the criticism never challenges the system of power. *ABC* has monarchist leanings and *La Vanguardia* stresses Catalan aspirations, but they are almost indistinguishable in their general emphasis from the Catholic Action and the Falange newspapers. *ABC* is alleged to have the largest circulation of all the more or less serious journals.

The censoring of foreign news coming into Spain is done partly by the controlled national news agencies, such as EFE, which buy American and other news-service material and sift it for Spanish consumption. Naturally enough, the emphasis is shrilly anti-Communist and habitually critical of any government which tends to "compromise" with the Soviet Union. The whole world is threatened by One Great Conspiracy centering in Moscow. Every menacing development throughout the world which has a Communist tinge is emphasized and re-emphasized. Simultaneously, every statement made abroad which can be construed as a compliment to the Franco regime is underscored. The doubts about Franco expressed by foreign commentators are eliminated from dispatches. Catholic propaganda is automatically sandwiched in with the general news, and every papal pronouncement is featured.

There has been one striking exception to this rule of kindly treatment for papal utterances. That was in 1937 when the encyclical of Pius XI, *Mit Brennender Sorge* was almost suppressed in the Spanish press because it was considered too hostile to Hitler. Actually, it was a very mild document, but Franco did not at that particular moment in history wish to disturb his friendly relations with the Nazis. He was an ally of Hitler and believed that Hitler was going to win the war. So he never permitted the Spanish people to see an adequate treatment of that famous, mildly anti-Nazi encyclical.

Sporadic Enforcement

No editor of a standard Spanish daily ever needs to be told by the government censor that favorable Protestant and Jewish news stories of a religious character are taboo, or that anything anti-clerical is also taboo. Occasionally some treatment of news is permitted in a Catholic or university journal which is anti-clerical in its total effect, but never if it is doctrinally anti-Catholic or doctrinally pro-Protestant or pro-Jewish. Literary criticism is similarly restricted. No book reviewer may praise too warmly any literary work offensive to the regime. "The only activities open to public blistering by unofficial critics," says Mildred Adams of the *New York Times*, "seem to be the bull fight and the football game; sports writing therefore becomes a refuge for pens repressed in other fields." Incidentally, football (soccer) seems to be replacing the bullfight as the favorite subject matter for the excitement of the Spanish masses.

Occasionally some criticism is permitted of the operation of some government department if the philosophy of the regime itself is not challenged. Usually the permitted publicity is carefully timed to allow an almost immediate anouncement of a necessary reform which has been accomplished by an ever-watchful and humane dictator. Thus the impression is created that a benevolent government is quickly rushing to assuage the sufferings of the people.

There is a kind of double double standard in the enforcement of this censorship of the press. The expensive periodicals are less likely to be censored because the masses cannot afford to buy them. It is assumed that the propertied classes cannot be too easily seduced by revolutionary information. Also there is a double standard in dealing with the foreign press which is published in foreign languages. Unless a foreign periodical happens to use the Spanish language or happens to be published in a Communist country, it has a far better chance of acceptance than a local publication. Since American magazines are both expensive and published in the English language, they sometimes enter Spain with material that no local Spanish paper would ever be permitted to print. Also American correspondents may enter Spain quite freely and include in their dispatches many items that would be excluded from Spanish newspapers.

In this field the most irregular standards of censorship obtain. A lazy local censor in Barcelona may sleep so late one morning that he permits the *New York Times* to describe in considerable detail the growth of revolutionary sentiment right in Barcelona at the very moment of a general strike—that is what happened one morning in June 1959 when I was in Barcelona at the time of the abortive general strike in that city. I was able to read in a copy of the *Times* at a Barcelona newsstand a realistic and provocative account of the forces of social discontent in Barcelona at the very moment when every mention of the powerful underground movement in that city was being suppressed or distorted by all the Spanish papers in the city.

The foreign journals never know how Franco will treat them after the publication of an item of sharp criticism. The *New York Times* and *Time* have both been victimized, particularly when they printed any personally derogatory reference to Franco. Generally the owners of American journals feel that any protest to Franco would be so futile that they do not even bother to report the suppressions and confiscations to the American Embassy.

On June 23, 1959 the *New York Times* published an editorial, "Dr. Salazar's Portugal," in which it said: "Unlike Generalissimo Franco, he did not take a barbarous revenge on enemies."

Nothing irks Franco more than an unfavorable comparison with Salazar. The censors promptly decided that the Spanish people should not be permitted to read such an outrageous falsehood. Accordingly all subscribers to the *New York Times* in Spain were notified that that particular issue of the offending paper was nondeliverable. No reason was given for the blockage in distribution.[5]

Of course, the final decision concerning exclusion of foreign journals is made by agents working directly under Franco himself, and sometimes his decisions are shrewdly Machiavellian. In June 1960 the aspirant to the Spanish throne, Don Juan, was quoted in *Life* magazine as saying: "We must find a new and better regime. It certainly will not be a dictatorship. The monarchy must not return to Spain with a desire to destroy—but rather to open Spain's windows and unify the country." The censorship immediately banned *Life* for this mild and rather equivocal comment, but Franco overruled the ban.[6] "Gentlemen," he said, "if the Count of Barcelona (Don Juan) wishes to commit political suicide, I shall not prevent him. Let the magazine be publicly sold." Franco's strategy in this case was based on the desire to keep the monarchists divided and uncertain, with one portion of the upper classes committed to Don Juan, and another portion to his son, Don Carlos, and both committed to Franco himself because of increasing anxiety concerning what might happen with any change of government.

Incidentally, *Life* is very unpopular with the Franco-controlled press. In February 1961, *ABC* headed an editorial, "With Spittle and With Bile," charging that *Life* had "amassed a fortune through sensational propaganda, profiting by petty vilenesses and reiterated journalistic perfidies." [7]

Nominally Spain continues full wartime censorship of personal mail. Every letter from abroad and every letter addressed to a foreign recipient is technically subject to mail censorship. Every book from a foreign country may be unwrapped and examined. A minor official in the postoffice can hold up a letter for as much as fifteen days without any special order. In practice, only those letters addressed to or coming from a few suspect individuals are ever held up, and usually these are retained in the post office for only a few hours. Single books sent to ordinary Spanish citizens or foreigners whose names are not on any list of suspects are likely to come through the mails untouched.

Both Protestants and socialists whom I met in Barcelona and

Madrid in 1959 told me of tapped telephone wires and pre-inspected mail, handled so carefully that sure proof of the spying was almost impossible. Letters going out of Spain which contain systematic factual material derogatory to the regime are likely to be held up and confiscated if they are sent by an identified Spanish critic. But, like most things in Spain, the rules are elastic. An important anti-Franco journal like *Iberica,* published in New York, is able to smuggle out regular news hostile to the regime. American correspondents of the great news services regularly send out uncensored dispatches. Of course, if their dispatches become too annoying, they can be excused from further residence in Spain.

The tourists find unusual freedom for themselves, particularly American tourists, since they bring millions of welcome dollars into the country. For these tourists there is virtually no censorship at all if they do not attempt any general distribution of anti-Franco material. They may bring with them—as I did—great crates of "subversive" material ranging from pro-socialist to pro-Protestant suasion, and no one will even open their luggage at the border. But let any person of Spanish citizenship attempt the distribution of any "subversive" importations, especially if they have a Masonic or Communist flavor, and he will find no mercy. His literature will be confiscated and he himself will be sent to prison, probably without trial.

Catholics Censor Catholics

The Spanish censorship system is primarily a system operated by pro-Vatican and pro-Franco Catholics with the object of controlling those liberal Catholics who question authoritarian rule. In the internecine struggle it is the younger Catholics who want freedom and the older Catholics who plead for discipline. The top rulers of the Church are unanimously pro-censorship, and they cooperate gladly with the economic and military aspects of that censorship in order to secure protection for their own privileged position.

The purely religious justification for the Spanish literary censorship goes back to Canon Law itself, supposedly binding on all Catholics throughout the world. Under Canon 1399 no Catholic may read any book or periodical which defends those errors proscribed by the Holy See, which disparages ecclesiastical discipline, or treats any Masonic organization as useful or ridicules any Church dogma, or favors the right of divorce, or promotes any heresy.

This basic philosophy of censorship is impressed upon all the students in Spain through their classes in Catholic faith and morals. The students are told that Catholic law is very specific about which books and periodicals can be published, read, owned, borrowed or sold. The grades of sin are meticulously defined and the guilt is apportioned according to the directness of responsibility for the publishing or the handling of sinful works. If there is any dispute about the right to read, publish or circulate any particular sample of critical literature, permission must be secured from the bishop, who has a right to pronounce a ban on any questionable reading matter. The publisher who knowingly publishes or the bookseller who knowingly sells a forbidden work is subject to excommunication. In Spain, as in Ireland, this means complete financial ruin for any individual dealing with the public.

Within the Church itself, under Canon 1386, priests are forbidden to publish any material on any subject without episcopal permission. If they are caught contributing anonymously to a somewhat liberal Catholic youth paper, they are likely to be sent to some mountain monastery. If they sign their own names to any criticism of a political or ecclesiastical nature, they are equally certain to be disciplined. Because of this tradition of internal thought-control, the Church is the strongest arm of the government in the national censorship system. Spain is now the only country in the world today in which every book on the *Index librorum prohibitorum* of the Vatican is officially suppressed by the government. (I say "officially" because the actuality does not come up to the rule.) Even in the Irish Republic the Church does not dare to go that far, and in Italy the Pope would be completely powerless to impose such a regulation.

In Madrid I was able to see, after a great deal of pleading, the actual censorship list of the banned books in the central office of the book censor. Although the prohibited index of current books is officially secret and is never mentioned in the press, I was able to see that a number of titles on the list were officially banned for purely ecclesiastical reasons, such as "Index" and "offensive to the Jesuits." When an official saw that I was copying down these reasons for suppression, the list was immediately taken from me.

Incidentally, the number of new banned books in Spain each

year is not large, because the publishers and the authors do not care to risk the time and expense involved in submitting a manuscript which is almost certain of rejection. Probably not more than sixty or seventy titles a year are banned by the central office in Madrid. Many times that number are withheld from publication; the authors do not write them and the publishers do not accept them.

One of the serious impediments is the length of time it takes to get a decision from the censorship office, especially if a book comes from a "suspicious" source. Three or four months is quite common; one author told me of a delay of more than six months in getting a permit for public release after all the material had been submitted.

As might be expected, the actions of the censorship office are frequently inexplicable and confused. An early Boris Pasternak, I noted, fell by the wayside with a book about Marilyn Monroe; and the two were joined with one of the more heretical books about Albert Schweitzer. Two Erskine Caldwells were coupled with one Somerset Maugham. A Stendahl was labeled simply "Index." Theodore Dreiser's *The Titans* was rated immoral along with a treatise on the charms of Brigitte Bardot. James Gould Cozzens shared the "immoral" category with a Gide and a Havelock Ellis.

There is a double screening for books, the screening of the manuscripts and the screening of books *after* publication. If error is not caught in the early stages, it may be caught in the bookstores. All bookstores must be licensed, and if they wish to retain their licenses they must obey government instructions about the display of books. Imported books must bear a stamp telling the purchaser the name of the importer. The general rule is that the stamp of approval, required for every book published in Spain, is never forthcoming if that book is directly disapproved by the hierarchy. When, in 1956, the Spanish police took 20,616 copies of New Testament extracts and 4,812 other books from the Madrid branch of the British and Foreign Bible Society, the ostensible reason for the seizure was that the books did not have the required stamp of approval from a Spanish censor. In this case everybody knew that the real policy was established by the Church and that the King James versions of the Bible were banned because they are forbidden for Catholics under Canon 1399.[8]

This type of priestly censorship is much more irregular and

unsystematic in Spain than it is in Ireland. Old books on the Catholic *Index* are not suppressed as rigorously as new works, and many works on the *Index* are overlooked. The National Library in Madrid still carries Thomas Paine's *The Rights of Man,* and several books by Victor Hugo, Dumas and Anatole France in spite of the fact that they are on the Vatican *Index.* The recently banned works of Jean-Paul Sartre are more carefully banned from this library since he has high standing in the Spanish revolutionary underground and is considered a present danger.

Although the National Library carries no general books attacking Catholicism or Franco directly, it is very charitable toward broadly philosophical works which do not have a specific application to present day Spain. John Dewey is permitted to slip in, with some of Voltaire. But while the National Library has found enough money for Carlton Hayes's egregiously pro-Franco book, *The United States and Spain,* no funds for Claude Bowers' far more perceptive, but anti-Franco, work, *My Mission to Spain* were available. One of the most powerful exposures of the Franco regime written by any Spaniard, Madariaga's *Spain, A Modern History* is not available in the National Library or in the bookstores, since it states quite bluntly some very important truths concerning Franco. (I was finally able to discover that the National Library possessed one copy of this work marked *Reservado.*) In general, the Spanish libraries have been swept clean of any works that present current arguments for anti-clericalism or anti-Francoism or which give a reasonably fair version of the Civil War.

The strictures against anti-Franco material are more severe than against liberal theological material. In the National Library I could find none of the best books on the Spanish Civil War written by Americans. When I mentioned this fact to the kind lady at the desk who had charge of certain reference material, she showed surprise and asked me which books I had in mind. I gave her a list of books by Americans which, in my opinion, represented the best American criticism of present-day Spain: Emmet J. Hughes, *Report on Spain*; Claude G. Bowers, *My Mission to Spain*; Herbert Matthews, *The Yoke and the Arrows*; Lawrence Fernsworth, *Spain's Struggle for Freedom*; Charles Foltz, Jr., *The Masquerade in Spain.*

The lady looked confused and, after due search, reported that these books were not available.

The younger Catholics in Spain resent this government mechanism for thought control very deeply, and they have started a few mildly critical journals of their own. However, these Catholic magazines of mild protest have very small and uncertain circulation as over against the 850 Catholic-oriented journals in the country. They are censored almost as severely as the genuine left-wing journals. "Our magazine," said one young Catholic editor to me, "must prepare two supplies of copy for the censors for every issue. Half of our material is rejected each month. The reasons? Well, they tell us that we must not say anything that can harm the government, or glorify youth organizations as such if they are not guided by the Church, or play up any movement of workers or students except under Falange or Church control. Most of us would like to see a Christian Democratic party in Spain after Franco, but of course no such organization can be mentioned now." The young editor's magazine incurred the wrath of Franco in 1957 because it published the statements of an American Catholic criticizing the dictator, together with an editorial commenting favorably on the criticisms. The next two issues of the journal were almost obliterated by the censor, and the severe censorship was still continuing two years later.

Above the Law

There is only one journal in Spain that is officially outside the power of all government censors and that is *Ecclesia,* the weekly organ of Catholic Action published in Madrid. Perhaps it is a misnomer to call it the organ of Catholic Action because it is too sober and ecclesiastical in style to reach the Spanish masses. It is essentially a documentary of the Spanish hierarchy, dry, academic, unillustrated, and filled with official Vatican documents and tedious repetitions of the Pope's addresses to visiting pilgrims at St. Peter's. It has a possible circulation of 25,000. (Catholic Action has five daily newspapers in addition to *Ecclesia* but they must submit to ordinary censorship rules.)

The Vatican, in its 1953 Concordat, specified that the Church must have independent rights of communication with the Spanish faithful, and the unique status of *Ecclesia* guarantees that the faithful can be reached by any message from the papal throne. The journal specializes in sober, priestly items designed for the Church both in Spain and in Latin America. It is extremely cautious in its pro-Franco policy since the bishops are conscious of the fate of those Church members who took sides against the Republic in the Civil War, and they know that anything appearing in *Ecclesia* might ultimately be used against them. *Ecclesia* was definitely committed to Franco in the 1947 plebiscite which gave the Caudillo lifetime rights as Chief of State, but for the most part it is content to endorse the regime obliquely and to repeat routine platitudes on moral values and the preservation of internal peace in the country.

Once, in 1954, an editor of *Ecclesia,* Father Jesus Irabarren, burst out in eloquent indignation against the whole system of thought control in Franco's state.[9] His indignation was directed partly against the Falange, which at that particular moment owned about one-third of the daily newspapers in Spain, but it also included the whole system of suppression. "A Catholicism must be weak and a national unity shattered which have to be protected day by day," said Father Irabarren. He criticized the Spanish government for treating the Spanish people like mental minors. His punishment came swiftly. He was summoned to the office of the Spanish Minister of Information, Gabriel Arias Salgado, and told that his dismissal would be demanded. For reasons of pride the Cardinal Primate suspended him "temporarily," but he was ultimately dismissed.

Franco permits the Church to engage in some public laments concerning the poverty of the poor and the corruption of minor officials so long as the fundamental structure of the dictatorship is not criticized. Perhaps he reasons that carefully worded descriptions of the pitiable poverty of Spain constitute good propaganda for more foreign financial aid and at the same time help the Church to create that image of paternalism which may save it from destruction later on.

Below the level of state censorship there is a whole network of Catholic lay censorship which branches out into publishing houses and distributing agencies. A fanatically Catholic distributing firm controls the distribution of literature at railway stations and exercises its own supplementary censorship of literature. The exclusions of works of literature on supposedly theological grounds are sometimes astounding as well as annoying. The works of

Tolstoy have been banned for several years; Balzac's "complete" works are reduced to two volumes; and Kant and Descartes are severely cut.

The top censor told one leading publisher in Spain recently, concerning the permissible limits of sexual comments: "Everything is permissible that an educated couple can read without blushing or getting excited." In practice the extreme Puritanical standard is not actually applied, either in Spanish magazines or in the foreign imports. Hollywood publicity magazines enter Spain with very little cutting. Presumably the priests never see them.

As we have already seen, the Church is given a very substantial dialectical reward for cooperating with the government censorship system. It is allowed to publish pamphlets attacking Protestantism, whereas the Protestants cannot print or distribute pamphlets attacking Catholicism. In 1959 a very successful publishing house in Barcelona, working under Catholic auspices, was distributing thousands of copies throughout Spain of *Espana Antiprotestante,* devoted primarily to eloquent exposures of "Protestant treason." Any formal attempt to answer such propaganda in print would be instantly suppressed as against the national interest.

In July 1960 some five hundred delegates from many countries attended a Congress of the International Catholic Press Union in Santander, a city on the northern coast of Spain.[10] The delegates were reluctant to come to Spain in the first place because of the joint Catholic-Franco censorship which seemed to them to be contrary to all the concepts of a free press. Some relatively liberal Catholics within Spain prevailed upon them to have the Congress in their country in the hope that it might spur the regime to improve conditions. American Jesuits took advantage of the congress to send out from Santander a strong appeal for more press freedom, and the *New York Times* carried a large headline: "Catholic Editor Asks Free Press; World Congress In Madrid Applauds Father Davis As He Calls Liberty Vital." The headline referred to an address by Father Thurston Davis, editor of the Jesuit magazine *America,* in which the American priest said bravely that: "Without this essential freedom [of the press] there can be no authentic public opinion, for wherever the Catholic press or the press in general is muzzled, public opinion has no means of self-expression." Readers were not told that this talk was either suppressed or distorted in the Spanish newspapers to prevent the Spanish people themselves from knowing that non-Spanish Catholics were critical of Spanish censorship. After Franco had seen the headlines in the American newspapers, the next Catholic congress in Spain, "The 20th Social Week of Spain," cancelled its session on "Information in Contemporary Society" because the question "had already been discussed."

The Films, the Air and the Human Body

American readers are quite familiar with Catholic censor-ship of motion pictures and periodicals in the United States through the Legion of Decency and the National Organization for Decent Literature.[11] Both organizations are controlled by the hierarchy, and all the final policy decisions are made by the bishops of the United States. The Legion of Decency is important for both the United States and Spain because it operates primarily in the capital of world film production, Hollywood, and its judgments affect the parallel verdicts by Catholic Action in all parts of the world. At the present time all Catholic censoring organizations of films are linked under the general supervision of the Pontifical Commission for Motion Pictures, Radio and Television, with headquarters in Rome, now headed by an American archbishop.

The literary importations from the United States into Spain are trifling; the film importations are very large and important. Perhaps this is the reason why the Church in Spain insists on oper-ating its own independent film censorship agency outside of the national system. Although Catholics and only Catholics man the government film censorship office, and there is a Church represen-tative on the national film censorship body, the bishops feel that the government's strictures are not quite severe enough to suit the Church. So the Church has set up a film censorship system which operates slightly to the right of the government in the moral and theological spectrum.

For the theater owners and the film distributors the existence of the two rating systems for films is very confusing, and tends to create a certain amount of anti-clerical bitterness. "They have just made three cuts in 'Daddy Long Legs,'" said a mournful theater owner to me in northern Spain, describing the three little "cut" strips that had come with his American film. "The chief source of our trouble is the local censorship representative of the Catholic family organization. He is a bachelor and he seems to be afraid of a skirt. So he gives me a little extra Church censorship beyond that of the government, and he is worse than Madrid."

"Why don't you defy your bachelor censor and see what would happen in court?" I asked.

He looked at me incredulously. "I wouldn't have a chance even to get into court in this country," he said. "If a Church representative in this town says 'No,' the police go along with him every time. If I went to trial I would simply lose my license."

Sometimes, in practice, the separate Church film censorship officials rate a film below the government rating, and the theater owner still assumes the risk and permits its exhibition. The government film office uses only two categories, "Todos" for general consumption, and "Mayores" for adults only; and all film advertisements are obliged to carry these ratings. The Church uses four categories of its own which permit finer shadings of approval and condemnation. While many newspapers carry these Church classifications, in addition to those of the government, they are not legally obliged to do so. The Church, of course, always carries its own ratings in its own press, and Catholic Action groups in each diocese are directed to see that the warnings are obeyed.

It is a sin to take a child to any but a No. 1 film, or any young person to a film graded 3 R. As in the United States, the Catholic film ratings are posted on church doors each week to remind the faithful of their obligations. This clerical system of censorship has acquired special dignity within the Church since Pius XII in his 1957 encyclical, *Miranda prorsus,* imposed upon bishops the responsibility for moral supervision of both air waves and films.

Everywhere in Spain the Church tries to enforce its special category of modified condemnation called "3 R," which means acceptable for adults with reservations. In the country districts the priests are quite successful in preventing the showing of such films; in Madrid and Barcelona they are not. On a certain day in July 1959, I counted seven films with a Church 3 R classification still being exhibited in Madrid. Of course, if a film receives absolute condemnation—a No. 4 rating—from the Church, the government censors will not permit its showing.

Films imported from abroad—and most films exhibited in Spain do come from abroad—are subject to a double and triple modification. To begin with, their language may be altered in the spoken script as the Spanish is dubbed in. Sometimes the most fantastic changes are made in the dialogue to make an American film

conform to Catholic decency standards. The most famous altera-
tion was that of a noted film made in Africa in which the unmarried
lovers who drifted through the jungle without chaperons were
made into a brother and sister. The baffled Spanish audiences
could not understand why there was anything exciting about the
plot.

American films must also run the special gauntlet of Church
objections to pictures glorifying divorce, or exalting any religion
other than the Catholic faith, or picturing the Spanish Civil War in
a way unfavorable to Franco. In 1959, Franco indignantly blocked
the production of an American film starring Ava Gardner because
it did not meet his view of a sound treatment of the Spanish Civil
War. The producers finally moved on to Sicily. When *Gentleman's
Agreement* was banned from Spain by the censors in 1948, the ecclesiastical member of the censorship body, according to the *New
York Times,* explained that the Christian duty to stimulate love
among individuals did not necessarily extend to Jews. This statement was finally disowned by an embarrassed hierarchy after some
criticism, and the film was exhibited in Spain with only slight modi-
fications.

Today the Spanish film censors rarely give exclusively religious
reasons for banning an American film. (The most popular films
are American, but every Spanish theater owner is obliged by law
to fill in his program with 25 per cent of domestic films, which are
usually quite second rate). American commercial importers, of
course, know that they cannot import into Spain any film that
might come under the ban against public manifestations of a non-
Catholic faith in the 1953 Concordat and the 1945 Spanish Charter. Sometimes Spanish Protestants attempt to show films in spite
of this ban, but their attempts usually result in failure. In 1957
the pastor of Madrid's First Baptist Church, Reverend Juan Luis
Rodrigo Marin, knowing that he could not secure a license for
an official public showing of a film on Martin Luther, quietly
showed the film in his own church behind closed doors. He
promptly received a communication from the police denouncing
him for showing an unlawful film without a license. He protested
strenuously that the private showing of such a film to the members
of one church was a private affair, not subject to censorship. His
protest was in vain, and he was fined 5,000 pesetas on January 5,
1957, for holding an "illegal meeting" and for "projecting a non-
authorized film."

It cannot be said that Church censorship of films in Spain is either successful or popular. There is widespread resentment against the standards of the priests in the handling of sexual matters on the screen. *Ecclesia* complained in an editorial in 1959 that there were fewer than half as many films fit to show children in that year as in 1957.[12] There were only ten films exhibited in all Spain in 1958 that won the Church's No. 1 rating, and many films were shown in spite of the Church's protests. In recent years the protested films have included such American productions as *Separate Tables, While the City Sleeps, Raintree County, Bus Stop,* and *Witness for the Prosecution.*

Regardless of one's opinions concerning the merits of such films, there can be no doubt that the importation of American films has a very salutary influence on the Spanish public. The Spanish people see other peoples with a standard of living far above their own and this helps to create a social discontent. On the whole, the American world they see on the screen is relatively free, even when the landscape is overcrowded with pistol-packing gunmen. It is not a Catholic world, or a world ruled by dictators. So the Spanish people rush to see American films far more hungrily than their American counterparts go to see those same films in the United States. In fact, Spain has nearly twice as many cinema seats as the United States in proportion to population, and they are filled far more frequently.

Although television in Spain is still in its infancy, the radio has enormous coverage, and Franco makes desperate efforts to fill the air waves with pro-government propaganda. Probably radio is more completely censored within Spain than any other medium in the country, since it reaches so many of the illiterate masses who could most easily be stampeded by rumor. There is pre-censorship of every program, and the broadcasting of any material not acceptable to the censor brings immediate discharge for any employee who is responsible.

But in this area of radio, the Franco censorship has been partially defeated. No one can prevent Spaniards from tuning in on French radio programs and the BBC. Probably the most powerful single anti-Franco force in Spain today is the daily Communist program being broadcast from Prague under the label *Radio Espana Independiente.* Everywhere I went in Spain I found that it was the most popular radio program among underground leaders, even though they were quite aware that its facts were doctored and that its management was controlled by the Communists. On this so-called "Radio Pyrenees" the Communists pour out fiction with consummate skill, making adroit use of the Catalan and other regional languages. Naturally enough they specialize in anti-American as well as anti-Franco propaganda.

The Spanish theater seems to be freer than the screen or the air. Perhaps one reason is that it is wholly urban and the people of Madrid and Barcelona are relatively sophisticated. There is a strong strain of French influence.

Although there are definite rules excluding obscenity and the human navel, almost every type of contortion and costume is permitted on a Spanish music-hall stage. The Catholic bishops rage in vain. Through their theater censoring bureau, a part of the Church's official censorship office, they frequently condemn a stage play in an urban theater, and the police calmly allow the show to go on in spite of the condemnation. Even a condemned No. 4 rating in the pages of *Ecclesia* does not stop a legitimate theater performance.

When pressure from the bishops becomes very strong, the government censors often visit the first performance of a censored play, observe carefully that it has eliminated all suggestive lines, and then conscientiously remain away from all subsequent performances. This is what happened to *Look Back in Anger* when it recently came to Madrid and was accepted after months of wrangling in the censor's office. Some frank words about infidelity, the female neckline and a possible interruption of pregnancy were eliminated from the first performance. After that performance, the play returned to its original form.

America Supports Censorship

In the struggle for free speech inside of Spain the agents of the United States government almost never take any positive, public position in favor of freedom. They explain that they cannot interfere in domestic matters in a foreign country. This explanation might carry some weight if our American representatives were in fact neutral in regard to Spain's internal struggle. In practice they are committed to Franco's dictatorship by virtue of their frequent public appearances with him in friendly poses. In the world of literature, also, they collaborate with his censorship without public protest. (The political aspects of this collaboration are discussed in a later chapter.)

The information services of the United States government in several parts of Spain were accepting Franco's censorship standards for their own American publications and libraries in 1959 when I visited them. They were withholding from the Spanish people those books and magazines which Franco and the Church wanted withheld, and they were helping to circulate those books and magazines about Spain which pictured church and state in a favorable light for American visitors. Anyone touring the country could test these charges by visiting, for example, the Casa Americana in Madrid, adjoining the United States Embassy, or the USIS information center in Barcelona. (The USIS is the overseas branch of the United States Information Agency, and together they have an immense program for the publication and distribution of books overseas, mostly concerning America, embracing 166 libraries in 70 countries, receiving about 250,000 books a year.) The USIS libraries in Spain were at that time deliberately excluding candid and scholarly American books on Spain in order to please the Franco regime and were accepting books about Spain which projected a pro-Franco image.

The American visitor who goes to the Casa Americana in Madrid, with its small and excellent library, is given a card which says:

> This library is designed for Spaniards who seek information about the United States. . . . The library is part of the United States Information Service program in Spain. There are also libraries in Barcelona, Bilbao and Sevilla. They bring the story of the United States and its policies to thousands of Spaniards every year. . . .

Although the American official libraries profess that they do not carry books about Spain for Spaniards, this claim is not true. They carry quite a number of books about Spain, both in Spanish and English, and these books are selected in such a way as to exclude many scholarly works that criticize the Church and Franco.

I have already mentioned in discussing the National Library in Madrid, five books by American authors about Spain which I consider important and scholarly and which have been excluded from Franco's National Library because they tell unpleasant truths about his regime. The literary and political credentials of the authors of these works are quite impeccable. Emmet J. Hughes,

Claude G. Bowers, Herbert L. Matthews, Lawrence Fernsworth and Charles Foltz, Jr., have records that would entitle them to a place in any American library. They have been, respectively, the Press Attache of the American Embassy in Madrid; the United States Ambassador to Spain; the chief correspondent of the *New York Times* in Spain; a correspondent of the *London Times* in Spain; and bureau chief of the Associated Press in Spain. It would be hard to find anywhere five men and five books which could tell the Spanish people in more authoritative language what informed Americans think about freedom and the lack of freedom in present-day Spain.

All of these books were excluded from general circulation by the Library of the Casa Americana in Madrid in 1959, while many lesser and more pro-Franco books were exhibited on the same shelves. The Casa Americana had shelf space to carry two pro-nationalist works, one by the American Catholic convert and former United States ambassador to Spain, Carlton J. M. Hayes: *My Wartime Mission in Spain* and *The United States and Spain*. It also carried the most pro-Franco and pro-Catholic modern book about the regime, *This is Spain*, by Richard Pattee of the National Catholic Welfare Conference.

When I asked about the omissions and apparent discriminations, I was informed: "We have such books as you mention, of course, but they are not for the general public. They are controversial. They are for the use of our staff only." I was taken into a private room and shown the library cards for many books about Spain which the embassy staff could read for itself but which Spanish visitors to the Casa Americana could not secure. Among the reserved books were Bowers' work and Madariaga's *Spain, A Modern History*. In a separate library for the embassy staff exclusively, not available to the general public, were almost all the works about Spain that a student could desire. A similar but modified type of American collaboration in censorship was apparent in the so-called American Club in Barcelona, where an American information library is used eagerly by Barcelona students.

In partial defense of the American policy of submission to Franco in American libraries in Spain, it should be said that in the present Spanish state *all* libraries are subject to the most severe censorship under an old statute which was written for nationalist territory before the Civil War came to an end. The job of cleaning up these Spanish libraries was assigned to a commission that included a university dean, a professor of philosophy, a representative of the Church, a representative of the army, a Falangist and a representative of the heads of Catholic families.

These library cleanup commissions had as their legal purpose the withdrawal of "books, pamphlets, magazines, engravings, and leaflets which may contain in their text illustrations or utterances expressing dissident ideas, immoral concepts, propaganda of Marxist doctrines, and anything showing the lack of respect for our glorious army, contempt for the unity of the fatherland, contempt for the Catholic Church, or opposition to the aims of our Great National Crusade." Three classes of literature were forbidden in libraries: obscene literature, revolutionary literature and literature which, although it might have some scientific or literary merit, could be "ideologically harmful." The first two classes of literature were to be destroyed outright. The last class was to be kept in a non-visible location which could not be easily reached by the public. The United States has accepted for its own public libraries in Spain the concept of "the non-visible location" for all candid literature that directly attacks the dual dictatorship of church and state.

9. THE LABOR-CAPITAL STRAIT JACKET

Catholic power and fascism are more completely blended in Spanish industry than in any other aspect of Franco's controlled society.

We have already seen how the fascist development of economic life in many European countries was partially based on Pius XI's famous 1931 encyclical *Reconstructing the Social Order*. That encyclical is the moral foundation for Franco's brand of fascism today. In that encyclical the Pope argued cautiously, and somewhat ambiguously, for the general principle of national vertical "corporative organization" which would include both employers and employees in one collaborating, united body controlled by a powerful state.

Pius XI did not commit himself for or against the specific tyranny of Mussolini's state, nor did he commit himself on the side of democracy. He left Catholics and others throughout the world to draw the conclusion from his favorable remarks about the Italian structure of power that he was quite willing to see democracy destroyed if "social order" could be preserved. Although he disagreed with Mussolini concerning some aspects of fascist society, he did not question its dictatorial forms or its enforced incorporation of organized labor into the fascist state.

The timing of Pius XI's encyclical on social reconstruction was as important as the language itself. The date was 1931, after Mussolini had been in power almost ten years. The Pope virtually endorsed the principle of fascist vertical control of industry at a time when that system of control was being recognized by the liberal world as a ruthless tyranny. His acceptance of the structure of power of the new society gave it respectability and moral standing at a time when fascism needed such endorsement most desperately.

Was this the price the Pope had to pay to stay healthy within a fascist nation and to receive the financial and other benefits of the 1929 Mussolini-Vatican agreements? Whatever may be the answer to that question, the Catholic people of Europe paid a terrible price for the Pope's limited collaboration with Mussolini. The rather ambiguous words of the 1931 encyclical were widely interpreted as a papal blessing for the fascist labor scheme. The Pope described the fascist syndicates of Italy in such vague and friendly language that their most objectionable features were concealed. He began his description rather cautiously:

> Within recent times, as all are aware, a special syndical and corporative organization has been inaugurated, which, in view of the subject of the present Encyclical, demands of us some mention and opportune comment.
>
> The State here grants legal recognition to the syndicate or union, and thereby confers on it some of the features of a monopoly, for in virtue of this recognition, it alone can represent respectively working-men and employers, and it alone can conclude labor contracts and agreements. Affiliation to the syndicate is optional for everyone; but in this sense only can the syndicate organization be said to be free, since the contribution to the union and special taxes are obligatory for all who belong to a given branch. . . . It is true that it has been authoritatively declared that the legal syndicate does not exclude the existence of unrecognized associations.[1]

There is no mention in this last sentence of the basic fact that independent trade unions were completely destroyed by fascism, and many of their leaders were murdered. Nor is there any mention in this famous encyclical of the fact that workers under the fascist system were forbidden to elect as their representatives any open enemies of the fascist system. The Pope proceeded:

> The corporations are composed of representatives of the unions of workingmen and employers of the same trade or profession, and as true and genuine organs and institutions of the State they direct and coordinate the activities of the unions in all matters of common interest. Strikes and lockouts are forbidden. If the contending parties cannot come to an agreement, public authority intervenes.
>
> Little reflection is required to perceive the advantage of the institution thus summarily described; peaceful collaboration of the classes, repression of Socialist organizations and efforts, the moderating influence of a special ministry.

Pius XI was both an economic reactionary and a skillful politician. Realizing the great risk involved in making a direct endorsement of fascist organizations, he sandwiched into his approving descriptions several precautionary phrases which could later be used to defend the Vatican in case fascism happened to be defeated. He called for "Catholic principles and their application" in the development of fascist forms of corporative growth. He deplored the "excessive bureaucratic and political character" of the new organizations. He reminded the Catholic world that although socialism "if it really remain Socialism . . . cannot be brought into harmony with the dogmas of the Catholic Church," it might be that "the tenets of mitigated [non-Marxist] Socialism" could be reconciled with Catholic policy. He assumed a generally benevolent tone in discussing labor organizations.

Naturally enough, when Franco finally realized his opportunity to establish the fascist system of industry in Spain in 1939, and when he had smashed the socialist, anarchist and independent trade unions by executing their leaders, he sought to give respectability and moral glamor to his reformation by using the name and the words of Pius XI. He needed the authority of the Church for such a drastic reorganization of Spanish life, and he found the verbal tools ready at hand in Pius XI's language.

Hybrid Labor Fascism Today

Today, after more than twenty years of clerical, semifascist rule, there is not a free labor union or a free employers' association in all of Spain, nor is there any free labor or industrial press. All strikes are forbidden as crimes, and any attempt to organize an independent labor movement is treated as a conspiracy against the state. The conspiracy is punishable by summary process without a formal civil trial.

Officially the employers are as completely bound into the strait jacket of the syndicate system as the workers. They cannot legally form their own self-governing trade associations; they cannot discharge any employee without governmental approval; and they cannot declare any lockouts. But there is a fundamental difference between their status and that of labor. The Franco state itself is essentially a semibenevolent capitalist dictatorship which not only preserves private ownership of the wealth of the country but also grants major economic control of the nation to five great centralized banks whose officers are often called the silent rulers of Spain.

Business has paid a price to Franco for its security, but the cost of the payment is not uniformly distributed. Little business has surrendered both independence and power; big business has surrendered some independence but not ultimate power. Labor has suffered forced absorption into the syndicate system without any corresponding compensation in terms of power.

It should be emphasized that this syndicate system is not all bad—otherwise it would not endure in Spain. The system has been used not only to tyrannize over the economic life of the nation but also to supply a certain type of stability and some protection for the workers. It is a system of paternalism as well as tyranny, and the paternalistic features are so well advertised by a controlled press that many of the workers actually accept the system's estimate of its own merits. Thus the defects of the system are partially concealed. The loss of liberty is partly balanced by the fact that the standard of living of the workers is improving slightly. The system, with generous American aid, is scoring some minor economic gains. In 1959, for example, a drift toward runaway inflation was halted by the abrupt and arbitrary imposition of a Stabilization Program which devalued the peseta and at the same time lowered the living standard of the Spanish workers. The economic price paid by the Spanish workers was appalling, but panic was prevented and collapse postponed. With all its inefficiency, the industrial system has raised the per capita product of Spain quite sharply since 1950.

The Franco "labor movement" has no recognized status even among Catholic trade unionists outside of Spain. The official Catholic labor movement with headquarters in Utrecht, known as the CISC, claiming more than 2 million members in Italy, France, Belgium and the Netherlands,[2] refuses to cooperate with Franco's syndicate system. If it did, it would lose all chance of friendly relations with the chief instrument of democratic and anti-Communist labor in Europe, the International Confederation of Free Trade Unions.

In the United States, the AFL-CIO, which is affiliated with the ICFTU, has been bitterly hostile to Franco's syndicate system from the beginning. "To American labor," said an AFL-CIO statement on "United States Labor's International Role" in May 1960, "the first test of totalitarianism of either the left or the right has been this simple yardstick: Does the government in question permit its workers to practice the principle of freedom of organization?" [3] By that test Spain has had no labor movement since 1936.

In December 1960 the ICFTU meeting in Brussels asked all its affiliated organizations to work for the discontinuance of all aid to the Franco government in view of its opposition to a free labor movement. In 1958 the Confederation had issued a manifesto of its objectives which included the following demands for political and labor freedom in Spain:

Establishment of a non-partisan provisional government of all democratic and anti-totalitarian forces, to guarantee to the Spanish people the exercise of its fundamental freedoms and to prepare in the shortest possible time the way for free elections in which the Spanish people will be able to determine what kind of government should rule the country.

Immediate repeal of the legislation instituting the discredited falangist syndicates and restoration of free trade unionism, independent from control by government and employers.

Establishment of the right of association and of the exercise of all individual freedoms. [4]

Such statements never reach the workers within Spain, except in an occasional Communist handbill distributed by the left underground, and the Communist source of the news gives the government an opportunity to discredit it by saying that the whole story was manufactured in Moscow.

How does Franco maintain his syndicates in the face of such near-unanimous condemnation by the world of Western labor? The first answer, of course, is that he uses physical force. He controls the army, the secret police, all the newspapers, magazines and local radio stations which could produce a counterrevolution based upon economic discontent. Any labor leader who insists on ordinary free speech in opposition is jailed as a "Communist."

The second answer is that he has been clever and far-sighted enough to use the Falangist syndicates as instruments of benevolence. By dovetailing an elaborate system of social benefits into his system of labor control he has been able to give the total amalgam an appearance of paternalism. The government grants of health insurance, family allowances and old-age pensions—such as they are—come to the workers through the syndicate system. And the third answer is that he has had the active support of the Church in imposing the system on Spanish labor.

In daily practice the Church's collaboration with the Franco syndicates is partly effected through priest advisers for each labor group, appointed by the bishops of each diocese. These priest advisers are helpful to individual workers in attempting to correct individual abuses, but they never challenge the repressive system itself. Their presence is taken as eccelesiastical approval of the system. The bishops constantly stress the claim that the only Spanish alternative to Franco's syndicate system is Communism. For this reason they even oppose the organization in Spain of Catholic trade unions affiliated to the CISC.

In the United States the Catholic press, with some honorable exceptions, tends to gloss over the cruelly repressive features of the Spanish syndicates. In the March 26, 1960 issue of the Jesuit magazine, *America,* Fernando Fugardo Sanz, Spain's syndicate representative at the International Labor Office in Geneva, published the following amazing description of the labor-capital strait jacket in Spain:

Regardless of what people in the United States think, the workers in Spain express their will through elections, with a direct and secret ballot. They decide who are to be their representatives from the companies they work for. They determine how their intermediaries are to be charged with watching out for their interests in the unions. They choose their own representatives for the social struggle and the achievement of economic social gains in the municipal governments. These men are there as citizens to defend the interest of a given town and to find out how the money of the taxpayers is being spent. Finally, in the Cortes, which corresponds to the United States Congress, these representatives see to it that the laws possess that social content which laws, if they are to be human and just, should embody. These organizations are elected by a system of universal suffrage, which means by direct and secret vote. . . .

I know of no country in Europe or in the Americas where the unions can exercise on the life of the nation a force so powerful as that possessed by the unions or syndicates of Spain. This is one of the secrets that explain why in Spain we do not have strikes to defend the interests of the workers. The workers have leaders elected by the workers themselves, and the function of these representatives is to see that the law is respected and fulfilled for the benefit of all.

I repeat that we are elected with complete freedom, and certainly not with the system of the raised hand that prevails so much in certain countries where they boast of being revolutionaries.

This description is almost wholly fraudulent. No leader of Spanish labor can occupy any place of influence in the Cortes or the syndicates without approval of Franco and the Falange. If a leader of Spanish labor dares to challenge this system of dictatorship, he goes not to the Cortes but to prison.

Northern European Catholic labor leaders do not like their Church's acquiescence in Franco's industrial tyranny. When I visited the Utrecht headquarters of the CISC a few years ago and engaged in a frank discussion of Catholic labor policy with its chief executive, I found him as skeptical of Franco's labor aims as any socialist could be. He was quite aware of the inconsistency of the Vatican in endorsing liberty for labor in the northern part of Europe, and collaborating in its suppression in Spain.

Probably the great majority of Catholic workers in Spain would agree with that critical judgment if they had any means of securing knowledge of the outside world. As it is, they tend to accept the inevitable, and their acquiescence is primarily a matter of desperation. They often use a question in discussing the system which is popular in Spain: "No hay remedio?" which roughly means: "What can you do anyway?" If they do not care to accept Franco's syndicate system, they can starve or die in battle.

The Economic Masquerade

The present organization of Spanish economic life is so different from anything existing in the United States that ordinary words cannot convey a real picture of it to most Americans. The trade union side can best be described as a type of company unionism. The capitalist side evokes some memories of the NRA, but without any genuine freedom for objection or reform. The industrial relations machinery contains the essence of compulsory arbitration, but the arbitrators are not chosen impartially. The whole economic scheme is built into an amalgam in which the single political party of Spain, the Falange, is the nominal controller of everything.

The Church is the cautious advocate of the whole scheme and its spiritual adviser. The army stands in reserve as the only power capable of suppressing any protest. In actual practice the whole scheme is a power instrument in the hands of one man, the Caudillo. All the democratic and semidemocratic features of the scheme are merely items of camouflage designed to give the arrangement some much-needed public respectability.

The suave Spanish diplomat who explained the whole scheme to me in Madrid gave me many statistics. The government publications informed me that national production is going up (it is slightly); they told me how the per capita income is rising (it is, but there is doubt about *real* income because of inflation); they told me how the nation is using more fertilizer and tractors (it is, but the increase seems miniscule by American standards); they told me how more fish are being caught, etc., etc. All this could be true, although all Franco statistics are subject to doubt. But since the whole Western world is moving ahead in economic growth, it would be almost a miracle if Spain should actually be receding.[5]

The alleged democratic features in the vertical-syndicate system are quite mythical. The Spanish workers in the 24 vertical syndicates in the scheme allegedly cast more than 5 million votes for their "industrial leaders" in 1959, about 4 million of them directly, and the rest obliquely. In 1960 it was alleged that 10.5 million were taking part in a five-month series of elections to choose about 500,000 officials and representatives among both workers and employers, with about 300,000 committee members for the 24 vertical syndicates, including about 80,000 shop stewards. These elections take place about every three years. In 1957, since some of the ballots were actually secret, some real anti-Franco revolutionists found their way into the shop-steward movement. The protest was quite futile, since the top 130 officials in the organization are appointed by the Franco regime, and any shop steward who carried his resistance to the point of open agitation would be sent to prison as guilty of subversion.

If the visitor points out to his Spanish host that the whole scheme is based on coercion, he receives the polite and evasive reply that the system is not yet "complete." Meanwhile, the descriptive terms applied to the system by its own leaders in addressing their own people assume that the ideal *has* been accomplished. Said the Secretary-General of the Social Council of Spanish Syndicates in 1959: "We have an authentic organized democracy, so perfect that there is nothing similar to it in any country in the world." [6]

The Falange Declines

In the first stages of the development of the vertical-syndicate system, everybody of importance had to be a member of the Falange, Spain's single political party. The Falange dominated virtually all labor organizations. Demonstrations of marching men in their red berets and blue uniforms were almost as common in Spain as the corresponding Fascist demonstrations in Italy. The Falange took over boldly from Italian Fascism some of its mystique of violence and idealism.

The Spanish Falange movement had been founded in 1933 as a kind of counterrevolutionary agency to undermine and ultimately overthrow the Republic. In 1934 it was joined with the JONS (Junta de Ofensiva Nacional Sindicalista), another right-wing body. This was a rather strange marriage since the JONS was originally quite anti-clerical. By one of the accidents of history, one of the most popular early leaders was Jose Antonio Primo de Rivera, son of the old monarchist dictator. After the triumph of the left-wing popular front in the Republic in 1936, he was arrested and shot as an enemy of the state. The manner and the timing of his death made him a national hero. He was, in fact, a rather rattlebrained and impulsive young man who produced during his short career more bathos than sense.

At first the Falange movement—now universally known in Spain simply as The Movement—combined the familiar mixture of idealism and swagger apparent in the Fascist Party in Italy and the National Socialist movement of Hitler. But it never acquired the mass following of the German and Italian movements. Perhaps the chief reason for this was that the Falange was not the primary instrument in Franco's victory. That distinction rested with the Spanish army, and the army has always taken a slightly patronizing and distrustful attitude toward the Falange blueshirts.

In the beginning of Franco's reign the blueshirts and their Fascist salute were almost as conspicuous and annoying in Spain as the corresponding manifestations in Italy and Germany. Then the army and its adroit master, Franco, gradually maneuvered them into decline, always claiming loyalty to the Falange principles in a loud voice. In a sense, Franco bought out the Falange, giving it state financial support for its activities in exchange for policy-power, and making it what H. R. Trevor-Roper has called a "great system of jobbery." [7]

Until the collapse of Fascism in Germany and Italy, the Falange held the loyalty of several million young Spaniards. Then it rapidly dwindled to about one-third of its former strength. Now its reunions seem a little pathetic and its faded blue uniforms quite dated. Today many of Franco's highest officials have dropped out altogether, apparently without rebuke from their chief. The few idealists left in the movement are bitter against both the Church and Franco, the Church because it is an important institutional rival and Franco because he has been an acquiescent pro-capitalist in his policies.

Originally the Falange was far from being pro-capitalist. Its original aims were humanitarian, somewhat socialistic, extremely imperialistic—and all confused. In its *Twenty-Six Points* in 1934, the organization declared: "We have a will to empire. We demand for Spain a pre-eminent place in Europe." Then the Manifesto went on to say: "Our state will be a totalitarian instrument in the service of National integrity. The family, municipal and syndical channels are to be the means of participation in the life of the state. Political parties are to be abolished."

The Falange insists that it is not a political party but a movement. Actually it is both. It uses the phrases of democracy as confusingly as the Communists do. Its published theses remind one of the statement of the famous Spanish philosopher, Ortega y Gasset: "Fascism wears an enigmatic face because its content is so contradictory. It affirms authority, and at the same time organizes revolt. . . . Whichever part of fascism you take hold of, you find that it is a thing and also that it is its opposite—it is A, and at the same time it is non-A." In its original Manifesto it not only condemned class warfare but also advocated the nationalization of the banks and repudiated "a capitalist system that ignores the needs of the people." Today the Movement is in alliance with totalitarian capitalism.

From the beginning of the Falange there has been official co-operation with the Church, but also continuous institutional rivalry. The original Falange Manifesto pledged the movement to "incorporate the Catholic spirit in the national reconstruction." Then it went on to say: "The state will tolerate no interference with its own dignity or the national dignity." That was a warning to all organizations, including the Church, to remember that Falange power should come first.

The Church was uneasy because there was, particularly in the beginning, a considerable amount of anti-clerical sentiment in the Falange movement. The Falange leaders looked upon themselves as more practical moral leaders than the bishops. They established various youth organizations to undermine the Church's associations and to indoctrinate Spanish youth with their own concepts.

Gradually the Church manipulated events against the Falange, and in the long run it won. As in Italy, it did not want a lay body which might supersede Catholic Action, more particularly in the organization of youth. When the Falange leaders tried to capture the schools of Spain for themselves, the Cardinal Primate tartly served notice on Franco that if the Church did not regain its dominant power over the school system, he would publicly resign from the Cortes and denounce the whole Falange educational plan. Franco squirmed, but finally capitulated.

Since then, Franco has watched the power struggle between the Church and the Falange with considerable relish. He has kept alive the workers' organizations of Catholic Action and simultaneously allowed the Falange to sabotage them. The rivalry over this situation broke into print in December 1960 when the aged Primate, Cardinal Pla y Deniel, warned the Falange that it must not suppress the independent Workers Brotherhoods of Catholic Action. Said the headline in the *New York Times*: "Primate of Spain Warns Franco Church-State Conflict Looms." [8] A casual reader might have believed that the Church was standing for labor rights against the dictatorship. Not so. An analysis of the bill of particulars revealed that, as in Italy and in Germany under Mussolini and Hitler, the Catholic complaint was not directed against dictatorship as such but against discriminatory treatment of the Church's own labor groups.

One of the conditions of the Church's approval of the state syndicate system in the first place was that the Church's own propaganda and social organizations for workers should be allowed to conduct their own activities. The Falange, because of jealousy, has been working against these Catholic Action "cells" in its syndicate bodies since the beginning.

Today the relationship between the syndicates and the Falange itself is confusing. The syndicates, organized in 1940, are nominally a department of the Falange. Both organizations constitute monopolies which are partly political and partly industrial. The Falange is the only political party allowed in Spain, and the syndicate system is the only labor-employers system allowed in Spain. Frequently the syndicates are called Falange syndicates, and the description is correct as far as it goes, but the syndicate and the Falange are two entities. Recently they attained a new kind of temporary unity when one man, Jose Solis Ruiz, became chief executive officer of both organizations simultaneously. Franco remains official head of the Falange.

The two organizations are partly fused in their political power in the Cortes, since that third of the 577-member Spanish parliament "elected" by industrial, economic and municipal groups is essentially Falange representation. Only members or friends of the Falange can secure positions as chosen leaders in this political-industrial framework. The parliamentary statistics of the masquerade are so meaningless that they are scarcely worth recording.[9] Of the 577-member Cortes—often described as 540 members because of different ways of reckoning ex-officio members—the syndicates have 181 *procuradores,* of whom 39 are ex-officio, 30 are elected by the employers, 24 elected by technical employees, 34 elected by workers and 34 elected by the above four groups. Of the national Falange representation, 50 are elected by the Falange, 50 appointed by the Chief of State, and 39 are ex-officio. From the municipal and provincial governments there are 52 ex-officio representatives, 50 elected by municipal councils, and 50 elected by provincial councils. But the whole elaborate setup has only advisory meaning. The elections are not free, and no opposition party or labor union is permitted. The Cortes has no power to upset the decisions of the dictator.

The powerful syndicate leader in Bilbao who described the facets of Falangism and the syndicates for me at great length was especially emphatic in underscoring the ecclesiastical roots of the whole system. This, he assured me, is a Catholic country and its ideals are Catholic. Both the Spanish corporative organizations and the Portuguese corporative organizations come essentially from the teachings of Pius XI, with slight variations in execution. They give freedom and justice to the Spanish people! Each Spaniard is allowed to choose his work career. Naturally, having chosen that career, he is bound to conform to the rules. Workers may express some discontent if their criticism is "constructive." He waves a small Communist handbill which has been picked up on the Bilbao street and says: "We do not permit things like this." In the end, as always, he returns to the threat of Communism as the reason for continuing dictatorship.

Ironically enough, the whole scheme of the national strait jacket for labor and capital is sanctioned by a so-called Charter of Labor, adopted in 1937, which allowed the old Falange to take over all the free and independent labor unions of Spain. Simultaneously it allowed all the real leaders of the new syndicate movement to be chosen without democratic process. The old Charter has been amended and amplified several times since 1937, but the restraints imposed upon labor are the same now as they were at the end of the Civil War.

Insecurity and Security

The over-all insecurity and poverty of the Spanish workers under the syndicate system is truly appalling. The average annual per capita income of Spain is less than $400. That is not even one-fifth of the figure for the United States, or one-half that of Great Britain, although it is better than Portugal. In 1959 the official legal minimum wage per day was, in American terms, about seventy cents, but this did not cover the great body of Spanish workers who are agricultural workers. They receive less than the seventy-cent average. However, industrial workers are considerably better off, partly because of a scheme for paying two large bonuses at Christmas and at mid-summer, and partly because of semisecret additions to their pay by employers who are in desperate need of skilled labor. If they are fortunate, some Spanish skilled workers can earn as much as three or four dollars a day.

The appallingly low wages of the system are cushioned a little by a compensating system of social insurance, administered through the syndicates in such a way that the "system" gets part of the credit. The Church, with its philosophy of large families, has been primarily responsible for incorporating benefit schemes for those families into social insurance legislation. The Labor Charter provides that the family is "the natural unit" of social life, and in practice this means that the heads of families are given some favored treatment in both political and industrial life. After the first child, the family allowance system gives rewards on a point plan, seven points for a man with a wife and two children, fourteen points for a wife and five children, and so on. Each extra child adds a few pesetas to the family income, but not enough to maintain the child with a decent standard of living.

In the factories the family-allowance fund is distributed not by the employers themselves but by a committee of the workers, with a management representative as the chairman. So the child-lessness of workers cannot be used by employers as a device for acquiring a cheap labor force—there are no low-wage factories exclusively for bachelors and spinsters. Any increase in the family beyond four children brings the parents an extra allowance for each child, and if the family goes beyond seven children the system provides an extra-extra allowance. In addition, the system encourages married workers by giving them special price concessions in purchasing goods. Engaged couples receive a grant for starting their household at the time of marriage if the woman promises not to work after marriage. There is a special prize for the two largest families in Spain each year.[10]

Neither the employers nor the workers are particularly happy about the present combined Falange-syndicate system. The limitation on the employer's right to discharge prevents the laying off of the inefficient, and it may be one of the basic reasons for the marked inefficiency of Spanish industry. Officially the Law of Labor Contracts allows employers to discharge workers without penalty for any one of eleven stated reasons, and many of these reasons include matters of production and efficiency.

The workers do receive a considerable amount of protection against unfair treatment by the employers under the present system. If they are wrongfully discharged, they can appeal to labor courts, manned by seventy-six reasonably expert labor magistrates. Although these magistrates dare not permit any individual or group within the system to rebel against the system itself, they are reasonably fair in preventing any individual employer from imposing unfair conditions upon individual workers. They have the power to reinstate a worker with back pay and also the power to compel the employer to grant him indemnification for the loss of his job.

The two classes of workers in Spain who get the least protection under this scheme are the agricultural workers and the members of the middle class. The farm workers constitute about forty-nine per cent of the nation's total labor force, and they are outside the vertical syndicates altogether. The great majority of them are illiterate, and their village priests are not much above their cultural level. Much of their back-breaking labor is hand labor—or mule labor—hand sowing, hand reaping and hand flailing of the grain. One expert has estimated that Spain needs 200,000 tractors to revive its agriculture.

Part of the tragic depression in agriculture is caused by the nation's tragic climate, with too-low a rainfall and too-mountainous a terrain in a large part of the nation to permit real cultivation. In addition there is tyranny and monopoly in land ownership. In a land of starvation there are still great baronial estates, often controlled by absentee owners, with masses of peasant laborers living on the estates in abject poverty. The per capita consumption of meat in Spain is less than one-fifth the consumption in the United States and less than one-fourth the consumption in France. A Spanish child has less than half the chance of an American child of getting enough milk to drink. The basic cause is low income. To buy one kilogram of bread in Spain, a Spanish worker must work an average of 59 minutes; an American 11 minutes; an Englishman 12; Dutchman 19; a Frenchman 21; a German 26; and an Italian 40.[11]

In the cities the economic squeeze affects middle-class workers most severely. For government workers and for many other middle-class workers the double job is the only answer. Probably no other city in the world has so many persons holding two jobs a day as Madrid. The government closes its eyes to the double-shift system because it knows that many of its civil servants could not live without it.

Coupled with this system of quasi-legal double-shift labor, is the universally practiced system of tax avoidance. In Spain, as in Italy, it is the thing to do to circumvent the tax collector if possible. Public opinion jeers at the conscientious businessman who is completely honest in his tax returns. The commonest form of tax swindling occurs in social security payments. The employer gives the employee an unrecorded bonus which is kept "confidential." Then neither the employer nor the worker is compelled to pay the required percentage on that bonus to the government welfare fund. A scientist of my acquaintance in Madrid was typical of the whole system. He received 5,500 pesetas a month, of which only 1,100 was recorded; the rest was received under the counter in order to escape welfare taxes.

In addition to this personal, welfare swindling, the tax structure itself is twisted to favor the rich in many ways which seem quite incredible to an American. The stiffly graduated individual income taxes of the United States are unknown. The great corporations, controlled by the inner circle of pro-Franco industrialists, are exempted from profit taxes altogether "in the national interest." When a Franco program of economic reconstruction was announced in August 1959, an analysis of the exemptions for special companies showed that 202 corporations were protected from profits taxes by a special order. A critical writer in *Iberica* commented:

> One can state without the slightest shadow of a doubt that not a single member of the oligarchy has been let down in this matter of having his firm's investments declared tax exempt. Could you imagine what would happen if the United States Government were to follow the Spanish example, and declare the members of the Board of Directors of the United States Steel Corporation, or the Gulf Oil Company, or the financial interests of the Rockefeller or Mellon families to be tax exempt? [12]

The corruption and economic inequality have become so notorious that some Catholic commentators both in Spain and in the United States have not been able to repress their feelings. An Irish Catholic observer writing about Spain in the Jesuit magazine *America* in 1954 said, "The workers work poorly, knowing that their best efforts will give them no share of the goods." He declared that there is a "great lack of confidence between the government and the business world. In order to escape taxation, falsified company reports are quite usual. . . . The same lack of confidence contributes to making all government statistics untrustworthy, especially if they refer to production or power consumption. Graft, intricate in method and on an immense scale, is a normal part of business."[13]

A 1957 study of the Spanish economy published by the International Federation of Metal Workers, estimated that 70 per cent of the Spanish people receive only 30 per cent of the national income but pay 60 per cent of the total taxes.[14]

Of course, these shortcomings in a clerically oriented fascist society are not specifically or exclusively Catholic; they are human. They exist in many non-Catholic nations that are under-privileged and under-educated. The thing that makes them relevant to a study of church and state in Spain is that the Church is a sustaining partner in the whole economic scheme of repression and control. While professing to stand for free trade unionism and free enterprise in the United States and in Northern Europe, the hierarchy gives sanction and respectability to a labor-capital strait jacket which denies and contradicts the basic requirements of freedom.

10. UNHOLY ALLIANCE

The most common question addressed by any Spanish liberal to any American liberal who visits Spain is this: Why does
your great, democratic country support the dictatorial regime of
Franco? That question was put to me in a hundred different
forms in Spain in 1959. Sometimes it was asked in anger; more
often it was asked in honest amazement. Frequently it was followed up with the challenge: What right do you have to present
yourselves to the world as an enemy of Communism and a champion of freedom when the semifascist type of tyranny that we have
here in Spain is playing into the hands of the Communists? Occasionally a more offensive form of the question was asked: How
does it happen that your United States is the *only* great foreign
military ally of the Franco dictatorship when you pretend to be
more democratic in your ideals than any of your associates?

The worst implications in those questions are all true.
Franco's Spain is the most fascist nation in the West today. His
dictatorship is playing into the hands of the Communists by identifying the United States with fascism and so providing fresh am-
munition for Communist propaganda, and the United States is the
only great military friend Franco has left. Portugal is a friend
also, but it is not great and it is not powerful in military terms.

When such questions were asked of me by anti-Franco Catholics, I tried as best I could to explain—but not to defend—the
American government's position. Millions of good Americans, I
said, despise Franco and his tyranny and want the regime overthrown. There are even good Catholic journals in the United
States which constantly publish denunciations of the Franco regime. Then I would quote the best denunciations I could remember from American Catholic journals. I would point out that too
often under our form of government, the Pentagon generals serve
political functions and the politicians are so fearful of McCarthyite

174

flank attacks that they dare not assert their own personal convictions.

But it was perfectly clear that my explanations were not satisfactory to the Spanish liberals I met. The liberal Spaniard sees just one side of America in his country, the side that Franco is willing to have him see. The great American bases are there, filled with American soldiers under the nominal chieftanship of a Franco military officer. Also, we have had a series of ambassadors in Madrid in recent years who have lent themselves to the service of pro-Franco publicity.[1]

The Spanish people, of course, never hear of anti-Franco American views in their own press. As far as they can see, the United States is a full partner with Franco in economic and military tyranny. The United States is jointly responsible with him for the regime which suppresses all opposition parties and labor unions in the name of "national unity." It does not protest when he censors newspapers and forbids all democratic elections. It talks about the lack of religious freedom in Hungary but not about the lack of religious freedom in Spain. To many a Spaniard we seem to be worse than the Soviet Union because we appear to be more pious and hypocritical. We claim to be apostles of freedom and simultaneously support the leader who is destroying it. The Communists, at least, make no pretense of believing in democracy. It does not help matters to explain to Spanish friends that our government is also inconsistent in helping other dictators.

The explanation for the unholy alliance between the most fascist nation in the world and the most democratic nation in the world is not a simple one. Roman Catholic influence has played some part in the alliance, and possibly a determining part, but there have been many other factors not connected with religion. Military oversimplification has probably been more important than Catholic pressure. The Pentagon has committed us to the wrong side in a great struggle for the future of Spain partly because generals have mistakenly oversold Spain as a bulwark against Communism. Also, generals have a way of subordinating political to strategic considerations while describing this subordination as wisdom.

The American and Spanish Images

It cannot be said that the United States and Spain have ever been natural allies. The English hostility to Spain was transmitted to our ancestors, the English colonists, in the early days and it has persisted throughout our history. In the English tradition the conquistadors were accepted as the bad men of the Western Hemisphere who were trying to take the hemisphere away from the good men, and the good men were not only Anglo-Saxons and Protestants, they were also a little whiter than the bad men who had conquered Latin America. The conviction of the Anglo-Saxon white Protestants who occupied the northern part of the hemisphere was strengthened by the fact that they succeeded in producing a standard of living far above the Latin American level. Thereafter, economic jealousy played its part in the north and in the south.

When the Spanish colonies in Central and South America successfully fought for their independence in the first two decades of the nineteenth century, and the United States took their side against Spain—and later against a Portugal which was losing Brazil—this did not endear Americans to either the Spaniards or the Portuguese.[2] When the Monroe Doctrine was enunciated in 1823, it strengthened the ties between the United States and Latin America, but to Spain and Portugal the doctrine represented swashbuckling American nationalism asserting itself against Spanish and Portuguese rights.

The four-month Spanish-American War did not improve the Spanish image of the American or the American image of the Spaniard. Before and after the war Spanish rule in Cuba was pictured in the American press as little better than genocide, and Protestant-Catholic tensions played a considerable part in creating antagonisms on both sides. American Protestant churches were almost unanimously in favor of the militant American policy, while American Catholic newspapers were, for the most part, cautiously anti-war. They demanded that the whole dispute be arbitrated by the Pope. For most American Protestants the Pope seemed to be the last person in the world to be called in, in such a dispute, since the Church was a major partner in the whole Spanish imperial enterprise in Cuba, Puerto Rico and the Philippines.

Said the Presbyterian *Evangelist* in March 1898: "And if it be the will of Almighty God that by war the last trace of this inhumanity of man to man shall be swept away from this Western Hemisphere, let it come!" Said the *Northern Christian Advocate* a month later: "Methodism will be ready to do its full duty. Every Methodist preacher will be a recruiting officer." At least one Protestant paper went a little further and recognized the war as a divine instrument for striking at that "system of iniquity, the papacy." [3]

Spain's defeat in the Spanish-American War was all the more humiliating because it was so easy. As a world power Spain was discredited. It had lost the last of its major colonial possessions, and the young arrogant victor was the United States. Both Spanish and Catholic humiliation were kept alive by the long struggle which followed in the Philippines between Catholic and Spanish elements on the one hand and American and Protestant elements on the other.

Even in the struggles between the United States and Mexico in the twentieth century, the sympathy of the American people with anti-Catholic and anti-Spanish Mexico played a part in widening the gap between Spain and this country. Pope Pius XI virtually called for American intervention in Mexico[4] in three famous encyclical letters directed against the anti-clerical policies of that nation, although he was careful to say that he was appealing only for peace. It was partly American Protestant opposition that prevented a full-scale American-Mexican war in 1926, 1927 and 1928 when President Calles was enforcing the anti-clerical provisions of the 1917 Mexican Constitution in an attempt to throw off the Church's control of Mexican education. While *cristeros* burned public schools and murdered federal teachers, the Mexican Church declared a three-year "strike."

Spain, of course, was anti-Mexican and anti-American and anti-Protestant in this long struggle. The Vatican used such American organizations as the Knights of Columbus in an attempt to swing American sentiment toward the Spanish and Catholic policy as opposed to that of the Mexican government, and it was noisily supported by the Hearst press. A full-scale American-Mexican war to rescue the Mexican people from "atheism" was narrowly averted, partly because American Protestant sentiment was skeptical about the Catholic Church as a bona fide champion of religious liberty either in Mexico or in any other country.

When Alfonso XIII was overthrown, there was enough

traditional anti-monarchical sentiment left in the United States to make the majority of the American people rejoice. But as soon as Azana had announced his anti-clerical measures, and it seemed that the Spanish religious orders would be stripped of their property, the American Catholic press followed the cue of the 1937 pronouncement of the Spanish bishops and became violently anti-Republican. The presence of the Communist contingent supporting the Loyalist government was used in American propaganda to brand the whole regime as "red." Congress felt the pressure from almost every Catholic parish in the United States, partly because the Catholic population in the United States had grown by that time to very substantial proportions.

The great American policy triumph for Catholicism came during the Spanish Civil War, when Roosevelt's administration was forced by Catholic pressure—or believed that it was forced by Catholic pressure—to retain the embargo on arms shipments to the Spanish Loyalists. That maintenance of the arms embargo has been described by many critics as one of the fatal blunders of modern history. It made possible the triumph of Franco, and Franco's triumph in turn encouraged Hitler and Mussolini to form their fascist Axis. France and Britain shared guilt with the Vatican, but Vatican pressure seemed most important in the United States.

The two German and Italian fascist leaders poured in supplies and men to help Franco to victory, while the United States and Britain withheld their supplies and men at the very moment when only a little help might have tipped the scales of battle. The Soviet Union entered the picture relatively late in the day, and the Spanish Republicans were compelled to grant the Communists a substantial part in their enterprise because they needed outside help so desperately.

This gave the Catholic Church the opportunity to issue its oversimplified description of the Republic as a "red" enterprise. The Church declared that to help such a government would be a sin against God and civilization. "Lift the Spanish embargo," said the Jesuit magazine *America* in 1938, "and the United States is on the sure road to war. Let us keep out of Spain! Let us refuse to make bloody dollars through munitions profits. . . . Lift the embargo and this country becomes an ally of Communism abroad and a tool of Communism here at home." [5] It should be noted that *America* took exactly the opposite line about intervention and aid to Spain when Franco came into power. It revealed no twinge of conscience concerning the shipment of American arms and men to a Catholic totalitarian regime.

Throughout the Spanish Civil War the Catholic pressure against American help for the Loyalist government increased in intensity. The famous film *Blockade,* which exposed some of the horrors wrought by Franco's bombing of Spanish cities, was denounced by the American Church as pro-Communist and pro-atheist. Professor F. Jay Taylor has told vividly the story of this period in *The United States and the Spanish Civil War.*[6] When sixty members of Congress cooperated in sending a telegram of good wishes to the Loyalist Cortes in Valencia in January 1938, they were denounced for showing sympathy with "a government which has absolutely proscribed the exercise of religion in the territory which it governs" by Monsignor Michael J. Ready, chairman of the National Catholic Welfare Conference. American Catholic opposition even prevented Basque refugee children from coming to the United States, although the Basques were good Catholics as well as being strongly anti-Franco.

John W. McCormack of Massachusetts who was then, as now, the chief spokesman of the Vatican on Capitol Hill, led the pro-Franco drive in Washington. (After the Civil War, he also led the fight for recognition of the Franco regime.) The National Council of Catholic Men organized a "Keep the Spanish Embargo Committee." In Chicago, Cardinal Mundelein, who was Roosevelt's chief priestly adviser, urged the retention of the embargo on arms; in Philadelphia, Cardinal Dougherty directed all Catholics "to sign immediately protests and letters and forward them to Congress protesting against the removal of the embargo on munitions to Spain."

The fate of Republican Spain was sealed in 1938 when Roosevelt decided that he did not dare to challenge Catholic sentiment at home and lift the Spanish embargo in an election year. As Harold Ickes pointed out in a 1938 entry in his diary: "He [Roosevelt] said frankly that to raise the embargo would mean the loss of every Catholic vote next fall. . . . This proves up to the hilt what so many people have been saying, namely, that the Catholic minorities in Great Britain and America have been dictating the international policy with respect to Spain." Hugh Thomas tells about the background of the Ickes entry. Secretary of State Hull, he says, had agreed in May 1938 that the American embargo on arms to the Republican Spanish regime should be lifted. "Immediately, the new American Ambassador in London, Kennedy [Joseph P.], a Catholic and a firm supporter of Chamberlain's Government, telegraphed his alarm lest this measure should cause an extension of the Civil War. The Catholics in the United States made passionate protests against such assistance to 'Bolshevists and atheists'. Roosevelt, on a fishing holiday in the Caribbean, told Hull to delay and, when he returned to Washington, the decision to end the embargo was reversed." [7]

Roosevelt's judgment as to the unanimity of the Catholic vote was quite wrong. In 1938, as now, America had millions of liberal Catholics who resented the alliance of their Church with Franco, or with any other political dictator. Some of them, notably *Commonweal* and the Chicago *New World,* published anti-Franco articles and editorials during the Spanish Civil War, but their voices were almost lost in the pro-Catholic, pro-Franco chorus. The American hierarchy, which produced the many million copies of the diocesan weeklies that entered American Catholic homes, pictured the Franco rebellion as a Christian Crusade against atheistic Communism.

The American Catholic press was so successful in its campaign of indoctrination concerning Franco that more than three times as many American Catholics as Protestants supported him. In 1938 an American Institute of Public Opinion Poll showed Catholics favoring Franco in the ratio of 58 to 42, while Protestants opposed him 83 to 17. The poll showed that the strongest pro-Franco bloc in the American population was that of the Catholic priesthood.[8]

America and Spain, 1939 to 1953

Although most non-Catholic Americans were disappointed to see Franco emerge as victor in the Spanish Civil War, they were soon too busy and too much concerned about a possible Axis victory in World War II to pay much attention to Franco. Spain, it was assumed, belonged with the Axis powers in general sympathy. It was assumed also that Franco might stay out of the war as an ally of Germany for a price. The potential contribution of Spain to either side was not given a very high evaluation.

Although the Vatican itself tended to be much more pro-Axis

than pro-Ally in the beginning, there was no indication that it wanted Spain to enter the fighting. The American hierarchy fought desperately in 1939 and 1940 in its American diocesan newspapers to keep America out of the war, but when the war had been declared the American Church cooperated fully with the government—as did the Italian Church with Mussolini.

All through Latin America and the Philippines in the early days of World War II, before the entrance of the United States, the monasteries and convents, with Franco pictures on their walls, were centers of pro-Axis sentiment.[9] In the fall of 1940 the Hispanidad Council was created in Madrid to restore Spanish—meaning pro-Franco—and Catholic influence in Latin America. The spirit of this movement was distinctly anti-American. It was even inspired by a faint hope of revived Spanish imperialism. As late as 1941 the Falange announced in Madrid that if Hitler and Mussolini won the war, the Philippines would be returned to Spain.[10] After America's entrance into the war in December 1941, Spanish imperialist propaganda became less aggressive.

Roosevelt maneuvered skillfully during the war to keep Spain neutral. From 1942 to 1945 he placed in the American Embassy in Madrid a Catholic convert, Carlton J. H. Hayes, who became almost a professional apologist for Franco. Hayes scored a technical success in his campaign to keep Spain out of the war, not because Franco had any love for Great Britain or the United States but because Hitler would not pay Franco's price for entering the war on the German side. Emmet J. Hughes, who served under Hayes in Madrid, has told in his *Report from Spain* how strenuously Franco tried to help Hitler's cause during the war up to the minute when he saw that Hitler was likely to be defeated. Then he began to hedge. The pictures of Hitler and Mussolini behind his desk in the Pardo finally came down, and he reminded Allied representatives that he had not actually entered the war on the Axis side, and that he had even supplied the Allies with some materials.

America's chief interest in Spain in those years was to keep Spain from interfering with Allied landings in North Africa and Italy, to prevent a German march through Spain to Gibraltar, and to stop Spain's flow of key war products to Germany.[11] The American apprehensions were quite justified, not only by Franco's pro-Axis conduct on many occasions but by the knowledge that Franco was actually an ally of Hitler and Mussolini in an open pact of friendship. Also, he had made secret agreements that granted to Hitler the use of Spanish ports and naval facilities under certain conditions. As Professor Arthur Whitaker has brought out in his *Spain and Defense of the West,* Franco submitted a note to the German ambassador on June 14, 1940, when everything seemed to be going gloriously for the Axis, indicating that he was willing to come into the war on the German side if he got Gibraltar, French Morocco, a slice of Algeria and some additions to Spanish territory in Africa south of Morocco. Many of the facts about Franco's maneuvers during this period came out officially after the war in a White Paper on Spain, published by the United States Department of State under the title, *The Spanish Government and the Axis.*

Hitler promised to let Franco have Gibraltar, but he hedged on the other Franco demands. Franco was especially anxious to have Morocco, but Germany and Italy also wanted Morocco. After a meeting at Hendaye on the French-Spanish border in October 1940, subsequent to the fall of France, Spain's entrance into the war seemed virtually certain. But Franco hesitated and haggled. He failed to take the final step only because he did not get his final price. He contributed his famous Blue Legion of 14,000 men—later increased to 28,000—to Hitler's German forces when the war started against the Soviet Union, and he seemed to share Hitler's illusion that Russia would be defeated easily. Even the entrance of the United States into the war did not shake his optimism.

When defeat finally came to the Axis, Franco was a disappointed and somewhat frightened man. The Spanish liberals were correspondingly optimistic. They thought that Franco was doomed by Allied victory and that he would soon be forced out of power. Franco himself shared that conviction for a time.

But the Allied nations that had won the war were too busy or too divided, too stupid or too tired, to spend any time in the elimination of Franco after they had finished such a shattering war against Hitler and Mussolini. Perhaps they thought that the anti-Franco forces within Spain had sufficient energy to take care of the task for themselves. They waited and talked and passed resolutions.

On March 4, 1946, the major Allied powers condemned the Franco regime and its "repressive measures," assuring the world that: "So long as General Franco continues in control of Spain, the Spanish people cannot anticipate full and cordial association with those nations of the world which have, by their common effort, brought defeat to German Nazism and Italian Fascism." The United States withdrew its ambassador from Spain as did other Allied powers represented at the San Francisco conference. Spain was refused admission to the UN and a sub-committee condemned the regime in language so severe that it now seems incredible that this same Franco regime was later admitted to this same body without changing so much as a syllable of its totalitarian principles. Said the UN subcommittee—and the United States agreed in this condemnation:

> Incontrovertible documentary evidence establishes that Franco was a guilty party with Hitler and Mussolini, in the conspiracy to wage war against those countries which eventually in the course of the World War became banded together as the United Nations. It was part of the conspiracy that Franco's full belligerency should be postponed until a time to be mutually agreed upon.
>
> Convinced that the Franco Fascist Government of Spain which was imposed by force upon the Spanish people with the aid of the Axis powers in the war, does not represent the Spanish people, and by its continued control of Spain is making impossible the participation of the Spanish people with the people of the United Nations in international affairs;
>
>> Recommends that the Franco Government of Spain be debarred from membership in international agencies. . . .
>>
>> Recommends that . . . the Security Council consider adequate measures to be taken in order to remedy the situation. . . .[12]

Franco must have breathed more easily when, after all that fiery language, no definite measures were taken against him except the withdrawal of ambassadors—a token measure that meant little except loss of face. Spanish anti-Franco liberals were bitterly disillusioned. They had hoped for the kind of sanctions against Franco that would have forced the collapse of his regime. What they got over the years was increasingly tepid condemnation of Franco in the UN, and, in the end, complete cooperation from the most powerful member of that body, the United States.

The story of the official American attitude toward Franco since that time has been the story of steady change from hostility to tolerance to friendliness to open alliance. At each step of change, the American Catholic press has rejoiced and encouraged more concessions. During the entire change, Franco, although he accepted some American suggestions for economic reform, did not budge an inch in the direction of democracy or freedom for the masses. His rule of Spain today is just as fascist as it was in 1946.

In 1947 the Political and Security Committee of the UN Assembly renewed its condemnation of Franco 29 to 6, with twenty abstentions. The United States abstained. The opposition to Franco was beginning to crack in spite of strong American labor antagonism to him, and much stronger British labor enmity. In 1949 a move to send ambassadors back to Spain failed by only two votes to get the required two-thirds in the UN Assembly. The Vatican, Portugal, the Irish Republic, and eight of the predominantly Catholic nations of Latin America had already sent ambassadors to Madrid. The United States had also lifted its ban on private credits to Franco in 1948.

In 1950, with American help, the UN General Assembly voted 38 to 10 to revoke the ban on ambassadors and admit the Spanish government to the specialized agencies of the UN. Congress had already, over President Truman's strenuous objection, voted a large loan. Spain was seated in the United Nations in 1955, and the United States has been working strenuously for several years to get the Spanish government admitted to NATO. The effort would have been successful if it had not been for the strong opposition of the British Labor Party and the socialists of Belgium, Norway and Denmark. Actually, Franco's exclusion from NATO is of little importance now so long as he has American military support.

The American Bases

The crowning glory of the process by which American democracy and Franco have moved into an alliance came in September 1953, when the United States and Spain signed the bases agreements under which we secured the privilege of building on Spanish soil four—or three-plus—air bases and a naval base in return for $200 million for the Spanish economy, plus a great deal of military aid to the Spanish armed forces.[13] Franco had been hinting at his willingness to lease land for bases for several years, and the negotiations themselves had taken two years.

The American Catholic press was much more enthusiastic

about the bases agreement than were the leaders of Spanish Catholicism. The Spanish bishops dreaded the influx of alien influences into a nation that had been protected so long in cultural isolation. Fiery old Cardinal Segura of Seville stormed against the notion
that the Spanish Catholic conscience could be sold for "heretical
dollars." The sting of the cardinal's criticism was somewhat reduced by the fact that the bases agreement was negotiated for Spain
by the former head of Catholic Action, Martin Artajo. Nevertheless, as Herbert Matthews of the *New York Times* pointed out:
"One of the difficulties in the negotiations for the bases was that the
hierarchy of the Spanish Church objected to the fact that so many
Protestants were going to be introduced into Catholic Spain."

The advertised initial cost of the venture was only a small
fraction of the ultimate cost to American taxpayers. Altogether we
have spent more than $2 billion on economic aid, on the bases
and on military help of one sort or another for Franco's Spain.[14]

What have we secured? Physically our assets are impressive,
although technically the land on which the bases are located does
not belong to us. (That limitation to leasehold occupancy is fairly
common in arrangements for bases.)

At Torrejon, eighteen miles northeast of Madrid, we have a
great air installation, a command post for all air bases in Spain, and
a small American luxury city for those fortunate Americans who
are permitted to bring their families to Spain and live far above
the level of the Spanish people. At Moron, near Seville, we have a
less impressive air base with a depot in San Pablo, also near Seville. At Saragossa, two hundred miles northeast of Madrid, we
have a twin air base, and at Rota, seven miles across the bay
from Cadiz, we have the largest United States naval base in Europe, built to serve the American Sixth Fleet operating in the Mediterranean. In addition we have fuel-ammunition facilities at El
Ferrol, Cartagena and Mahon in the Balearic Islands. To serve
ourselves and the bases we have a great oil pipeline running 485
miles from Rota up through Spain to Saragossa.

Incidentally, the great gap between our luxurious standard of
living and that of the Spanish people creates constant bitterness
and friction. An ordinary American sergeant gets twice as much as
a Spanish general; an American secretary at Torrejon starts at
three times the wage of a Spanish secretary who uses English
fluently.

The very effective air force publicity which is used to defend these Spanish bases stresses their readiness to launch an attack or counterattack on the Soviet Union from a location nearer than the United States mainland. This was the theme of a great anniversary celebration held in Spain in March 1961 with the joint participation of Spanish and American air officers. "With their nuclear bombers always poised for take off, the alerted three-man crew units are always together," said the *New York Times*. "The extreme degree of readiness is evidenced by the fact that the crews—in full flying gear—always have the table nearest the door of the officers' mess. The importance of the bombers based in Spain is readily summed up in one officer's laconic observation that 'these are the planes they'd have to stop.' " [15]

The less obvious but unpalatable fact for Spanish liberals is that these might be the planes *they* would have to stop if they set out to make Spain a genuine part of the free world, because under the bases agreement, planes are not only supplied to the United States for bombing the Soviet Union but also nine squadrons of F-86's are supplied to Franco's air force. No democratic rebellion could get started against such a force. From the point of view of the Spanish liberals, American military power and Franco military power have been dovetailed into a completely hostile amalgam. In fact, the so-called American bases have been misplaced in Spain in order to satisfy Spanish rather than American concepts of strategic defense.

Although the primary cohesive force in the American-Franco alliance is sincere opposition to Communist domination, the actual effect of the alliance within Spain is to unite the military power of the United States with the army of the fascist dictator. The underground revolutionists know that the air bases would be the first line of defense of the Spanish army against any revolt of the Spanish masses. And they take it for granted that if they should attempt a revolt, Franco would succeed in describing it to the world as a "Communist" attempt to destroy his legitimate government.

Probably most American taxpayers think that the United States actually owns "our" air bases in Spain and is free to decide all policy questions concerning their use. Actually the base agreement gives only occupation rights for ten years, plus optional extensions. Even symbolic control of the American bases is exercised by subordinates of Franco, and the American flag may not be flown over "our" bases.

When a Catholic congressman from Connecticut, Frank

Kowalski, visited Spain in 1959 he was "amazed and disturbed" to discover the rule about the American flag.[16] Former Ambassador John Davis Lodge reported that the flying of the flag "would cause difficulties with the Franco government." Snorted Kowalski: "I cannot believe that the American people who have contributed almost one and one-half billion dollars in military and economic aid to Spain [the amount is higher now] should have to accept this humiliating decision." Kowalski wired President Eisenhower: "I urge you as commander-in-chief of our great nation to initiate steps to restore to our fighting men the right and privilege of seeing our flag fly over the bases at which they serve." This, of course, was mere political elocution but it is not without some significance.

Americans in the armed forces in Spain are still surrounded with many restrictions. They are not permitted to wear American uniforms off the base. As we have seen, Protestant armed forces chaplains at the bases are forbidden to make contacts with Spanish Protestant congregations; and there are strict limitations upon mixed marriages even for American servicemen.

All these irritations are minor compared to the fact that the very control of the bases is not in our hands. We have not only surrendered to Franco on minor points; our use of the bases in time of war is conditioned upon his consent. Imbedded in the 1953 agreements is a clause which says that the time and manner of war-time use of the bases "will be as mutually agreed upon." The option is left to Franco as to whether, in the event of attack and counterattack, he would come in on the American side. Without his wholehearted cooperation our military position would be untenable.

Meanwhile, with the development of intercontinental ballistic missiles and the Polaris-carrying submarine, *all* foreign bases have become somewhat less important in the scheme of things.[17] The United States was not deeply disturbed in 1960 when it learned that it would have to evacuate four great air bases in Morocco by 1963, after spending $500 million on them. Since we can now point a fatal blow against an enemy directly from the continental United States, the military experts feel that most of our foreign bases are expendable.

Whatever anyone may say about these strategic considerations—and no one can deny that American bases have *some* strategic value—the military alliance with Franco has proved a moral disaster. It has made us suspect among the liberal, labor and social-democratic forces of Europe upon which we should be able to rely as the chief bastion of defense against Communist aggression. This suspicion and hostility among the labor and liberal forces of Europe became clear on two occasions, in 1959 and 1960 when President Eisenhower visited Franco in Madrid, and when it was disclosed that West Germany, without consulting its allies in NATO, was attempting to negotiate bases on Spanish soil with Franco.

Eisenhower, of course, was cordial and vague in his public utterances during and after his brief visit to Madrid since he realized that he could not commit the United States to all of Franco's concepts. But the reaction within Spain and throughout Europe was one of anger and shock that the foremost symbol of the free world should publicly acknowledge friendship with one of its most notorious enemies. Murray Marder, reporting to the *Washington Post* from Madrid, remarked: "Every American act of assistance to Spain, every action which increases Spain's respectability in the West, is counted by Franco's many critics as a blow to their cause. The United States cannot have it both ways in Spain. Its military bases here, its economic and defense assistance for the Caudillo's government, for good or ill, identify it with his dictatorship."

During Eisenhower's visit in Madrid the roads along his route were manned with Franco's cheering forces. Thousands of "suspicious" characters—meaning persons likely to advertise the people's grievances in President Eisenhower's presence—were temporarily jailed or told to go away. Probably Eisenhower never saw a pathetic little letter from the Christian Democratic Party of Catalonia addressed to him through the United States Embassy in Madrid. It reminded him that Franco was the last survivor of the friends and accomplices of Mussolini and Hitler, a dictator who was a shame to the free world. In a toast to Franco that night at a state dinner in the Oriente Palace in Madrid, Mr. Eisenhower declared that neither Spain nor the United States "is impelled by an atheistic philosophy to degrade human beings into economic tools of the state." [18]

Early in 1960 the European liberal press was horrified when it learned that West German Defense Minister Franz-Josef Strauss was secretly bargaining with Franco for supply depots and air force training facilities in Spain. A great Danish newspaper remarked: "The thought of a Bonn-Madrid Axis is so detestable one might think it was fostered by the Kremlin. Adenauer could not find anything worse to do than try to make secret agreements with the only surviving Fascist dictatorship in Europe." [19]

The West German negotiations were promptly broken off, but they raised a pertinent question. Is the alliance between the United States and Spain any more justifiable in moral terms than the proposed alliance between West Germany and Spain?

Just before President Kennedy was inaugurated, fourteen distinguished Spanish leaders, including Gil Robles and Dionisio Ridruejo, wrote him a letter that well expressed the Spanish liberal challenge to America. "We wish to remain permanently in the free world," they said, "hence we consider it dangerous to keep Spain under non-democratic forms of government. . . . Obviously it would be most inept to permit Russia to be the sole champion of Spain's liberation. . . . We hope that your administration will find the right way by which to give Spaniards the opportunity for which they are asking to express their opinions and move pacifically toward a democratic situation." [20]

These Spanish liberals were horrified when Secretary of State Dean Rusk, in December 1961, made a conspicuously friendly visit to Franco in Madrid. Rusk praised Franco warmly, and even suggested a possible triangular alliance between the United States, Spain and Latin America, without once criticizing, directly or indirectly, any of Franco's anti-democratic policies.

The Curtain of Incense

The continuation of the alliance between the United States and Franco Spain has been made possible by a stream of pro-Franco propaganda from two sources within our country: the Spanish Embassy in Washington and the controlled agencies of the American Catholic hierarchy. Technically our own State Department is passive in the matter. It is forced to admit that Franco's regime is wholly undemocratic. In its memorandum on the subject it says: "Although Spain is officially a monarchy . . . the processes and institutions of the Spanish Government are controlled by General Francisco Franco, who has been Chief of State since 1936. . . . The present Spanish Government has been supported since its origin by the Army, the Church, the Falange Party, and by wealthy commercial interests." This statement represents the present limit of derogation to which our government is willing to commit itself in describing the realities in Spain.

The State Department is not willing to make any counter-moves, either at home or abroad, against the prodigious pro-Franco propaganda campaign carried on in the Catholic press. It uses the Voice of America to condemn totalitarianism of the Communist brand; it never permits the Voice of America to engage in any critical exposure of the totalitarianism of either Franco or Salazar. These regimes are protected by what one writer has called a "curtain of incense."

That curtain of incense, fortunately, does not apply to America's greatest independent newspapers and magazines. It does not even apply to all the American Catholic newspapers. A few journals, such as *Commonweal,* edited by Catholic laymen, and *The Criterion* (formerly the *Indiana Catholic and Record*), have been caustic in criticizing the Spanish and Portuguese regimes. Occasionally the Jesuit magazine *America* assumes a critical role.

But the great diocesan weeklies, which are directly controlled by the bishops, and the magazines of such organizations as the Knights of Columbus (which altogether claim a circulation of almost 25 million) continuously manufacture a prettified image of Franco's Spain. They conceal the persecution of Protestants and the discrimination against Jews, and they justify the dictatorship in very frank language. Here, for example, is what the *Tablet,* official organ of the diocese of Brooklyn, says about the morality of dictatorship in Spain in the words of Father Raymond J. Neufeld, who conducts its regular "Question Box."

Q. Is a dictatorship as a form of government morally wrong in the eyes of the Church?

A. A dictatorship is a form of government in which one person comes into, or is appointed to rule with absolute authority. Such a form of government can be morally good or evil depending on the justice or the injustice of its rule. First of all, the dictator must have a right to his position. If he came by his power unjustly, then his dictatorship is morally wrong. Secondly, the government under a dictator must acknowledge God as the supreme author of all law. No man has authority except it come to him from God. Thirdly, the inalienable rights of the subject of the government must be respected and preserved. Dictatorship as it operates in Russia, as it operated in Germany under Hitler and in Italy under Mussolini, is morally wrong. These three isms are based on the Karl Marx theory of government in which the State is supreme, going so far as to deny the existence of God. The rights of the citizenry are denied, since, under this kind of rule, especially as it is exercised in Russia, the individual person is the property of the State.

The dictatorship in Spain, on the other hand, is morally good, certain areas of public opinion notwithstanding. The Franco government was established in defense against the Russian influence in Spain. Though Franco is a dictator, he acknowledges the existence and the supremacy of God, and he respects the God-given rights of his people.[21]

The most industrious defender of Spain and Portugal in the American Catholic press is Richard Pattee, author of *This Is Spain* and of a pamphlet circulated by the National Council of Catholic Men, *The Religious Question in Spain*. Pattee, for long an employee of the National Catholic Welfare Conference, is especially skillful in understating the facts about religious discrimination under Franco.

Needless to say, real union of Church and State does not exist in Spain at all, and cannot exist in a Catholic country.[22]

The precious heritage of religious unity means that Spain is not doomed to internal strife because of the irreconcilable divergences of religion. The problem to the contemporary Spaniard is why he should sacrifice this unity that exists for a wider freedom of public worship which can easily lead, given the inherent passion of the Spanish temperament, to violence and discord.[23]

Mr. Pattee justifies the right of the Spanish Church to prevent the opening of new Protestant chapels in these words—and simultaneously fails to tell his readers that old chapels are being closed without due process:

The reason for this denial is that the number of churches in Spain today for Protestants is more than sufficient to fulfill the needs of the existing Protestant communities. The new ones that are going up are not to meet an existing need, but to propagandize among Catholics and against Catholics. This distinction is very clear, very proper and completely logical.[24]

Mr. Pattee dismisses the whole problem of the legal difficulties of former Catholics in mixed marriages with a single sentence: "There are certain complications in the case of mixed marriages, and especially of lapsed Catholics." [25] Of burial he says: "Another problem frequently raised is that of burial. In almost every Spanish town and even in many villages a second cemetery exists for those who die outside the Church, for non-Catholics and the like. On this score it is difficult to see what real problem is raised." [26]

The work of the Spanish Embassy in Washington is dovetailed with the American Catholic press and the American Catholic schools. For many years the chief official purveyor of Franco's point of view to the American press has been the former Spanish ambassador to the United States, Jose M. de Areilza, ably supported by his chief, the present Foreign Minister of Spain, Fernando Maria Castiella y Maiz, who was formerly Spanish ambassador to the Vatican. Before the days of Castiella the chief burden of pro-Franco propaganda was assumed by the Spanish Foreign Minister, Alberto Martin Artajo, who was once head of Spanish Catholic Action.

While serving as Foreign Minister in 1956, Senor Artajo received an honorary degree from the Jesuit head of Georgetown University in Washington for "long and clear-visioned leadership in Catholic Action in Spain," during some of its most militant years. Senor Artajo, said the president of Georgetown, has championed "those Christian principles and social doctrines in which alone reside our hope for a truly peaceful world." [27] Senor Castiella received the Memorial Award for distinguished service from the Georgetown University School of Foreign Service in 1960 with similar encomiums.

It is appropriate that the names of these two leading Spanish officials should be joined in describing Spanish and Catholic propaganda in the United States. They are joint authors of a book, *A Vindication of Spain,* in which they saluted the wartime alliance with Hitler and Mussolini, and declared:

Spanish soil was the melting pot where the heroism of three poor countries, Spain, Italy, and Germany, were joined, nurtured by the fresh sap of the modern concept of the world, founded on the exaltation of vital values, before the decadent and moth-eaten edifice of the French and British Empires, gluttonous for wealth, rotten in their moral texture.[28]

It was partly as a result of this passage and partly as a result of Castiella's support of Spanish claims on Gibraltar that the

British government refused in 1951 to accept him as ambassador to London. One factor in the rejection may also have been the fact that Castiella served under Hitler on the Russian front during World War II in the famous Spanish Blue Division. For this he received Hitler's Iron Cross. He has consistently defended his participation in this enterprise ever since.

When Senor Castiella appeared in Washington in the spring of 1960 and was received by President Eisenhower at the White House, very few political leaders dared to challenge his credentials as a friend of freedom. One exception was the courageous congressman from Oregon, Charles O. Porter, who introduced into the *Congressional Record* a brief analysis of Castiella's past with the comment: "One of his jobs in Spain today is to blacklist Catholics who indicate a dislike for Franco. Communication is necessary between all governments. However, it is to be hoped that the President realizes that, for this gentleman and his despotic government, the formal handshake, not the warm embrace, is appropriate." [29]

Mr. Porter climaxed his brief speech with a quotation from the aforementioned book by Castiella and Areilza: "No belligerent, Spain does not conceal her fervent cordiality toward one of the two sides in the war which was unleashed on September 1, 1939, five months after we achieved our victory, in an act of indescribable insanity by the British and French democracies against the Third Reich under the Fuehrer, Chancellor Adolph Hitler."

Senor Areilza, during his long period of service as Spanish ambassador to the United States, consistently pictured Spain as a country where "real" freedom existed for the people. Speaking in 1956 at Creighton University, a Jesuit institution in Nebraska, he said:

The right to popular representation and the exercise of the basic liberties of man are active in the minds of those who govern Spain today, men of deep political and cultural insight. . . . The feeling of freedom in the Spanish people is so deep and substantial that, in spite of the formal and legal restrictions, I do not believe there is in Europe today a more outspoken democracy, with greater freedom to criticize, analyze, approve or disagree with its leaders, on the street or in any other public or private place.[30]

Most American Catholic bishops do not go quite so far in praising Franco as Senor Areilza went, but there is no doubt that the statement of Professor William Ebenstein of Princeton is true: "From the outbreak of the civil war in 1936 to this day, the spokesmen of the Roman Catholic Church in the United States, from Cardinal Spellman downward, have consistently and enthusiastically supported the Franco dictatorship." Franco is deeply appreciative of that support. On June 9, 1960, the Cardinal received from the Franco government its highest political decoration, the Grand Cross of the Order of Isabella the Catholic.[31] It was conferred upon him in behalf of Franco by Ambassador Areilza in the presence of the Vatican Apostolic Delegate to the United States and Archbishop Patrick O'Boyle of Washington, currently the administrative head of the Catholic bishops of the United States. On November 30, 1961, Cardinal Spellman received the highest award of the Portuguese government, the Grand Cross of the Military Order of Christ, from Portugal's ambassador in Washington "for outstanding services rendered in defense of the sacred principles of Christian civilization." [32]

11. FROM THE INQUISITION
   TO SALAZAR

The narrow little country that stretches for 360 miles along the Atlantic Ocean on the western shore of the Iberian peninsula has little to remind the visitor that it was once one of the world's greatest powers. Today it has the lowest standard of living in Western Europe and the highest illiteracy rate in all of Europe.[1] Inhabiting a total mainland area about the size of Indiana, its population of 9 million is growing too fast for the national terrain.

For the purposes of this study the primary significance of Portugal is that, although the Portuguese and Spanish people are naturally hostile to each other, Spain and Portugal are linked together as Catholic-fascist twins. They are the last great strongholds of fascism in Western Europe, both ruled by Catholic dictators whose philosophies of government and religion are strikingly similar. They are so similar in their outlook and practices that many of the features of Portuguese life which would otherwise deserve separate analysis in this book will be passed over lightly in order to avoid duplication.

I have called these two countries Catholic and fascist twins, but they are not Siamese twins. They are not joined by any indissoluble bond, and the two fascist and Catholic dictators, although they are united in a military alliance, are not deeply affectionate friends. Between the people of the two countries there is mutual and corresponding suffering under dictatorship without a great deal of mutual esteem. Spaniards look down on Portuguese, and the Portuguese respond with some envy and some fear. Spanish kings did rule Portugal once for about sixty years (1581 to 1640) and it *might* happen again.

The anti-Francoists in Spain and the anti-Salazarites in Portugal share one thing that creates a kind of unity of fear. Both agree that they are facing what a Portuguese opposition leader has called "Peninsular fascism," and they know that a revolution in one country would be crushed by a fascist invasion from the other country unless it succeeded in the first few hours. Franco and Salazar are bound by the Iberian Pact to help each other against any "Communist" rebels. If an attempted revolution should occur, all rebels would be promptly identified as "Communists" regardless of the accuracy of the label, as they are today in the propaganda of both dictators.

Portugal is, in many ways, the favorite Catholic nation in the world, exalted in Catholic journals in the United States as a model Catholic country and lauded by the popes who regard the Concordat with Portugal as perhaps the most skillful document of adjustment produced by the Vatican in negotiations with any modern state. The American Catholic press even describes Portugal as a model of the "separation of church and state."

It is also a model of the wrong kind of imperialism, a nation that persists in maintaining a nineteenth-century colonial regime in the middle of the twentieth century. The world was reminded of this fact by the great explosion in Angola in 1961. Today the primary significance of Portugal among the nations is that it stands almost alone among the nations of the West in openly defying the African drift toward national independence. It is attempting to protect the largest remaining empire in the world with the slogans of an outdated paternalism.

The overseas holdings of Portugal are more than twenty-two times the size of the mainland nation. They include the Azores, with nine islands, and the Madeiras with three; the fourteen Cape Verde islands off the shore of Africa, with their "black Portuguese" people; Timor, near Indonesia, very small; Macao, a five-mile square inset near Hong Kong; also Goa and two tiny enclaves in India until December 1961. Far more important are Angola in West Africa, fourteen times the size of Portugal; and Mozambique in East Africa, eight times the size of the motherland. Also, there are relatively small Portuguese Guinea, and Sao Tome and Principe, two islands off West Africa near the Equator. The events of 1961 demonstrated that these overseas possessions of Portugal threaten to become as critical and annoying for the Western world as the Congo and Cuba.

Faith and the Sword

The Ministry of Information in Lisbon hands out a little mimeographed summary of Portuguese history which contains one illuminating sentence about Portugal's past: "Missionaries and businessmen sailed to all the Continents bearing with them Christianity and civilization." In a sense that statement could be applied to all the great colonial powers of the West, but it is particularly appropriate for Portugal. Faith and the sword have been so closely associated that church and state power have gone forward together as joint symbols of civilization. Religion has been a basic factor in Portuguese history from the very beginning.

The nation was born out of the Christian crusade against the Moors in the eleventh century, and this circumstance has helped to join religious and political policy ever since then. In the twelfth century Alfonso I was pleased to declare his nation a vassal state of the Papacy, and to pay the Vatican symbolic tribute of four ounces of gold each year. In a sense, the upper classes of Portugal have been paying that tribute ever since.

It was Catholic missionary zeal, as well as gold and land, that inspired the Portuguese navigators and soldiers in their early conquest of much of the world. Portugal's most famous sailor, Prince Henry the Navigator, secured the resources of the Order of Christ to support his pioneering in the fifteenth century.

The popes were pleased to grant spiritual favors to the nation's warriors and to bestow on Portugal sovereignty over the lands that the warriors and religious orders captured in their joint campaigns. In 1502, Pope Alexander VI confirmed King Emanuel I in his title: "Lord of the conquest, navigation and commerce of India, Ethiopia, Arabia, and Persia."

The Church and the imperial flag went together to India, after Vasco da Gama had reached it by sea in 1498; to Brazil after it was discovered in 1500; and to other parts of the Western world after Magellan made his first trip around the world in 1522. (Vasco da Gama today is the nation's greatest historical hero.) Goa, the Portuguese enclave in India, became the hub of a great Catholic missionary wheel which, through the Franciscans, Dominicans and Jesuits, branched out into East Africa, China, Japan and the Malay Archipelago to claim the heathen world for Christ and the Portuguese monarchs.[2] The missionaries became businessmen as well as politicial representatives of Portuguese imperialism, and their profits from the exploitation of the natives did not all go to the glory of God.

By the middle of the sixteenth century, the Portuguese empire stretched from Brazil to Morocco to the East Indies. And everywhere the Roman Catholic Church was built into that empire at next to the highest level, bringing Church and state into a union of piety and imperialism. There is an old English saying: "Where the English settle they first build a punch house, the Dutch a fort, and the Portuguese a church."

Part of this built-in fusion of politics and religion was based on the fact that the nation has always had just one religion, the Catholic faith, and that faith was organically connected with the Portuguese monarchy for about eight hundred years. The Protestant Reformation never caught hold in Lusitania, and Judaism was crushed as ruthlessly as Protestantism. Most Portuguese Jews were exiled, enslaved or forcibly converted to Christianity about the time Ferdinand and Isabella were driving them out of Spain. Although the Portuguese Inquisition never became as famous as its Spanish counterpart, it was ruthless enough to accomplish the same purpose. As Salazar has said: "We were born as an independent nation in the heart of Catholicism." It took Portugal five centuries to eliminate the Moors, and in a sense they never have been completely eliminated.

Although Portugal did not have a formal Protestant Reformation—Eduardo Moreira says that a few Christians who did not recognize the existence of a Pope were exterminated between 1502 and 1516[3]—the nation could not escape the winds of rationalism and heresy that swept over Europe in the seventeenth and eighteenth centuries. There were several stormy attempts at anticlerical reformation and they left a deep mark on the national culture. That is one reason why some of the worst evidences of Catholic dictatorship in Spain are not present in Portugal today. Anticlerical liberalism held sway in the nation longer than in Spain, and the memory of those liberal days remains.

The most important and most significant of the anti-clerical leaders was a man who, oddly enough, is still commemorated in a great statue at the head of the Avenida da Liberdade in Lisbon, the Marquis of Pombal. Shortly before our American Revolution he sought to save the throne from Church domination by driving out the Jesuits and breaking Vatican control over government departments. He happened to be the leader of the government at the time of the great Lisbon earthquake of 1775, and that is one reason for Portuguese adulation of him today.

In many ways he was a ruthless dictator, but he had an extraordinarily modern outlook on the nation's future. He succeeded for a time in importing into his country the ideas of the French enlightenment, and he fathered the first law for general education. He fought against the exploitation of native peoples by Catholic religious orders and even dared to put a bishop in jail for eight years when the bishop tried to establish Catholic censorship over books. In 1751 he broke the power of the Inquisition sufficiently to require that every inquisitorial sentence be reviewed by the crown. In 1759 he drove the Jesuits out of all Portuguese colonies, and a year later he ordered the Papal Nuncio of the Vatican to leave Lisbon. The *Catholic Encyclopedia* says of him bitterly: "He forged those fetters for the Church that still paralyze her action."

From the days of Pombal to the present the anti-Vatican policy which he represented has not been forgotten. Several times during the nineteenth century the anti-clerical spirit of the people produced crude rebellions, which were usually short-lived because they were so ill prepared. Since the overwhelming majority of the people were illiterate, they were not ready to take advantage of any upheaval in the government.

In the long chaos of changing Portuguese governments which stretched through the nineteenth century, monarchism, Catholicism and the army were usually on one side, and the divided democrats and anti-clericals were on the other. As in Spain, the large property holdings of the religious orders were primary causes of friction. In 1834, in a wave of economic and anti-clerical animosity, the monasteries were dissolved and their property expropriated.

In spite of such eruptions, the Church preserved its firm and profitable alliance with the state right down to the republican revolution of 1910. Catholicism was the official state religion and all other religions were tolerated only if their services were "not practiced in a building having the exterior form of a church." The Catholic catechism was part of the curriculum of primary schools and most high school education for boys was in the hands of the Jesuits.

The Concordat of 1886 between the Vatican and Portugal

gave the government the power to nominate each bishop, who was thereafter appointed by the Pope and paid by the state. The parish priests were appointed by the Minister of Justice—often for political reasons—after being certified for fitness by their bishops. This joint operation by Church and state made it inevitable that when a revolution came, it would affect the fortunes of the Church. It remained for the Portuguese revolution of 1910 to create an anticlerical republic that succeeded for the first time in the nation's history in disestablishing religion and bringing in the separation of church and state as a formal policy.

The Anti-Clerical Republic

The story of the sixteen-year, anti-clerical Republic of Portugal which preceded the regime of Salazar is almost never told in a non-partisan fashion. Many of the aging anti-clerical republicans whom I met in Portugal in 1959 regard the period as a shining symbol of democracy and enlightenment, a golden age of religious freedom. They contend that their great experiment was destroyed by the machinations of the rich, the army and the Church. The government's and the Church's propaganda, on the other hand, pictures the period as the worst in Portuguese history, replete with assassinations, graft and incompetence.

No one can doubt that the sixteen-year record was one that included assassination, graft and incompetence. The idealists who had brought about the revolution were soon overwhelmed by chaos and confusion. Their handicaps were enormous; they had a population at least 70 per cent illiterate and an upper class accustomed to rule by repression and manipulation. Nevertheless they moved the Portuguese masses toward a free culture farther than the people had been moved in the previous century. They abolished the throne and forbade all titles of nobility. They staged a great drive for popular education whose effects are still being felt today. They forced teachers who wanted to remain in the public school system in the great cities to spend some years in the desperately poor country districts away from Lisbon and Oporto, which had almost a monopoly on education. Although they did not succeed in bringing about the complete separation of church and state, they demonstrated that the power of a great and reactionary church could be broken.

Under the Republic there were eighteen changes of government in nine years, many of them preceded, accompanied or followed by violence. The Republic itself, although it probably represented the wishes of the majority of the people, was ushered in originally without a plebiscite by the assassination of King Carlos and his eldest son on a Lisbon street in 1908. It won a popular majority in an election in 1910, and then proceeded to "clean up" both government and Church.

On April 20, 1911, the new Republican regime published the Law of the Separation of the Churches and the State. The Church, which had been receiving public revenue, was dropped from the national budget. Diplomatic relations with the Vatican were suspended. All ecclesiastical holdings of every sort, including both churches and seminaries, were declared the property of the state. The union of church and state, which had existed for eight centuries, was declared dissolved. A system of boards of laymen was created—at least on paper—to control the property of every church in the future. Obligatory religious oaths were abolished; doctrinal classes were eliminated from the public schools; the faculty of theology at the university at Coimbra was abolished; divorce was permitted; civil marriage ceremonies were required for everybody, although religious ceremonies were still permitted; and certain holidays of the Church were made into working days.

Public worship was allowed but only inside the churches. The control of some of the Church's functions was taken away from the hierarchy. The Jesuits were expelled from Portuguese territory and other members of religious orders were directed not to live together in community life. Priests were legally allowed to marry and quite a few of them did marry—but they were promptly excommunicated.

The Vatican, of course, struck back swiftly at the anti-clerical Republic. Pope Pius X in a bitter encyclical defied the Portuguese government and declared its whole legal program on church and state null and void.[4] In effect those who supported the Pope became subversives in the eyes of the new government, and every Catholic church became a center of anti-democratic rebellion.

It was natural that the extreme anti-clerical measures of the Republic—especially the expropriation of Church property without compensation—should create extreme reactions. Several royalist rebellions occurred, backed unofficially by the Church. Several heads of government were murdered by terrorist leaders, and the assassinations were followed by a considerable amount of political chaos. President Sidonio Pais led the retreat from anti-clericalism when he assumed office and abrogated many of the anti-clerical laws which had caused so much bitterness. He allowed the cardinal patriarch to return to Lisbon and resumed diplomatic relations with the Vatican. But he was assassinated in 1918, and thereafter compromise became increasingly difficult. Under financial pressure and panic, the escudo dropped to about one-nineteenth of its value in 1910.

World War I followed and Portugal entered it as an ally of Great Britain. Several presidents thereafter were deposed by military revolts and the country was in a badly disorganized condition when, after an election, General Antonio Oscar Carmona was proclaimed president on April 15, 1928, two years after the virtually bloodless revolution of May 28, 1926 had established the so-called New State.

What happened in 1926 and 1928 was actually a counter-revolution in answer to chaos. Out of it came a slender young professor of economics of the University of Coimbra named Antonio de Oliveira Salazar. He began to cooperate with the new military junta, as a financial expert, but drew back when he failed to win acceptance of strict economic reforms. He wanted nothing to do with a regime that would plunge the country into economic chaos again. Finally the military leaders were forced to accept him on his own terms to save the economy (although he did not become Prime Minister until 1932).

The new regime borrowed heavily from Mussolini's counter-revolution, which had occurred four years earlier, but it had little of Mussolini's histrionics. Salazar himself had no party except a small Catholic party, and no popular following. He was put in power as a financial strong man at a moment when the nation was virtually bankrupt, but he came into office not only as a financial wizard but also as a devout Catholic determined to erase the record of the anti-clerical Republic.

Even before he rose to power he had served his Church as leader of Centro Catolico, a Catholic Action political group whose purpose was to defeat the anti-clerical Republic and gain "recognition and rights of the liberties of the Church." The Church had taken a very important part in preparing for the National Revolution, and its political operations had steadily undermined the Republic. One basic reason why Salazar rose to power was that he had satisfied the Church concerning his loyalty.

In a rare pamphlet[5] from those early days there is still extant an address that Salazar, as a young professor of thirty-three, gave in 1922 to the Central Catholic Congress of Portugal outlining his concept of religion and politics. This was four years before he had assumed any position of power in the national government and six years before he became dictator. He declared that "we intend to follow in the politico-religious policy of the country the instruction and advice of Rome, without betraying the basic interests of the country." "Perhaps," he added, "we interpret the wishes of Rome badly, but if so Rome will speak again by way of instructions."

Salazar, the Catholic

From the very beginning Oliveira Salazar has carried out the spirit and the letter of that 1922 declaration. He has been a Catholic ruler of his country, executing Catholic policy. He has used religion as a political instrument to turn Portugal to the right and to keep himself in power. His announced belief that "the people has less need of being sovereign than of being governed" is essentially that of his Church.

One of his first acts when he established his New Corporate State in 1926 was to announce that that state would have as its foundation the most famous encyclicals of Leo XIII and Pius XI concerning a new social order. As Richard Pattee, one of Salazar's most ardent defenders, has said, in discussing Salazar's ideas about the organization of state and industry:

Where do they come from? They come from traditional Christian [Catholic] thought first of all and, to anyone familiar with the social encyclicals of the Popes, the terms and even the phrases are quite recognizable. . . . Certainly Salazar got many of his corporative ideas from the Catholic sociology that propounded them as possible solutions of the social problem. . . . Salazar's analysis was in no wise different from that of Leo XIII and in general his thought runs along the lines proposed by the Church.[6]

In one of his most authoritative works, *Doctrine and Action,* Salazar has a passage about government by the masses that might well have been taken directly from Leo XIII's *Christian Constitution of States:*

> In order to have the true interests of the people nearest our heart, and to stand for their material and moral advancement, it is not necessary to believe that authority is to be found in the masses, that justice is ruled by numbers, and that the administration of the law can be carried out by the mob instead of by an elite whose duty it is to lead and to sacrifice itself for the rest of the community. . . . It is not necessary that liberty should form the basis of every political scheme.[7]

Leo XIII's famous parallel sentences were: "The origin of public power is to be sought for in God, himself, and not in the multitude. . . ." And Leo had declared, in scoring democracy: "The sovereignty of the people, however, and this without any reference to God, is held to reside in the multitude, which is doubtless a doctrine well calculated to flatter and to inflame many passions, but which lacks all reasonable proof and all power of public safety and preserving order." [8]

Salazar, born in 1889, has lived an almost monastic life. He is often called "the little priest," and he actually began his youthful career by studying for the priesthood. His stern and Puritan habits as a bachelor and partial recluse have added to this priestly legend. It is a legend of a man who is pious, frugal to the point of asceticism, devoted to the national interests and, within limits, exceptionally honest. The son of an agricultural foreman, he has never been a man of great wealth and he is said to draw for himself a salary of only $130 a week, although he receives from the government in addition a summer palace and a mansion in Lisbon. He drinks very little and never smokes. There are no women in his life except two adopted daughters.[9]

How much of the Salazar legend is manufactured for political consumption and how much is reality it is impossible to tell. Probably the popular image of the personal ascetic is substantially accurate.

His reputation as a conservative economist may or may not be sound—he has succeeded in penny-pinching but not in development. He is as far from the Franco image of a rotund militarist as a Harvard president is from a Tammany Hall leader. For an almost absolute ruler of a country he is extraordinarily self-effacing in public affairs. He is the ascetic intellectual, elevated by the accident of history into a role which no man of his type has ever before occupied. He even prefers the fiction that he is not the chief of state—that function is exercised by a puppet President, Admiral Americo Tomas. He rarely appears at public functions and he leaves the ribbon cutting and the greeting of foreign monarchs to the President. His occasional public addresses are models of academic restraint, professorial in style and utterly lacking in flamboyance. Although there are pictures of him everywhere in Portugal, there is nothing in the public adulation of his personality to approach the German exploitation of Hitler or the Italian exaltation of Mussolini—or even the less conspicuous exaltation of Franco.

Indeed, Salazar's techniques of self-effacement are so pronounced as to arouse a suspicion that they are deliberately theatrical, like the all-too-conspicuous inconspicuousness of Greta Garbo in her later days. Some of Salazar's critics have branded the whole public image of the dictator as a pose designed to hide the reality of his ruthlessness. They contend that in spite of his scholarly, monastic image he actually imprisons as many democratic opponents proportionately as the most swashbuckling military oppressor.

In his original ascent to power he moved up into the dictator's chair so unobtrusively that many citizens of Portugal scarcely realized that they had in this young economics professor a potential dictator. When he moved from the university at Coimbra, he agreed to take over responsibility for improving the national economic debacle only if he received absolute power to control the expenditures of departments, to trim the national budget and to lay off unneeded government workers. The soldiers and professional politicians who had managed the country very badly for a long time were fascinated by the quiet audacity of their young professor. He clipped the national payrolls one-third the first year and another one-third the next year. He balanced the budget within one year—at least he was far more successful than his predecessors were in balancing it. The value of the escudo went up steadily. The army was quite content, finally, to give him the reins of power.

During the Salazar reign the nation has had several "elected" Presidents. General Antonio Oscar Carmona held the job more than twenty years. He was succeeded in 1951 by General Higinio

Craveiro Lopes. Nominally each President appoints Salazar as Prime Minister under the Constitution of 1933, but everybody knows that the Presidents are merely puppets and that the real dictator of the country is the suave, ingratiating "little priest" who lives in modest quarters and saves on heat bills by putting his feet in a blanket to keep them warm on chilly days. This quiet dictator has had the longest run of any Western political dictator of modern times. He announced in 1958: "Although I have suggested retirement, I have never insisted on it."

These are the basic elements in the Salazar success story. The other side of the legend may well be symbolized by two public statements he has made, one general and one specific. "I believe democracy is a fiction," he once said. "I do not believe in universal suffrage. I do not believe in equality but hierarchy." [10]

The other statement reported in *Time* on May 5, 1961, was made just after the troubles had begun in Portuguese Angola, when the bizarre "piratical" seizure of the tourist liner *Santa Maria* by Henrique Galvao and his associates had advertised the meaning of the Portuguese dictatorship to the whole world. It was at a moment when the United States had shocked the Portuguese rulers by voting against Salazar on the Angola question in the United Nations. "The Western bloc," said Salazar, "is being badly led by its natural leader, the United States. Whenever a country runs into trouble and most needs help from the Americans, they leave it to its fate. . . . On the other hand, the Russians are always ready to take action. The Americans go around preaching liberty for all the people of the world. But in every country where they implant liberty, they also implant Communism."

Salazar sees the whole world in terms of authoritarian papal concepts and political anti-Communism. He is constantly implying or saying in his public addresses that democracy may lead to disorder and disorder may lead to Communism. Hence the only safe type of government is "responsible" government dedicated to national unity and headed by "disinterested" statesmen. In a 1957 address he blandly defended the abolition of political parties by saying: "There is no doubt that political democracy in its parliamentary and party form has long ago entered upon a crisis of discredit and is in disintegration. . . . The system will drag out its existence for decades yet, but philosophically we may say that its foundations are already crumbling." [11] In a 1956 address on "Government and Politics" he confessed he had a "cordial dislike" for politics; and he added: "The careful observer will note that what goes by the name of political activity in the world of today is to a great extent nothing but excitement and this excitement is fed by primitive feelings and foggy ideas."

Salazar's enemies contend that his own ideas may be primitive but that they are far from foggy. They claim that he is an artful master of public relations camouflage who covers up the corruption and cruelty of an iron dictatorship with "entrancing public propaganda."

In an article about Salazar for the *Nation,* in 1960, Galvao stated the extreme position of the anti-Salazar critics about the "successful" dictatorship.

It is his talent for fraud which alone distinguishes Salazar from other dictators and gives his own dictatorship a different appearance. He has always been a constant and clever liar. . . . The Portuguese themselves, the victims of this success, are astounded to hear him described abroad as a sort of strict but just parent. This is what they hear of a dictatorship which, under the guise of paternalism, has robbed them of their fundamental liberties, degraded them to the status of a flock herded by police, sterilized them in spirit, and kept one-fifth of them in hunger and sickness.[12]

Galvao as a representative of Salazar's leading enemy, General Delgado, was not an impartial witness, but his words concerning Salazar were relatively mild compared to many other indictments made by anti-Salazar leaders who have had direct personal experience with his dictatorship. Delgado's representative in Latin America, Major Luis Calafate, declared in 1960 that Portugal's prisons were "overflowing with political prisoners" and that Salazar's humane treatment of prisoners "consists of such tortures as making the victim stand for days on end with their genital organs tied to a nail on the wall, burning out their eyes with lighted cigarettes, or inflicting other forms of violence which, in many cases, have left them permanently crippled or demented. . . . It is no exaggeration to say that as many as 50,000 have been killed, crippled, or permanently deranged."[13]

I cannot vouch for the particular details described by Major Calafate—probably no one could except the leaders of Salazar's political police, PIDE. Although I talked to many of Delgado's supporters in Lisbon whose tales were not entirely inconsistent with this description, most accounts of the Salazar methods of repression indicate a much more merciful attitude than Calafate's statement depicts. The total evidence seems to indicate that Salazar, at least in recent years, has been less physically ruthless than Franco. I met several Portuguese professors, for example, who had been treated in prison with reasonable respect. However, some of them assured me that PIDE (*Policia Internacional de Defesa do Estado*) was as ruthless as anything developed by Franco.

Although there may be less personal cruelty in the Salazar regime than in the Franco regime, the end product is quite similar. The members of the bureaucracy defend dictatorship without apology. They both adopt the familiar fascist line that it is "necessary" in the war against Communism and disorder to place the state in the hands of "responsible" leaders.

The Fraudulent Elections

Salazar has maintained himself in power through his National Union Party in elections that are as fraudulent as anything practiced by Franco. At the very beginning of his regime he made no pretence of maintaining the reality of consent which had, to a certain extent, existed under the Republic. He continued some of the outward forms of the Republic but suspended all those features which would have permitted the people to make an anti-Salazar choice at the polls. He acquiesced in the continued abolition of the monarchy because there was sufficient anti-monarchical feeling in the nation to endanger any Salazar-king combination. At present there seems to be no prospect of revival of the monarchical idea.

Salazar imposed a Political Constitution on his New State in 1933 without any meeting of a constituent assembly for discussion, after an arranged plebiscite.[14] It creates only a facade of self-government, a "unitary Corporative Republic founded upon the equality of all its citizens" in which no citizen can lawfully be put in prison without due process except under paragraphs 3 and 4 of Chapter II, Article 8, Section XX, sub-section 3. This sub-section covers all acts "against the safety of the state." Salazar is the only one who can define "safety of the state."

Under the system no independent judiciary exists to determine whether a citizen is performing acts against the safety of the state, and no ordinance promulgated by the President of the Republic may be called into question except by the National Assembly. This National Assembly is a creature of the only political party permitted in the state, the National Union Party, which is in turn a creature of Salazar. For the sake of appearances there is nominal permission for other political parties to operate so long as their program is within "the framework of the existing regime." No opposition party is able to function consistently outside that framework. There are some guarantees of freedom in the Constitution but no statutes have been enacted implementing the guarantees.

The chief of state is a President who is nominally elected by a plurality of voters past the age of thirty-five for a term of seven years, but when a considerable and embarrassing proportion of the voters failed to endorse the Salazar choice for President in 1958—about 23 per cent—Salazar immediately had the Constitution altered to abolish all popular elections for President in the future.

The change in the Constitution made little difference because the President has been for many years nothing but a figurehead. According to the little pamphlet, *Portuguese Political Organization,* given to tourists by the government information office: "The President of the Republic does not exercise governmental functions directly; he chooses a President of the Council of Ministers to whom, as to a chancellor, he delegates the actual power of government and administration." The President of the Council of Ministers is Salazar. It is the President of the Council, says the little pamphlet, "who lays down the general policy of the government and directs and coordinates the activity of all the Ministers. The Ministers are named by the President of the Republic after being proposed by the President of the Council, but it is to the latter that they are responsible." And the pamphlet adds, just to make sure that no one will mistake this framework of dictation for parliamentary democracy: "The Government is independent of Parliament. . . . De facto it may be assumed that the vote of the President of the Council generally prevails at meetings." It does!

The President can dissolve the National Assembly, which is composed of 120 deputies elected for four-year terms. The Constitution provides for an "industrial parliament" or Corporative Chamber of 12 sections, one "spiritual and moral" and the rest industrial and economic. This Corporative Chamber is wholly advisory. Says the little government pamphlet: "The dominant idea behind the Portuguese political organization is to secure an equilibrium between the liberty that it is possible for citizens to enjoy and the necessary authority of the State." When in doubt, Salazar chooses "the necessary authority of the state."

The various elections for President and for membership in the National Assembly since Salazar came into power have been so carefully rigged that it is rather surprising to find so many Portuguese citizens going to the polls at all. Many of them go because of the social and economic penalties involved in refraining from voting. In the 1949 elections for the National Assembly there were only two candidates in the whole nation who were not on the Salazar-National Union Party slate, and they carried only a few parishes.

After General Carmona had been returned three times as President without opposition—he died in 1951—opposition finally appeared in 1948 in the person of an eighty-year-old general, Norton de Matos. He made a feeble attempt to start a campaign but withdrew when the machinery of the government, both local and national, was used against him. He was not permitted to do any campaigning in time to affect public opinion, and the newspapers were forbidden to mention his name at the time when the mention would have aided him. It was alleged that he had once spoken of Communists as "patriots," and that his election might cause the Church to suffer further persecution.

In the June 1958 election, a dramatic and emotional rebel, General Humberto Delgado, startled the world and deeply wounded the feelings of Salazar by conducting a courageous campaign against overwhelming odds and officially winning 23 per cent of the total vote. Of course, Salazar's hand-picked candidate, General Americo Tomas, won easily, but I did not meet a single Delgado supporter in Portugal who believed that Tomas had actually won. The machinery of the election was so wholly controlled by the government that an accurate measure of the opposition vote was impossible.

The November 1961 elections for the National Assembly were even more farcical. The Salazar forces attempted to brand the democratic opposition as "Communist," and the Catholic bishops of Portugal issued a solemn warning against voting for "Communists or their allies." At the same time the bishops denied that the Church had been "compromised in any way with methods of totalitarian government." Five days before the election all twenty-five of the opposition candidates withdrew, declaring that Salazar refused to make the election "either free or clean." "The country," they said, "is under the rule of a government obstinate in its anti-democratic methods and processes."

Delgado himself is described by his enemies as a melodramatic publicity seeker, and by his friends as a robust and courageous champion of freedom. The government steadily promotes the notion that he is unstable to the point of insanity. A former Salazar supporter, Delgado was once Director of Civil Aviation in Portugal's air force under Salazar, and received the American Legion of Merit for service as a Portuguese military attache in Washington. His public pronouncements do not indicate a very mature political intelligence, but he is liberally endowed with courage. In the 1958 campaign he resisted the indirect and often the direct attempts of PIDE to ruin his meetings and suppress his movement. After his defeat, he was discharged from the air force and charged by the government with circulating "subversive" pamphlets. He decided, with probable justification, that his liberty and life were in danger. So, in January 1959, he fled to safety in the Brazilian Embassy in Lisbon; from there he went to Brazil to promote the Portuguese opposition from that country. Later he visited Britain, Sweden and the Netherlands, where he received warm support from labor and socialist groups.

The Portuguese opposition behind Delgado is motley and disorganized. The various factions are united in hating Salazar and demanding "democracy"; beyond that there is little unity. Generally four opposition groups are distinguished: monarchists, liberal republicans, socialists and Communists. Since they are all illegal under a strict interpretation of the Constitution, and all suppressed by the censorship, no one can tell how strong they are. The Communists, operating under the title "Movement for Democratic Unity," have received considerable publicity but there is no reason to believe that they have a large following. Their one great advantage is that they are definitely organized and well disciplined. The monarchists are allowed more latitude than the socialists and Communists, since nobody takes them very seriously and Salazar finds it occasionally convenient to have an opposition political force on the right. Although there are liberal Catholics in opposition, I did not find in Portugal many traces of a responsible Christian Democratic opposition. There are apparently fewer stabilizing middle-class influences in the Portuguese situation than in

Spain. It is the army, rather than a formal opposition party, which is most likely to displace Salazar, and there have been many signs of discontent in the army in recent years.

In April 1961 the army almost took over Portugal, not because its leaders wanted more democracy but because they became convinced that Salazar was not acting with sufficient energy in suppressing the natives in Angola. The nation's Supreme Council of Defense actually passed a vote of no confidence in Salazar and tried to get him dismissed, but Salazar saved himself by taking refuge in the headquarters of the loyal Republican Guard and reorganizing his cabinet to take the post of Defense Minister for himself.[15]

Censorship, Literary and Economic

"The Salazar regime," said a writer in the Jesuit magazine *America* in 1961, "has virtually outlawed politics as a subject of conversation above a whisper." [16] I found this to be true everywhere I went in Portugal. In fact, cafe conversation on politics seemed to be more restricted in Portugal than in Spain. The Portuguese censorship system resembles the Spanish system in all major particulars. The government controls all aspects of communications, including books, newspapers, motion pictures, radio and television.

Connected with it, at least morally, is the repressive system of industrial control that prohibits all independent labor organizations and outlaws any vocal or printed assaults on the basic system of economic or political power. The two systems of repression are interrelated. Although the corporative system in industry is not usually described as a censorship system, it is essentially that. Its alleged cooperative and democratic aspects are almost nonexistent. It is primarily designed to prevent organized discontent from being expressed through any anti-government labor unions or employers' organizations.

Early in the development of his New State, Salazar took complete control of the press through a series of arbitrary decrees, creating a censorship office, first in the Department of the Interior and then under more direct control by his own office. The restrictive laws on the press cover almost anything that any intelligent man would want to say against the government. The forbidden statements include "insults to Republican institutions" and "rumors or information capable of causing public alarm." Also forbidden are any statements "offensive to the dignity or decorum of the nation" or any "provocative language against the security of the state and its public order and tranquility."

Under a decree of 1933 the Censorship Board has pre-censorship rights over all newspapers and magazines, and even over billboards and posters if they touch on political and social matters. Radio is controlled in a similar manner, and the newly arrived television industry "enjoys" a completely controlled monopoly, with one-third of the stock in government hands. All broadcasting is quasi-government activity, operating by decree "within the moral and social principles instituted by the Constitution of the Nation." Although radio and TV programs are subject to pre-censorship, the censor rarely needs to exercise his authority in such a controlled society.

The most hopeful flow of information to the people comes from foreign radio, which the government cannot entirely block. Portuguese independent citizens enjoy the BBC and the French National Radio as they come in from London and Paris. They also enjoy 300 to 400 American films a year—more than half the total exhibited—although these foreign films are as carefully censored as the corresponding films in Spain.

Under the circumstances, it is not surprising that the total national circulation of Portuguese newspapers is small; only two have a circulation of more than 100,000. Only one of the Portuguese dailies has any genuine independence, that is the Lisbon daily, *Republica,* but its circulation is very small and its independence is limited to a few weeks before each national election. Then Salazar partially lifts the bans and allows the people to "express themselves." This last phrase is put in quotation marks because the claim is largely fraudulent, and *Republica*'s editors would be the first to acknowledge the fact. In the few free weeks just before an election, *Republica* is allowed by the dictatorship to publish some mild denunciations of the regime, but the editors must pull their punches so obviously that their range of criticism is less than half of the corresponding range of an American editor in an American election. However, this limited freedom is joyously welcomed by Lisbon readers, and the circulation of the paper always doubles in the "free" weeks. Those free weeks begin with a great headline on the front page: "Viva a liberdade!!!"

Republica's chief editor, a former professor, has been in prison under the Salazar dictatorship several times and he must be prepared to return again at any moment. His whole staff lives in a world of continuing police surveillance. Except in the era of modified freedom before each election, the paper's columns are so severely cut that no direct criticism of the dictator ever appears. Each issue must bear on the front page, even during the free period, "This has been seen by the Censor." When, at the end of the free period, it returns to complete censorship, the journal carries the headline, "Silencio! Portugal Returns To Its Sad Fate."

Meanwhile, during the period of partial freedom, the language of every editorial must be restrained. A certain nameless gentleman in its offices showed me the great pile of bundles of articles removed from the paper by the government censor after the type had been set up. They covered not only Portuguese affairs but also many foreign news items which might be disturbing. One of them was headed: "Castro Asks Land Reform In Cuba."

In dealing with foreign news and foreign newsmen the Salazar policy is erratic. Much Portuguese news is sent abroad which would never be allowed for Portuguese readers. News coming in from abroad is not carefully censored if it is published in a foreign language, but the dispatches published in Portugal itself are carefully winnowed. The Portuguese people are never allowed to understand the extent of anti-Salazar sentiment abroad. News stories are doctored or diluted not only when they concern the regime and Salazar, but also when they tend to expose Franco and his associated misdemeanors.

When, for example, President Eisenhower in September 1959 received in London the Spanish Foreign Secretary, Fernando Castiella, and the British Labor Party staged a great public protest against any American concession to a fascist dictator who had tortured political prisoners, the Portuguese newspapers reported the reception of the Spanish Foreign Minister and his request for more help, but carefully omitted the sensational news of public anti-Franco demonstrations in London. When, in January 1961, the *Santa Maria* was captured in the Caribbean, the reader of the Portuguese press might have imagined that the whole Western world was outraged not by the dictatorship against which the pirates were protesting but by the criminal activity of the protesters themselves.

If a foreign correspondent is particularly acute in exposing the Salazar regime, he may be excluded at the border when he seeks to return from a foreign journey. This is what happened in May of 1960 to one of the ablest of the American correspondents, Richard Scott Mowrer, correspondent of the *Christian Science Monitor,* the *Chicago Daily News* and other journals. His reporting was described by Salazar censors as "tendentious."

The censorship of books is less severe and less efficient in Portugal than in Spain. Perhaps one reason for this laxity is that so few of the people read books. Not even all the books on the Roman Catholic *Index* are prohibited in Portugal, although a feeble attempt to suppress them is made by the Church. Salazar permits publishers to print some liberal and mildly heretical works in Portuguese for export if they are marked, for example, "Edition destined for Brazil."

What does the Church think of this system of national censorship? In general it gives cautious approval. Here are a few of my notes, written down just after an interview in September 1959 with the editor of the only official Catholic daily newspaper in Lisbon, *Novidades.*

He is a short, balding priest with deep-set eloquent eyes, vigorous and cordial.

Q. Does Portugal have separation of church and state?

A. Yes, of course, since the Concordat of 1940.

Q. What proportion of the people is Catholic?

A. Perhaps 94 per cent.

Q. Is your paper censored by the government?

A. Yes, but very gently. The censorship is somewhat benign in dealing with us.

Q. Does the state suppress literature attacking religion?

A. The censorship applies to all that is against God and the family, as well as the state itself.

Q. Would a book advocating atheism be permitted?

A. Only to confound it, not to advocate it.

Q. What do you think of the censorship of the opposition daily, *Republica?*

A. It is not only anti-clerical; it is against God, and Salazar rightly says we should not allow discussion against God.

Q. Does your paper ever attack the government itself?

A. Not directly, but we try to maintain an independent attitude.

Q. What about that letter of the Bishop of Oporto criticizing the government? [See next chapter.]

A. That is a very complicated and delicate subject. Some of the things the bishop said were true, but it was scarcely appropriate for a bishop to say them in public. The bishop, you know, is not in the country now.

Q. Did Salazar send him out?

A. Oh no! It was the Holy See itself that sent him out.

Q. How do you feel about the censorship in general?

A. Some censorship is necessary. We are living in troubled times.

The so-called vertical unions or syndicates of Salazar's New State are so similar in principle to Franco's vertical unions that they do not merit any extended description here. The chief difference in the two syndicate systems is that Portugal's system is very much less developed than that of Spain. Portugal is still essentially a country of uncontrolled private enterprise, operating under nineteenth-century theories of economics, all sponsored by Professor Salazar. Salazar, like Franco, uses the "corporative" machinery of his vertical unions to confer some incidental benefits upon the workers, and these social benefits give the structure a facade of humane progress and social welfare.

If the Axis powers had won World War II, there is not much doubt that Salazar would have moved into a full-blown fascist state. He wanted his country to fulfill the dream of corporate unity expressed by Pius XI, and he attempted to take the first step toward that dream. It was a dream not unlike the dream of Engelbert Dollfuss who established in Austria in 1934 what he called the "German Corporative Christian State," described by one Catholic writer as "the first Catholic model government in Europe." When official fascism failed in Germany and Italy, Salazar modified his dream. In any case, as he discovered, he did not need full-blown fascism to keep the Portuguese workers in their place. Portugal had never had a powerful independent labor movement comparable to the movements in France, Italy and Germany. The militants in the working class have always been badly divided.

Under these circumstances, Salazar's syndicates, organized into a National Advisory twelve-section Corporative Chamber, are nothing but state-controlled company unions that serve to channel some welfare benefits to the workers and at the same time prevent the organization of any genuine opposition labor movement. No bona fide labor movement of Europe will have anything to do with them. No strikes or lockouts are permitted and nominally there is no wrongful discharge of any worker. But when I asked a pro-Salazar official of the bakers' union in Lisbon what would happen to him if he insisted on trying to raise the bakers' minimum wage of $1.12 a day, he looked around to see that no one was listening and then said.

"I would be sent off to one of the colonies to do some hard work."

"Would you be able to get back?"

"That would depend on my good behavior."

Meanwhile, almost the whole economic life of the nation is controlled by a small upper class whose support of Salazar is a kind of liability insurance against revolution. The leaders of this class give Salazar grudging admiration for being more honest and devoted than they are. Then they exact from him as a price for their support all that the traffic will bear in the way of tax dodging, corporate profits and government favoritism.

The poverty of the workers is appalling. The scholar who waits on me at the Lisbon Central National Library receives about fifty dollars a month. A woman working in the fields receives about the price of a cup of coffee at a leading Lisbon hotel. Although the economic condition of the people is improving slightly, and Salazar is sometimes balancing the national budget, the distance between the rich and the poor seems to be as great as ever.

Gabriel Gersh, writing in the Jesuit magazine *America* on April 1, 1961, described the class situation in Portugal under Salazar as follows:

At the top is a small rich class which, with the full blessings of the Salazar regime, controls the economy of the country. At the bottom are the hard-working, largely impoverished masses, whose politeness is charming but servile. Sandwiched in between is a nebulous middle class, comprised of teachers, doctors, lawyers, journalists and business men who, though prosperous, are chafing under the political and economic restrictions imposed on them by the regime. The critics of the government come mainly from the ranks of the middle class, which opposes the numerous restrictive and cautious policies of Dr. Salazar. Unrest is also the result of boredom induced by many years of one-man rule.

12. CATHOLICS, PROTESTANTS AND FATIMA

The Church which has emerged under the New State in Portugal as an ally of the army and Salazar is the pride and joy of the Vatican, but it has few qualities which endear it to Western democracy. In the eyes of Portuguese liberals it is thoroughly tainted by its quarter-century of association with political dictatorship. In the opinion of European labor it has done little to lift the Portuguese masses from poverty and ignorance. With a few exceptions, its bishops have served as handmaidens of a privileged upper class which has ruled the nation in conjunction with the dictator and the army.

The Catholic Church claims a nominal membership of about 90 per cent of the Portuguese people but the claim is based on baptismal statistics, not on church attendance. In a 1956 radio broadcast in Portugal a Catholic leader declared: "We would flatter ourselves if we found 30 per cent of the people within the life of the Church." A former Minnesota Protestant said to me in Lisbon: "I do not think Lisbon is as Catholic as St. Paul." When I told a prominent Catholic author that several anti-clericals had given me the estimate that only 25 per cent of the Portuguese people were in any sense genuine Catholics, he responded: "That estimate is too high. I should put it nearer 15 per cent."

My own impression is that the Church of Portugal is much weaker than its counterpart in Spain. The outward manifestations of success are all there. They range from the 92-foot statue of Christ the King on the south bank of the Tagus, which all visitors to Lisbon are bound to see, to the great, cemented plaza at Fatima in the north where hundreds of thousands of devout tourists and pilgrims from all over the world come to gaze in curiosity and homage. But many Portuguese critics assured me that the Church actually commands the loyalty of only the least literate quarter of the population. They dismiss the so-called loyalty of officialdom and the dependent professional classes as purchased loyalty which could easily be transformed into indifference or hostility if a revolution came. They believe that the south of Portugal has been quite de-Christianized through neglect and poverty.

I have never before encountered in any country more general skepticism concerning the sexual morality of the priests or more tales of general indifference to the Church among the male population. The Portuguese Church is the church of the womenfolk and the peasants. The poverty-stricken country priest is proverbial in his ignorance as well as his poverty; and there is a desperate shortage of priests. After eight centuries of establishment and a generation of political favoritism under a Catholic dictator, the Church today has only about half as many priests per capita as Spain, and the disparity with the per capita supply of priests in the United States is even greater.

Part of the weakness in the Portuguese Church is due to the sixteen-year domination of an anti-clerical regime. That anti-clerical hiatus in Portuguese history, lasting from 1910 to 1926, covered the youthful years of many of the present rulers of this generation. During those years the people were relatively free from clerical pressure, with newspapers that were quite definitely hostile to clerical ambitions. The people's schools were not operated then by the Jesuits and their universities were led by left-of-center philosophers.

Of course, this period of anti-clerical rule was preceded by a century in which Portuguese anti-clericalism developed under the inspiration of French liberal thought, a development which one scholar has called "an efflorescence of Positivism." The anti-clerical tradition plus the sixteen-year history have had an influence that is quite incalculable. Even Salazar has not dared to challenge all the innovations in the Portuguese way of life which flowered under the anti-clerical Republic. Divorce, for example, is still authorized in this Catholic country for those who were married in the days of the Republic. Also divorce is permitted today for all those who claim to be non-Catholics. Priests wear trousers instead of cassocks when they walk on the streets, in contrast to the Romanized practices in Spain. Protestants, as we shall see, are far freer in Portugal than they are in Spain—or at least they were until the summer of 1961 when the "troubles" in Angola created new tensions and downgraded the Protestants because they were associated with Angolan discontent.

The Unofficial-Official Alliance

Salazar reversed virtually every law of the Republic on church and state as soon as he could get his hands on the reins of power. He restored as much of the Church's property as could be disengaged from that of the state, and he brought Catholicism back into the national schools. He restored diplomatic relations with the Vatican by exchanging full ambassadors. He ordered a crucifix put in every primary school. Apparently he did not quite dare to make Catholicism the official and exclusive religion of the state in his new Constitution, but the position that he granted to the Church gives it a definite preferential status superior to the status of all other faiths. In terms of American concepts, he restored about 90 per cent of that church-state union which had existed under the monarchy.

Salazar wrote a special Chapter—Chapter X—into the 1933 Constitution entitled: "On the Relations of the State with the Catholic Church and the Regime of Worship." Although that chapter nominally guarantees freedom of worship and organization for all other religious faiths, it does not mention those faiths by name. The Catholic Church alone is guaranteed "juridical personality" under its own canon law. The state may grant juridical personality to other churches if it wishes, but there is no guarantee for those other churches. In plain English, this means that Protestant churches and Jewish synagogues exist on sufferance while the Catholic Church continues to be the actual church of the Portuguese state.

One of the transparent—and transparently unsuccessful—devices of camouflage used by the present regime to disguise this establishment of the Catholic Church is the claim that the nation has the separation of church and state. This language is used in the section on religion in the Constitution itself, which says: "The relationship between the State and the Catholic Church shall be one of separation. . . ." Then the Constitution continues the sentence by adding ". . . with diplomatic relations maintained between the Holy See and Portugal by means of reciprocal representation, and concordats or agreements. . . ."

There are only two respects in which Portugal has the separation of church and state; one is nominal and the other is substantial. The present Republic is not described in the statute books as a Catholic Republic; in this respect the constitutional nomenclature is slightly different from that in Spanish law. Also, the priests and bishops who function in mainland Portugal do not receive their full salaries out of the national treasury.

This last variation is significant. Anti-clericalism almost always strikes first at the economic status of an established church. After 16 years of anti-clerical agitation, with its emphasis upon economic justice, even Salazar did not venture to heap upon the poor any added tax burdens for maintaining their priests. The Church at home receives intermittent grants and many special favors, and the Church in the colonies gets full government financial support, but the homeland congregations must raise most of the money for their own priests.

The Vatican itself maintains the fiction that Portugal has the separation of church and state, and both American diocesan newspapers and American Catholic textbooks spread the same fiction. In 1948 the National Catholic Welfare Conference of the United States circulated to American Catholic newspapers a series of articles by Eugene Bagger which, in describing the details of the 1940 Concordat with Portugal said flatly: "The Holy See accepts the separation of Church and State." (The important provisions of that Concordat are printed in the Appendix. The full texts of Concordat and Missionary Agreement are in *Canon Law Digest, volume II.*)[1]

In view of this claim, it will be well to list a few of the provisions of that Concordat, especially since it is almost universally described by Catholic authorities as a model of church-state relationships in a modern society.

1. Before appointment the name of every archbishop and bishop must be submitted by the Pope to the Portuguese government for rejection or acceptance. Silence for thirty days is to be taken as acceptance. (In the *Catholic Encyclopedia Supplement* this arrangement is misrepresented as follows: "Under the Concordat of 1940, bishops are appointed solely by the Holy See without intervention of the Portuguese government, and parish priests are appointed by their bishops.")

2. The Catholic religion and only the Catholic religion shall be taught in all public elementary, secondary and intermediate schools to all children whose parents do not file an objection.

3. All religious textbooks and religious teachers in the public schools must be approved by the Catholic authorities.

4. All textbooks in Catholic schools not concerned with theological and philosophical subjects must be cleared with the government to see that their sentiments are patriotic.

5. Catholic marriage by a priest according to Canon Law is recognized, and no other religious marriage is so recognized. For persons married under a Catholic ceremony divorce is forbidden.

6. The Church has the independent right to annul any Catholic marriage, and this annulment must be recognized by the state.

7. The Church is granted a monopoly of state-supported missions in the colonies. (This will be discussed in the next chapter.)

American Catholic enthusiasm for the 1940 Concordat is not limited to the church-state arrangement involved. It spreads to the whole Salazar regime. The heading on one of Eugene Bagger's articles on Portugal in the *Catholic World* in December 1946 read: "Portugal, Anti-Totalitarian Outpost." Portugal, Mr. Bagger maintained, "is one of the few countries left where the fabric of our culture still remains intact. . . . Portugal, as the nearest and most hospitable Continental bridgehead and airbase for American power, is one of the three chief bulwarks of Vatican City. . . . Portugal is the most misrepresented country in the world. . . . The New State . . . stands at the opposite pole to totalitarianism."

"The result [of the Salazar regime]," said Gabriel Gersh, writing in the Jesuit magazine *America* in the issue of October 24, 1959, "however one may judge it in the abstract, seems admirably suited to the Portuguese temperament. The New State has brought riches and peace to the nation; it makes no attempt to steam-roller the individual; its methods of government are surprisingly flexible. The effect of Salazar on Portugal can be compared with Thomas Arnold's impact on the English public schools. Before Arnold there was freedom, indeed, but also anarchy and a sense of purpose which, to say the least of it, was haphazard. After Arnold there was order, but also a hampering rigidity of standards; there was purpose but also limitation of enterprise. This is the state of Portugal today. In an age of European decadence in the art of government, the Portuguese, on balance, are extremely lucky to have found their own Dr. Arnold to lead them out of the 18th century."

Mr. Gersh's analogy between the English public (private) schools and the achievements of the Salazar regime is particularly incongruous. The Catholic philosophy as demonstrated in Portugal before and after Salazar has resulted in a very low standard of culture for the masses and a very limited education for the elite. As in Spain, the Church seems to be interested primarily in giving the people enough education to remove the stigma of absolute illiteracy and provide some technical discipline without preparing them for independent thinking or independent citizenship.

In view of the pro-Salazar comments in *America,* it is refreshing to find in one journal edited by American Catholic laymen, the *Commonweal,* a vigorous dissent. In an article on "Salazar's Dream World," the Rome correspondent of this journal, Gunnar Kumlein, after a 1961 visit to Lisbon, said: "As far as Salazar's political views are concerned . . . they could be summed up this way: the world is being devoured from within by Communist agents, with the exception of only these nations: Portugal, Spain and the Union of South Africa." Mr. Kumlein declared: "If a free Gallup poll could be made in all the countries with dictatorial governments, my guess is that the present regime in Portugal would prove to be the most unpopular." [2]

The Schools and Censorship

Portugal is a rather striking example of Catholic educational theory in practice. As we have seen, education under that theory is the secondary responsibility of parents; the primary duty under Canon Law must be assigned to the Church (Canon 1374).

In a Catholic-dominated country like Portugal it is cheaper for the Church to incorporate Catholicism into the national school system than it is to operate an elementary system of its own. As in Spain and Italy, the Portuguese elementary schools are national and Catholic at the same time. The Church's chief educational endeavors are centered in the high schools.

The clerical pattern in education is protected by Article XXI of the 1940 Concordat with the Vatican in very specific language.

Under its terms the Church is the moral guide for the whole national school system. "The teaching ministered by the State in public schools shall be guided by the principles of Christian doctrine and morals, traditional in the country. Therefore, the Catholic religion and Catholic morals will be taught in public elementary, secondary, and intermediate schools to pupils whose parents and legal guardians have not lodged a request to the contrary." The Church's right to censor all textbooks in the national schools dealing with religion is acknowledged in equally specific language.

The Church has also successfully resisted efforts by advocates of public education to inspect its own schools as carefully as national schools are inspected, or to subject its teachers to equally rigid tests of competence. In 1949 when a considerable bloc in the National Assembly wanted to require priests to obtain normal professional diplomas before they were permitted to teach such subjects as literature and science, Catholic parents of the nation were rallied in protest. The Assembly lowered the disputed requirement to a mere "sound recommendation" from a priest's religious superior.

When state inspection of sanitation and hygiene in Church schools was proposed, this reform also was defeated in spite of the fact that the Concordat gives the state the right of inspection and supervision over such schools. It was argued that the Concordat guaranteed to Catholic seminaries and their ecclesiastical establishments that "their internal regulations are not subject to State control," and it was claimed that sanitation and hygiene were "internal" affairs.

As in Spain, the universities constitute the most liberal segment of the servile society. They are state-owned and, nominally at least, state-managed. The Church dominates them only obliquely. Students are not required, as in Spain, to pass a course in Catholic doctrine. Salazar, being a Catholic and a dictator, makes sure that no professor in a university is ever permitted to hold his position and to speak out specifically and openly as an anti-Catholic or as an opponent of Salazar. Within these limits, many variations are permitted. The university libraries, perhaps because they serve such a small class of the intellectually elite, are much freer than ordinary libraries and bookstores. At the University of Coimbra one may find many heretical productions that are never displayed in bookstores, including the most provocative works of Bertrand Russell, Alexandre Herculano, Ernest Renan, and even the explosive books of veteran anti-clerical Portuguese writer Tomas da Fonseca.

The general intellectual attack on orthodoxy by a philosopher or a novelist is more likely to be overlooked by the censors than anything specifically political. Bertrand Russell's *Why I Am Not a Christian* is being translated into Portuguese by a hopeful Lisbon professor. I saw Sartre's *Nausea* conspicuously displayed in Lisbon even after the important Catholic magazine *Lumen* had announced that "all the works of Sartre are condemned" under a Vatican decree of October 30, 1948. Papini's *The Devil* is also obtainable in Portugal although it is on the Catholic *Index* and cannot be purchased in Spain.

"They have put me in prison without notice," said the quiet retired professor of philosophy at the University of Lisbon when the door was closed. "I am a criminal, you know," he smiled wryly. "I supported Delgado; that was one crime. The police came and took me without papers and without trial. They were very gentlemanly and pleasant though. They do not treat university professors like Communists always, although they did search my house very carefully. Once they kept me eight days, once nine days. I suppose one reason was that I had signed a letter with a few other leaders asking Aneurin Bevan of the British Labor Party to come to Portugal and look us over. I never met Bevan, and he didn't come, but that was enough for Salazar." Earlier, in 1935, the regime had expelled thirty-three professors from the University of Lisbon for holding heretical political opinions, and in 1947 twenty-six professors had been excluded from public activity.

Catholics Against Salazar

Those professors and other leaders who were penalized for wanting to meet the late Aneurin Bevan were baptized Catholics. In a nation where almost every infant is baptized by a priest, this fact is not distinctive, but it should serve to remind the reader that not even sincere and devout Catholics are irretrievably committed to Salazar. There is a Portuguese Catholic opposition of sorts. It is not as powerful or as specifically Catholic as the Catholic opposition in Spain, since anti-clericalism has a proportionately larger following in Portugal than in Spain.

Nevertheless there is enough opposition among the younger

priests and the Catholic Youth Workers, especially in Oporto, Portugal's second city, to cause Salazar some anger and anxiety. This youth organization has circulated a strong protest against the atrocities of the political police and has called for a more independent Church policy. Although the highest clergy remain firm in their allegiance to Salazar, they are plagued with anxiety. They recall the fate of their confreres in the sixteen-year anticlerical Republic, and they do not regard the future with equanimity.

The Cardinal Patriarch of Lisbon, Manuel Gonsalves Cerejeira, was once a roommate of Salazar in his student days, and he has continued to be a loyal supporter. But the vigorous and rebellious Bishop of Oporto, Antonio Ferreira Gomes, is a man of a different stripe. Since July 1958 he has become the most famous cleric in Portugal by virtue of a "private" letter which became public, protesting against the Salazar regime just before the June 1958, election.

Perhaps I should say "out of Portugal" instead of "in Portugal." The Bishop of Oporto was followed by the police for a time as long as he remained in Portugal, forbidden to visit his own mother, and then he was quietly deported. Salazar forbade any civil servant to attend any public function attended by the recalcitrant Bishop. In October 1959, the Pope appointed a new "apostolic administrator" to replace him while the Bishop went to South America, Rome and other places for a "vacation."

The Bishop of Oporto's letter of protest was not the kind of letter that would have created any great stir in a democratic country.[3] He was careful to say that he was writing not as a representative of the Church but simply as an individual. For the most part, it was a mild moral censure of the type indulged in by many preachers in many countries. Salazar, however, suppressed it angrily. (I was able to get a copy in the Bishop's home town only after a considerable amount of sleuthing.)

"I have always given the greatest attention to the words of Your Excellency," wrote the Bishop, "but they have not given me satisfaction in the fields either of political philosophy or sociology." The Bishop argued that sound social peace must be based on justice, that strikes should not be automatically listed as crimes, and that the workers could not be expected to take their ideas at second-hand from the employers. He championed the "natural right of association" of workers and he criticized Salazar for attempting to tie the Church to the corporative system. He ended his letter by a familiar appeal for the right of Catholic organizations to undertake education for a more Christian social order. His most important points were made in the form of quiet and courteous questions:

1. Does the state have any objection to the Church's teaching its social doctrine freely and by all the means at its disposal, chiefly through the organizations and services of Catholic Action and its press?

2. Does the state have any objection to the Church carrying out its assigned mission by counseling and stimulating Catholics to fulfill their civic and political responsibilities so that they can, with full enlightenment, know the problems of Portuguese community life and meet those problems as Catholic citizens?

3. Does the state have any objection to Catholics defining, publishing and propagating their programs even though the programs touch on present-day politics, since politics can scarcely progress without awakening people to bold and meaningful innovations in the present climate of opinion?

4. Does the state have any objection to Catholics initiating a minimum of political action and organization as they see fit, so that they can be ready at the next lawful election, or whenever they judge the time ripe, to take part in the voting for a specific program and for candidates they prefer?

Probably Salazar's anger was not caused primarily by the content of the bishop's letter. The protest was important chiefly because it represented one churchman's estimate concerning his, Salazar's future. As Salazar knew only too well, the Vatican, like any good strategist, hedges on future risks. The Bishop of Oporto represented the Church's political anchor to windward. Now, if the revolution came, the Vatican could swiftly transfer its loyalty to an anti-Salazar successor and use the letter of the Bishop of Oporto as "proof" that it had perceived the injustices in the Salazar regime all along. And, of course, the logical cardinal of a new revolutionary regime might, in due time, be the Bishop of Oporto instead of Salazar's old roommate.

The prospect so annoyed Salazar that he threatened in a public statement in December 1958 to revise his whole church policy. In 1959 he kept the newly appointed Lisbon Papal Nuncio wait-

ing for months before receiving him officially,. He even had a
Lisbon priest arrested for allegedly conspiring with others to overthrow the government in a secret plot. It was claimed that some
three hundred "conspirators" were arrested in this "plot."

In self-defense the Catholic bishops of Portugal, including the
Bishop of Oporto himself, issued a 3,000-word pastoral letter asserting that the Church had not become involved in party politics,
that it had no wish to become involved in party politics, and that
all bishops should obey the public authorities.[4] At the same time,
the bishops protested vigorously that the Church should not be
considered as a friend of the rich and an enemy of the poor, and
that Catholicism had a right to stand "prudently but firmly" for its
family and cultural ideals. The bishops insisted that Catholic Action members as individuals should have the privilege of engaging
in political activity. But there was not a word in the bishops'
statement to indicate any real objection to dictatorship as such, or
any support for a democratic regime. Also, there was no protest
against the measures taken to suppress the Bishop of Oporto.

The present eleventh-hour drift of some Church leaders toward social justice has probably come too late to save either the
Church's future or its reputation. The people have starved under
a Catholic-approved dictatorship for too many years. Also, a great
deal of the alleged Catholic opposition to the present regime appears to be mere anti-statism, based on institutional jealousy more
than readiness for freedom. The Bishop of Oporto made a statement himself in 1957 which was quite revealing: "It is a major
disgrace of our country, possibly the greatest disgrace of our history . . . that the State considers it its function to educate, as well
as to assist, the people and the nation." [5] The good Bishop wanted
his Church to be supreme in both education and welfare, and he
seemed much more interested in Church supremacy than in education and welfare themselves.

That doctrinaire and institutional philosophy of the Portuguese Church was well illustrated in a controversy over too-large
families which broke out in Portugal in July 1959, shortly after
the Bishop of Oporto had been banished. What should a hungry
family do when, year after year, a new mouth is added and the
children already born do not have enough to eat? That happens
to be a critical issue in many a Portuguese family today. The upper classes can buy their contraceptives in any Lisbon drug store,
and most of them have notoriously small families. Why should not

the Church permit contraception for the overburdened poor of Portugal, who have very large and poverty-stricken families?

Novidades, the official Catholic daily of Lisbon, jumped to the attack when the question was raised in 1959.[6] The problem, it admitted, was frightfully serious in Portugal with its appalling poverty and its oversized families. But the Catholic answer was the only divine answer. Pius XII had realized the difficulties and had said there was only one remedy. Good Catholics must "restrain their passions." Also, said Novidades, Canada has multiplied its production of corn thirty times. The day may come when even in polar regions corn and vegetables can be grown. Overpopulation is not a valid reason for birth control. It legitimatizes selfishness, and it is against God's law. An American visitor in Lisbon, reading the columns of Novidades, might have imagined himself in Boston.

The Protestants and the Jews

In respect to religious freedom the greatest single difference between Spain and Portugal lies in the treatment of Protestants.[7] In Portugal, Protestants are second-class citizens but they are not subversives or criminals. They walk conspicuously to church on Sunday mornings through the streets of Lisbon with their Bibles in their hands, and there is no shame on their faces. The police do not molest them and even the newspapers occasionally mention them with some respect. Although their churches are not usually impressive structures, there is no concealment about them. The buildings usually look like churches and occasionally they carry a cross on the outside. Sometimes, by raising technical building impediments, the authorities make it almost impossible for a new Protestant church to be erected, or an old church to be adequately remodeled, but this is not the general rule. Recently it took an old Presbyterian church in Lisbon eleven years of negotiations with the authorities to get permission for a new building, and in the end, after a long dispute concerning the right to have an external cross, the congregation finally bought an old garage and remodeled it.

There is, however, no legal prohibition on any statute book against building Protestant churches, nor is there any definite ban on the external accoutrements of a Protestant church. The old Protestant churches have no difficulty in remaining open and some Protestant church groups even publish their own small Protestant journals, always being careful not to attack the government directly. Lisbon actually has a Protestant book store, slightly disguised, and there are two Protestant seminaries, largely supported by American gifts: a large and important one near Lisbon, and a small one in Leiria. After coming from Spain to Portugal, it is quite startling to open a Lisbon telephone book and see the Presbyterian Theological Seminary listed openly in both English and Portuguese. Of course, this relatively free status for Protestants applies only to mainland Portugal. There is considerably more discrimination against Protestant work in the Portuguese colonies.

There are many explanations for the greater freedom of Protestantism in Portugal than in Spain. British influence is strong and has been strong for centuries. Brazilian influence is also strong and Brazil is relatively tolerant of Protestantism—it is said that there are nearly two million Protestants in Brazil today. Moreover, the slightly larger proportion of both Protestants and Jews in Portugal has been a protection to both groups. Probably the most important explanatory factor is that Spain had a bloody civil war in which Protestantism—along with Masonry—was definitely identified with the enemy. Salazar, on the other hand, moved into power after seizure of the government by a junta with almost no bloodshed. The small Protestant minority took no active part in opposing him.

The disabilities which Protestants suffer are extralegal rather than legal. In addition, there are a few minor annoyances. No Protestant minister in Portugal may carry a professional identity card. Such a card is immensely important in Portuguese life since it aids the holder in securing discounts in stores and many other favors under the law. No Protestant minister is exempted from active military service, whereas all Catholic priests are exempted under Article XIV of the Concordat.

When a Protestant is married by his own pastor, the ceremony does not count. It is permitted under the law, but it is purely ceremonial. Protestant brides and grooms are compelled to go through an independent civil ceremony that is legally binding. On the other hand, when a Catholic is married, the priest simply sends a carbon copy of the ceremonial document he has signed to the marriage register and the transaction is completed.

When Protestant children go to the national schools, the pres-

sure from other children and from Catholic teachers on behalf of
Catholic religious teaching, as in Spain, is so great that most Protestant parents succumb. No Protestant religion, of course, can be
taught in the government schools, but the Protestants themselves
are allowed to have some separate schools.

Although there is no law excluding Protestants from public
office, the political and journalistic discrimination against them is
universal. No Portuguese public official would dare appear at a
formal Protestant ceremony. The anti-Protestant climate is promoted in the newspapers by eloquent attacks upon Protestantism
by Catholic clerics, and there is never a published counterattack.
The British and Foreign Bible Society sells perhaps 200,000
scripture portions a year, but sometimes they are seized and burned
by orders of the local police. The children, instigated by the
police, have been known to cry out in front of Protestant book-
stalls: "These books are false and Communistic."

Burial practices in Portugal for Protestants are almost identical with those for Roman Catholics. Graves may be blessed by
either faith, and sometimes a Protestant is actually buried side by
side with a Catholic. This surprising tolerance goes back to the
anti-clerical Republic which abolished religious discrimination in
death.

Naturally enough, the Roman Catholic rules for mixed marriage apply in this Catholic country. No Catholic who wishes to be
rated as a married person is allowed to accept marriage by a Protestant minister as genuine marriage. However, there is no legal
barrier to mixed marriage outside the Church if the Catholic participant cares to accept excommunication for his "no marriage."
Oddly enough, this "no marriage" confers a slight privilege, the
right to secure a civil divorce. The Church contends that the sinful individual was never married in the first place and his divorce,
therefore, does not count.

It is estimated that altogether there may be about 10,000
regular members of Protestant churches in Portugal in a population of 9 million. There are perhaps 50,000 unattached sympa-
thizers who occasionally attend Protestant services. That is a trifling
number, but it is a higher Protestant proportion than in Spain.

Unfortunately for their own health and strength, the few
Portuguese Protestants are badly divided not only in theology but
also in national origin and in formal association. An editor of the
Christian Century once described Portugal as the land of least Prot-

estant cooperation among all the nations in the world.[8] This disparate character of Portuguese Protestantism is a fatal weakness. It is exploited at every turn by Catholic bishops who use the words of Protestants themselves against Protestants.

The Protestant faith is still for most Portuguese people an alien phenomenon. It comes on the wings of American dollars, British pounds, and Swedish kroner. The largest Protestant segment, the Assemblies of God (Pentecostals), is based in Sweden; the next largest is the Brethren, based in England; the most vigorous and aggressive bloc is Baptist, based in the United States and Brazil. There are also Presbyterians, Methodists, Lutherans, Congregationalists, Seventh Day Adventists and Episcopalians. Most of them receive some foreign mission support from other countries—there are at least twenty-four mission boards from abroad functioning in Portugal today.

The general tolerance for Protestantism was sharply reduced in 1961 after the uprisings in Angola, particularly the tolerance for any Protestant clergymen of foreign extraction who voiced any sympathy for African self-government. In the spring of that year two prominent non-Portuguese Protestant clergymen were suddenly imprisoned in Lisbon on charges which involved alleged opposition to Salazar's African policy. Other American Protestant leaders from Angola were held prisoners in Lisbon. The hostility toward Protestant seminaries increased. We shall see in the next chapter how the new policy in dealing with Protestantism is based largely on the opposition of American and British missionaries to the cruel policies of repression practiced against the natives of Angola. In a sense the new derogation of Protestantism should be accepted as an award of merit.

The social position of the few religious Jews in Portugal tends to be somewhat higher than that of the Protestants, because of a historical accident. Protestants are usually hornyhanded proletarians; Jews tend to be white-collar workers and businessmen. Until the latter part of the fifteenth century Portuguese Jews were treated very tolerantly under the rule of Islam, and they achieved a social and economic status unparalleled in Europe. That status has never been altogether lost in spite of the fact that officially all the Jews were driven out of the Peninsula under Ferdinand and Isabella of Spain and under John II and Emanuel I of Portugal.

Actually many thousands of the Jews who were supposed to

leave Portugal at that time, never left. They survived horrible persecutions, submitted to forced baptism, and finally they or their children, as "Christians," married into the best families. Biologically, therefore, when you touch a member of the Portuguese upper class you may be touching a man whose great-great-great grandparents were enslaved during the anti-Jewish persecutions of the Inquisition. Now he is almost certain to be a nominal Catholic, and he may even be unaware of his Jewish past.

The tiny non-Catholic Jewish community which is still loyal to the ancient faith probably numbers about one thousand in the whole nation, with only two synagogues—one in Lisbon and one in Oporto—and one cemetery. Portuguese religious Jews have the same disabilities concerning mixed marriage as the Protestants, but otherwise they have little to complain about. In Lisbon their one synagogue sits far back from the road behind a wall and gate, not because Salazar has ordered it so but because it was built before 1910 in the days when all non-Catholic houses of worship were excluded from public view. The synagogue is large and commodious, and its congregation is distinctly non-political, even more non-political than its counterpart in Madrid. "We do not proselyte," says the shamun almost proudly. He even suggests that if a non-Jew in Portugal should cross over to the Jewish faith his motives might be questioned, since the Jews are so "well established."

It is the Masons, rather than the Jews or the Protestants as such, who feel the full force of prejudice and oppression today in Portugal. They were violently outlawed in 1930 on the ground of past and continuing hostility both to the Salazar regime and to the Church. They are now paying the price for active support of democracy and for vigorous anti-clericalism during the last days of the monarchy and the sixteen-year life of the Republic. They face virtually the same treatment in Portugal that their confreres face in Spain. If they exist at all, they must remain far underground.

The Fatima Spectacle

Fatima—pronounced *Fat*-i-ma—is a tiny rural place about seventy miles north of Lisbon. It is located in a region of fearful poverty, a region which in 1917 was almost totally illiterate.

At Fatima on October 13, 1917, the Catholic Church claims that one of the most significant miracles of all time took place, furnishing a guide to the human race in its war against Communism. That alleged miracle is now the center of a great ecclesiastical-commercial campaign throughout Europe and the United States which includes in its scope television networks, the distribution of tons of literature, organized pilgrimages to a Fatima shrine, the sale of countless images of Our Lady of Fatima, and the development of a great Catholic tourist trade to Portugal. The central theme of the campaign is that Catholicism is the world's best protection against Communism and that the Virgin Mary made a direct revelation of this fact to three little Portuguese shepherd children in a series of personal appearances.

Although the educated people of Portugal regard the whole scheme of exploitation with distaste, there is no doubt that Fatima has become one of the most important financial and emotional assets of the Salazar regime and of the Catholic Church, both in Portugal and, to some extent, in the United States. It is a tourist attraction for thousands of devout travelers and it has become the main theme song for a great anti-Communist priestly organization in the United States called The Blue Army of Fatima. This Blue Army collects and spends very large sums of money in broadcasting anti-Communist addresses with a subtle, pro-Catholic emphasis, to the general American public and to the American armed forces. A whole body of literature in English has developed on the subject of the Fatima "miracle," and the Library of Congress in Washington now has seventy-five cards in its index of books about this "miracle" and its anti-Communist significance for the Western world.

The modicum of alleged fact in this great publicity enterprise is relatively simple. On May 13, 1917, in the midst of World War I, at a place called Cova da Iria in Fatima, three little shepherd children, Lucia, aged ten, Francisco, aged nine, and Jacinta, aged seven, who could not read or write and who had never been to school, said they saw in a field a vision of a "Beautiful Lady" who told them that if they would come back each month on the same day they would ultimately see something wonderful. Presumably this "Beautiful Lady" was an advance angel, not the Virgin herself. Half a dozen varying versions of the May 13 apparition include a flash in the heavens, two flashes in the heavens, a marvelous cloud, and many other variations.[9]

Although the children were told to keep the message secret, Jacinta told her mother, who promptly mocked her. Lucia's mother even threatened to beat her when she heard the story. But the rumors spread, and on each thirteenth of the succeeding months increasing crowds of peasants went to Cova da Iria with the children until on October 13, 1917, when a "great miracle" had been promised, it is said that there were 70,000 people present. It was raining. Suddenly the rain stopped. Lucia said she saw St. Joseph, the Holy Child, then Our Lady of Sorrows and Our Lady of Carmel. Then she saw "Our Lord, also in red, but only the upper part of His form." (I am using the language of the *Catholic Encyclopedia Supplement.*)

Something simultaneously seemed to happen to the sun. There was a rift in the clouds. It looked like a "silvery disc" and "emitted prismatic rays," seeming to rotate, pausing two or three times, coming nearer to the earth and "radiating a red light." During the special performance of the sun, Lucia said that she talked to Our Lady.

It has never been quite clear what the Virgin Mary was reported to have said on that October 13 to the three children. Lucia, who did all the talking, at one time said that the Virgin had directed the erection of a chapel on the spot and advised intensified Catholic devotion. Jacinta and Francisco both died shortly afterward in the great, worldwide influenza epidemic, and their testimony has never been available. Lucia became a Carmelite nun and is still living in a Spanish convent, so closely guarded in recent years that no one, not even a priestly author, can interview her without the express authorization of the Pope. And the Pope is extremely reticent on the subject. Lucia has been carefully guarded, almost as a prisoner, during all the years since the Vatican decided to accept and exploit the "miracle."

Portuguese students who had the opportunity earlier to see Lucia report that she is an introspective, not very intelligent, and quite possibly a very disturbed personality. She had a whole series of "visions" before and after the famous event of October 13, 1917. Lisbon newspapers at the time of the event described her gestures as "epileptic." Her various stories have been so confused that even the *Catholic Encyclopedia Supplement* admits that she "may have fused, modified, or amplified her memories."

Twenty-four years after the alleged event Lucia informed the world that the Virgin Mary had given her in 1917 a special prophetic political warning saying that a "horrible" war was coming unless the world was consecrated to her Immaculate Heart. Then the Virgin Mary is supposed to have added, and I use the words of Bishop Fulton Sheen in the final and climactic chapter of his *Communism and the Conscience of the West*: "If my requests are granted Russia will be converted; there will be peace. Otherwise Russia will spread its error throughout the world giving rise to wars and persecutions against the Church."

Pope Benedict XV, who was reigning at the time of the Fatima incident, and his successor, Pius XI, paid no attention to the story. Pius XII, who became Pope in 1939, saw its possibilities and finally launched a great pro-Fatima movement as an anti-Communist crusade. The village of Fatima itself was made into a Catholic, anti-Communist shrine, with a great basilica, a gigantic plaza for outdoor crowds, fifteen water taps yielding large quantities of "Fatima water," a large hospital, and more than fifty commercial shops selling relics and mementoes—which pay a very respectable income to the Church. The prelates who operate the shrine have attempted to make it a rival of Lourdes in the healing of the sick, but in this they have not been successful. As yet it is not as shocking or as commercial as Lourdes.

After visiting Fatima three times in 1959, observing the lines of despairing pilgrims in wheelchairs and the women with blood-soaked knees, and after talking not only with the leading anti-clericals of Portugal but with the chief "independent" witness promoted by the Church, I venture to list the following observations about Fatima. I am aware of the fact that it is now fashionable in the world of American scholarship to avoid all exposures of religious fraud as somehow beneath the dignity of serious literature. Intellectuals usually regard such phenomena with slightly amused —and irresponsible—condescension. In the case of Fatima and Portugal reticence does not seem justifiable because the total scheme of exploitation which centers in Fatima is being used to promote Portuguese clerical fascism in the United States as well as in Portugal. Fatima is a *political* racket and political rackets should not be allowed to hide behind a cloak of religious sentimentalism.

1. The original "message" of the Virgin to Lucia had nothing to do with Communism or Russia. It is not mentioned in any of the earlier works of the Fatima miracle. It was a political afterthought sandwiched into the story of the miracle so crudely that its absence in the original story is easily proved.

2. The actual prophecy which the children say they heard

was completely false as a prophecy. They said that the Virgin assured them that World War I would end *that very day*. This fact is not revealed in the literature sent out to most of the faithful, for obvious reasons, but the *Catholic Encyclopedia Supplement* admits that Lucia said four times that the Virgin had prophesied the end of the war "today," meaning October 13, 1917. The most authoritative early work on the miracle, published under the imprimatur of the Bishop of Leiria himself, who has been the chief local promoter of the project, bears out the fact that the original message from the Virgin Mary was an unfulfilled prediction and that it contained nothing about Communism.

3. The alleged physical phenomena connected with the sun on October 13, 1917 have no independent scientific support. The devout saw something unusual, although their descriptions are contradictory. Many persons present in the large crowd saw nothing more than an unusual sun-and-cloud formation, such as might follow any rainy squall near the ocean in warm weather. The *Catholic Encyclopedia Supplement* admits that the incident "must have been subjective, since no observatory recorded any disturbance." The Fatima region near the ocean has frequent cloud-and-sun phenomena. My wife and I, driving out to Fatima along the coast for the first time from Lisbon on a day in September 1959, saw something strikingly similar to the 1917 event, the sun bursting through a whirling cloud formation, great streaks of light seeming to move through the mist and the sun itself showing as a translucent disc. It was a miracle of beauty.

4. The chief alleged "independent" witness used by the Church, who says that he saw the physical phenomena of October 13, 1917, is Gilberto Santos of Lisbon. He is neither independent, scientific nor coherent in his explanations of the event. He is a retired grocer who now makes his living selling Fatima religious articles and writing very bad poetry as an avocation. In a long conversation with me, he was unable to explain why, although he was present on the great day, he kept quiet for nearly twenty years about the details. Then he came forward with a "firsthand" account which fitted in neatly with the Church's theses. Even he did not see the vision of the Virgin seen by Lucia. He claims that he had some special private visions of his own while the sun was "revolving."

5. The stories of the miracle told by Lucia, Francisco and Jacinta are full of detailed contradictions and alterations concern-

ing the costume of the Virgin, the costume of the Angel Messenger, the color of "Our Lord," and the words spoken.

6. Lucia's mother had read to her shortly before her 1917 vision a simple version of the familiar Catholic miracle of Our Lady of La Salette, which is a direct parallel to the Fatima story. In the La Salette story a shepherd girl and boy in the French Alps in 1846 had a vision of a "Beautiful Lady" dressed in resplendent garments who gave the children a message of moral warning and confided to each child a "special secret." Incidentally, the La Salette miracle was involved in fraud charges and the "special secret" transmitted to the Pope was so confused it was never made public.

7. Faithful Catholics throughout the world have been told for the last twenty years that Lucia gave to the Pope a special secret message, very ominous in nature, which would be made public in 1960. As the year of 1960 passed and the secret was not revealed, the Catholic press, in considerable embarrassment, warned that the message might be so general as not to need publication. It has not been published.

8. A veteran Portuguese anti-clerical scholar who was once one of the nation's leading members of parliament and a division head in the Ministry of Education, Tomas da Fonseca, has suggested the most plausible explanation for this whole Fatima phenomenon. The Fatima region had been full of tales of local apparitions of the Virgin for several centuries. The children had been brought up on those tales. (While I was in Portugal a competing "vision center" was being promoted only a few miles from Fatima, with a young Portuguese boy as the visionary, and when I visited the spot I found out that the bishop in charge of Fatima was very angry because of the competition.) In this atmosphere a beautiful and well-dressed wife of an army officer from the city walked through the Fatima hills one day where she could have been seen by Lucia and her little companions. Untrained childish imaginations, working under suggestions from La Salette could account for the rest. (Fonseca has written a book about some phases of the Fatima situation which Salazar has banned, but not before Portuguese intellectuals had hungrily bought up at least four thousand copies.)

I would not mention these eight points if they did not have a considerable political significance for the United States. The gigantic organization known as The Blue Army of Our Lady of Fatima, claiming 45 million adherents, not only promotes a great, essentially McCarthyite television program in the United States under the slogans of anti-Communism, but it couples its preachments with bare-faced, pro-fascist propaganda which is protected from newspaper criticism by its Catholic label.[10] While promoting Our Lady of Fatima as the "Queen of Portugal," it also promotes Salazar and the present regime as divine blessings. Here, for example, is the summary of Portuguese history in the light of Fatima published in the Blue Army's magazine, *Soul,* for March 8, 1960:

Unfortunately, Portugal in the early twentieth century had still to undergo an era of hate and appalling ugliness. After the 1910 revolution, the country became prey to all that was vile. Venal politicians and anti-God men ruled Portugal. Catholic Portugal endured a time similar to what countries under the Reds endure now. The Concordat with the Holy See was ignored. The press of the country fell into the hands of the corrupt and infidel. Sacred images were defamed, churches were looted, convents sold. Even far away missions were taken from the Catholics—and given to Protestants.

In sixteen years, Portugal had sixteen revolutions and eight presidents and great, great financial disasters. But from the first Apparition of Fatima dates a new era of clergy and rulers. Order followed chaos. Christian principles were restored to a grateful people.

Salazar and his aides have been distinguished and habitual patrons of Fatima for many years. In fact, the above summary of Portuguese history was published shortly after the head of the Portuguese state had reverently visited the Fatima shrine, and after the shrine had been visited also by Carmen Franco, wife of Generalissimo Franco, and Fulgencio Batista, former dictator of Cuba. In 1955, Salazar received the annual award of the Blue Army for "outstanding service for victory over Communism and for world peace." The award took the form of an ivory statue of Our Lady of Fatima on a gold case.

Thus, the whole cult of Fatima has become associated with powerful political forces important to all democracies. The manner in which this has come about, and its implications, are worth consideration

13. AMERICA, PORTUGAL AND
THE AFRICAN EXPLOSION

Until one fateful day in March 1961, the official relations between the United States and Portugal were reasonably friendly. When, on that day, a crowd of 20,000 Portuguese citizens stormed the United States Embassy in Lisbon, smashing windows and screaming anti-U.S. insults, the situation suddenly changed.[1] Portugal—or, at least, the governing clique that rules Portugal—was very angry because the United States had stepped on its colonial toes. And Portugal's colonial toes constitute the most sensitive part of the Portuguese anatomy.

Some of the "hate-America" slogans carried by Lisbon rioters on that day might well have been produced in Moscow, although they originated at the opposite end of the political spectrum. "Get Out Of The Azores," was the most militaristic. And slogans in a similar vein appeared nine months later on the occasion of India's seizure of Goa, when Portugal believed American protests to be too little and too late.

Until then Salazar's Portugal had been treated by the United States as a slightly disappointing ally, a member of the United Nations and NATO, which persisted in dictatorial ways in spite of the lofty freedom slogans of those organizations. The United States had accepted Salazar as an ally after World War II without very serious protests partly because the Pentagon had needed air bases on the Azores in the critical year of 1944, and Salazar had supplied those bases by a lease. The arrangement was renewed in 1951, and the bases are still considered a fairly important part of the American defense system.

Although the United States has never displayed toward Portugal that lavish generosity which has characterized its treatment of Franco Spain, our government has been consistently helpful, always in cooperation with Great Britain, as the British have for centuries been considered the primary international guardians of Portugal.

In terms of dollars American cooperation has totaled about 400 millions in all kinds of military and non-military aid, but very little economic aid has been given since 1951.[2]

The Portuguese people have never been a major factor in American life. In the nineteenth century the United States received a considerable influx of Portuguese immigrants, mostly via the Azores, who went chiefly to southern New England. Now the immigrant gates are shut, or almost shut. In Portuguese cities long lines of disappointed farmers and industrial workers form at the doors of American consulates whenever false rumors spread about an increase in the American quota. That quota is now only about 450 a year, and it is filled almost entirely by relatives of those already in the United States. If the American gates were opened wide, it is probable that millions of Portuguese would come over.

One of the chief aims of the foreign policy of the New State has been to keep the United States quiescent about Portuguese dictatorship and Portuguese colonialism in Africa. Catholic pressure within the United States has helped mightily to maintain the first objective; in the second Salazar has failed, although there has been the usual exchange of diplomatic amenities between the two countries. When President Eisenhower made a twenty-four-hour visit to Lisbon in May 1960, and publicly declared that the Salazar regime and the United States were "united in a common cause," Salazar accepted the compliment blandly, and immediately attempted to go beyond it.[3] He tried to persuade the American President to soften American anti-colonial policies in the United Nations. He succeeded temporarily, but when the Kennedy administration came in, the United States became for the first time an open and avowed enemy of Portuguese policy in Africa.

The *Santa Maria* and the UN

The spark that set off explosive repercussions between the United States and Portugal was the capture of the liner *Santa Maria* by anti-Salazar rebels in the Caribbean on January 22, 1961.[4] The less spectacular but more serious cause of friction was the vote of Adlai Stevenson in the Security Council of the UN in March 1961, a vote for step-by-step progress of Portuguese possessions in Africa toward full self-determination. "The United States would be remiss in its duties as a friend of Portugal," said Stevenson, "if it failed to express honestly its conviction that step-by-step planning within Portuguese territories and its acceleration is now imperative for the successful political and economic and social advancement of all inhabitants under Portuguese administration—advancement, in brief, toward self-determination."

This, in the eyes of the ruling faction in Portugal, was treachery and treason, especially since the United States actually voted with the Soviet Union against Portugal in the Security Council. The move would have been successful if Great Britain and France had not abstained. In Lisbon the *Diario da Manha* called the United States vote "an act of stupidity." That was the mildest of many Portuguese comments. In April 1961, Benjamin Welles reported in the *New York Times* that: "Pro-American sentiment which used to be taken for granted has disappeared overnight." The feeling against the United States became even stronger in June when Stevenson joined a 9 to 0 majority in the Security Council in condemning the "repressive" measures of Portugal in Africa.

Even before these incidents Portugal had been very sensitive —the sensitivity being commingled with guilt—about the anticolonialism of her leading allies. There had been bitter recriminations over India's claim to Goa[5] and the obvious American sympathy for Nehru's demands concerning that predominantly Hindu enclave. On November 11, 1960, the Salazar government had been denounced as a "menace to peace" in the Trusteeship Committee of the UN for refusing to submit reports concerning its "dependent areas"—and fifty-five nations joined in the censure. Salazar, angrily proclaiming that Portugal had no colonies and would produce no reports, spoke to his national Assembly in stern terms. He attacked "abusive interference by third parties in our internal affairs."

A year later, the vote of censure against Portugal in the Trusteeship Committee was 83 to 2, and only Spain and the Union of South Africa approved Salazar's intransigent stand.

The comic opera seizure of the *Santa Maria* was chiefly important because it advertised the grievances of the people living under Portuguese dictatorship in both the homeland and the colonies, and because it revealed the wide-spread sympathy for the anti-Salazar rebels in the United States and in Latin America. The seizure itself was melodrama of a high order. Henrique M. Galvao, posing as a wheel-chair paralytic, smuggled some seventy male tourist-revolutionists on board the Portuguese liner at Curacao, captured the vessel, and headed east toward Africa, proclaiming that he was not, as Portugal charged, a pirate but an official representative of the National Independence Movement headed by Humberto Delgado, who had been "elected by the people" of Portugal in 1958. Delgado, speaking from Brazil, enthusiastically endorsed his aide and announced that this was the beginning of an anti-Salazar revolution. The seizure, it was said, was a kind of Portuguese Boston Tea Party.

The United States and Great Britain were embarrassed. As allies of Portugal they could not encourage her enemies. The admiralty lawyers debated the piracy charge with contradictory citations while the American and Latin American press tended to be extremely sympathetic to the rebels. Because at least forty-two United States citizens were on board the *Santa Maria,* the United States government felt obliged to put on a show of stern disapprobation. Four American destroyers and eighteen planes trailed the *Santa Maria* across the ocean toward Africa, being careful not to attempt a capture. Finally, after twelve days of public negotiations and anti-Salazar advertising, Captain Galvao was persuaded to head for Brazil and surrender his ship to the Brazilian navy, with guarantees of safety for his "pirates" and his passengers.

Portugal was not only angry and humiliated; the government was apprehensive about the effect in Africa, and the apprehensions were quickly justified. An uprising began almost immediately in Angola. Indeed, Galvao, far from being a mere publicity seeker and clown, was an effective symbol of that anti-colonial discontent which had been seething below the surface in Portuguese Africa for a long time. Galvao, once a supporter of Salazar, had served as provincial governor of Huila in Angola, and Colonial Inspector.[6] He had been sentenced to sixteen years in prison by the Salazar regime in 1958 for political "crimes," meaning opposition to the Salazar system of forced labor and corruption. Seven years earlier he had gone to jail during an election campaign.

The Portuguese government and the Portuguese Catholic Church were annoyed by American "softness" toward Galvao. Spanish newspapers reported that Portugal would take revenge on the United States by terminating the leases for air bases in the Azores, but Salazar's controlled press did not go that far. The Church entered the picture when Manuel Cardinal Goncalves of Lisbon sent a handwritten letter to President Kennedy "on behalf of the entire Portuguese episcopacy" appealing for good treatment of the *Santa Maria* crew, noting that they were all Roman Catholics.[7] His critics naturally noted the fact that he had filed no corresponding appeal for the political prisoners of the Salazar regime either in Africa or at home.

In the United States the *Tablet,* official organ of the diocese of Brooklyn, denounced the anti-Portuguese colonial policy of the United States as a "sad mistake" and called the UN resolution asking for an inquiry into Angolan affairs "an incitement to violence." Richard Pattee predicted that if Angola and Mozambique were allowed to "go under," it would "push one more stable and sound nation straight into the kind of chaos the Soviet Union welcomes." [8] *America* called the UN move to investigate Angola "an unwarranted snub of a loyal NATO ally."

Foreign Minister Castiella in Spain backed up Salazar. He denounced that sterile and inconsistent "Monroeism" which permits the United States to claim certain exclusive rights in its own hemisphere, including rights to non-contiguous Alaska, while questioning the rights of Portugal "which has spread from Lisbon to Timor, across continents and oceans, for five centuries." [9] Castiella's protest served to remind the world that Spain still has an almost forgotten empire of sorts, a few remnants in Africa which include Spanish Guinea, the Spanish Sahara, the tiny enclave of Ifni on the Atlantic coast south of Morocco, and two cities in Morocco, Ceuta and Melilla. They are of primary interest to the world now as possible centers of African-versus-European friction. Morocco claims—very militantly—not only Ifni and the two cities but also the large and quite important Spanish Sahara, which is valuable because of potential oil.[10] Franco denies the Moroccan claims with equal militancy, and, like Salazar, says he has no colonies in Africa at all but only "overseas provinces." Together, Spain and Portugal by defying both the UN and the rising forces of African nationalism could seriously delay any constructive settlement of the issue of imperialism and freedom in the "dark continent."

Church, State and Education in the Colonies

The Lisbon cardinal's special plea for the crew of the *Santa Maria* served to remind the public that his Church had been for centuries an almost co-equal partner with the government in the development of the Portuguese Empire in Africa and Asia. It continues its partnership today through the Missionary Agreement between the Vatican and Salazar which accompanied the 1940 Vatican Portugal Concordat; and through the Missionary Statute of the following year.

The Portuguese Episcopate of the Catholic Church, meeting in a plenary session in January 1961 not only lauded this Missionary Agreement as "unique in contemporary history" and "a new investiture of the Holy See in the civilizing mission of the Portuguese Fatherland," but it also went out of its way to deplore the attacks on Portugal as a nation "not understood nor appreciated." [11]

Under Article 9 of the Agreement the Catholic missions throughout the Empire "will be subsidized according to needs by the Government of Portugal and the Government of the respective colony, independently of the help they receive from the Holy See." The Catholic missions are recognized as "institutions of imperial utility." The bishops are guaranteed "suitable stipends" and the missionary staffs are assured of retirement pensions. All approved missionary travel costs "within and outside the colonies" are paid out of taxes. Of course, no other missionaries of any non-Catholic faith receive tax support. (Key portions of the Missionary Agreement are printed in the Appendix.)

A detailed discussion of Portuguese policy in Africa is beyond the scope of this book. Fortunately, American readers have recently been provided with several penetrating analyses of Portugal's activities in Africa, and I shall draw upon them for background facts. The most authoritative and complete work is *Portuguese Africa* by Professor James Duffy of Brandeis University, published in 1959 by Harvard University Press. It covers thoroughly the story of Angola and Mozambique. Many of Professor Duffy's findings were confirmed in an anonymous article on Angola in *Harper's Magazine* for May 1961. Earlier, in 1955, the English author, Basil Davidson, had exposed forced labor in Angola and the Belgian Congo.[12] An important description of labor and educational conditions in Mozambique was written for the American Committee on Africa in 1958 by Professor Marvin Harris of Columbia. In the spring of 1961, Benjamin Welles of the *New York Times* brought the Angola story up to date in an authoritative series of dispatches from that colony.

Of course, the use of the word "colony" is the gravamen of the whole problem which the Western world faces in Africa. When is a colony not a colony? Professors Duffy and Harris prove by indisputable evidence that the 10 million to 11 million black Africans who are ruled by some 350,000 Portuguese whites and mulattoes in Angola and Mozambique have that oppressed and exploited status which is usually described as "colonial." Their alleged citizenship in the Portuguese New State is a publicity facade for a system which denies all the basic human freedoms.

Salazar, who was once Minister of Colonies for a short time in his early years, accepted the word "colony" in those days, but he has consistently rejected any responsibility for changing his colonies into independent nations. Although Portugal belongs to the United Nations, and Chapter XI of the UN Charter calls for periodic reports to the UN concerning all dependent territories, the Portuguese government has steadily refused to acknowledge this obligation, even after an adverse vote of 45 to 6 in the Genral Assembly's Trusteeship Committee in 1960.[13] Salazar was very angry when Franco gave in on the matter of colonial reports in November 1960 and, merely "as a courtesy," agreed to submit some facts about Spain's small African remnants. Salazar still claims that Portuguese Africa is an integral part of his New State.

It is understandable that Salazar should resist anything in the way of honest reports on Portugal's colonial practices. There is almost nothing to be said for those practices except the well-known charity of the white Portuguese toward the color line.

"A significant feature of the Portuguese colonies," says the *Catholic Encyclopedia Supplement,* "is the entire absence of a native problem." That astounding sentence was written by a genial and distinguished Catholic scholar whom I interviewed at great length in Lisbon. He would not dare to write such a statement today, since economic and social discontent in Africa is now quite definitely commingled with racial animosities. It is impossible now to deny that the caste system in both Angola and Mozambique is as much racial as it is political.

The *Catholic Encyclopedia* statement serves to remind us that, on the whole, the Church has been so completely and complacently a part of the system that it is rightly considered a moral sponsor of that system. Its friendly attitude toward biological racial mixture, an attitude exemplified particularly in Brazil, can scarcely excuse the hierarchy for collaboration with one of the world's worst manifestations of racial exploitation. The collaboration includes the most shameless misrepresentation of the Portuguese colonial system in official Catholic publications in the United States. The

1961 *National Catholic Almanac*, for example, which is prepared at the Catholic University of America in Washington, describes both Angola and Mozambique as existing under a system of "constitutional freedom." The Jesuit magazine *America* declared in its issue of March 4, 1961: "The native of Angola (and Mozambique) has the same rights as a white Portuguese living anywhere under the Salazar regime. In fact, whites, mulattoes and blacks have been living amiably side by side for 400 years. In this respect, Portugal has been almost unique among colonizing nations."

Incidentally, even the liberal attitude of earlier Portuguese settlers in Africa toward miscegenation seems to have changed appreciably in recent years. Angola, even before the 1961 disturbances, was beginning to adopt many of the racial prejudices of South Africa, particularly because there has been a new influx of white Portuguese manual workers who resent black competition.

Portuguese policy in Angola and Mozambique may be briefly summarized as typical of the Empire.[14] Both of these gigantic African colonies, together almost twenty-three times the size of the "mother" country, are mosaics of class distinction. Angola, three times the size of California, has perhaps 4.5 million black Africans working under the rule of about 250,000 "civilized" persons, meaning Portuguese whites and mulattoes with a tiny segment of "redeemed" natives. The word "civilized" is used to describe a special official Portugal classification in a three-layer society, which is ruled completely from the top by the central Portuguese government. That government is represented in each colony by an appointed governor-general who is almost a czar. There is no pretense of democratic machinery for the masses, either political or judicial. No government official of any kind in all of Angola is actually elected by the people. An advisory Legislative Council in Angola has a small "elected" section, but the African masses have no right to vote for those "elected" individuals. Says Professor Duffy politely: "While it is possible that all the members of the Legislative Council have the African's interests at heart, it is nonetheless significant that not one member directly represents the interests of the nine million Africans in the two provinces." The Portuguese natives are automatically rated as "civilized"; the native Africans by hypothesis are uncivilized or, at least, they were officially until the autumn of 1961 when it was announced that citizenship would be open to them automatically. But the new grant was hedged about by many conditions.[15]

The Negro natives who have not been artifically "evolved" are called *indigenas*. These *indigenas* may become "civilized" by learning the Portuguese language, acquiring posts of responsibility under the government and demonstrating Western manners. Then they are called *assimilados* and given new identity cards with improved treatment. Theoretically no *indigenas* are prevented from becoming redeemed *assimilados* by their color. Actually Angola, after more than four hundred years of Portuguese rule, has only 35,000 *assimilados*. This means that the colony has elevated to the rights of limited Portuguese citizenship about eight-hundredths of 1 per cent of the native Negro population.

The Union of the People of Angola (UPA), a native group, estimates that in all three of Portugal's major African colonies—Angola, Mozambique and Guinea—with a total population of perhaps 10.5 million, there are fewer than 300,000 persons who are "evolved." And it adds bitterly: "This figure gives a clear indication of what the so-called 'Civilizing Mission' of the Portuguese slave-masters has accomplished in five centuries of domination." By the most generous calculation, 6 per cent of the people in Angola have some civic rights: 94 per cent have none.

The key to the whole system of exploitation is planned undereducation of the natives. "Not only is there no provision for popular African education in Portugal's colonial schemes," says Professor Duffy, "but there is no attempt to create an educational elite." [16] The estimated illiteracy of the Africans in Portuguese Africa in 1950 was 99 per cent. The percentage has not changed appreciably since then.

The present role of the Catholic Church in this system of planned undereducation is primarily to take care of the special, three-year "rudimentary" schools supplied for a small minority of the black natives. (Until 1908 it controlled all educational activities in Angola.) The Church was "totally entrusted"—at government expense—with the rudimentary schools in the Missionary Statute of 1941. In these schools, which are essentially sub-elementary training schools, a tiny fraction of the children of school age get a little training in the Portuguese tongue, a little history and religion a la Salazar and the Church, a few facts about hygiene from textbooks designed for use in Lisbon, and a considerable amount of supervised labor in the fields. Professor Harris says that in Mozambique this labor in the fields on mission farms produces some revenue for the Church and the clergy. [17]

After this brief and distorted sampling of education, nearly all the pupils leave school forever. It is very rare for an African to reach high school. In all of Angola there were only thirteen native high school graduates in 1960. Professor Harris indicates that in Mozambique most black natives never even go beyond the first grade; the 1955 educational figures showed that less than 2 per cent passed on to the third grade. The entire province of Mozambique had in 1958, only one African with a university degree. (There are about 100,000 whites and 6,400,000 Africans in Mozambique.) Concerning the whole spirit of the Portuguese educational system in the colonies Professor Harris says:

There is no place in Mozambique for Africans who have been taught how to think for themselves. The present administration has no intention of hastening its own eventual doom by exposing its impressionable wards to that portion of the western world's intellectual heritage which was acquired after the 16th century.

The end-product of the system of planned undereducation is forced labor. Technically it does not exist in law; actually it exists wherever white overlords can seize able-bodied blacks and make them work for a few cents a day. The legal minimum for this labor is two to four dollars a month. The process begins in Angola when natives are allowed to work out an annual head tax of seven dollars by labor for one month. It is continued through the life of most of the natives by a system of pass books which must show that the card-carrier has worked at least six months of the preceding year or is now working. If the required fact is not recorded in the native's documents, he can be turned directly over to "public service," or indirectly to contract labor under private employers. By way of punishment, if he cares to defy his masters and the system, he may be beaten on the hands by the dreaded *palmatoria,* a perforated wooden paddle which raises great welts on the flesh. If he shows persistent signs of being an "undesirable," he may be deported without trial to the Portuguese African island of Sao Tome, where there is a notorious forced labor colony.

The legal definition of an "undesirable" in Mozambique is as follows:

By undesirable *indigenas* is meant those who may be considered by the administrative authorities to be a source of inconvenience with respect to the governing of the natives and to general order and discipline . . . and those who, having been condemned to correctional punishment, it would be prejudicial to permit to remain [in Mozambique].[18]

In Mozambique, as Professor Harris points out, there is a modern system of serfdom in cotton production operated by twelve private Portuguese companies which have received monopolistic concessions over vast areas. *Indigenas* within each concession area are simply assigned cotton acreage by the authorities, and they must plant, cultivate and harvest cotton wherever they are told, with an economic return just above the starvation level, while they bear all the risks of production themselves. The cotton is shipped to Portuguese textile mills.

Even during the 1961 riots and disturbances in Angola, Mozambique remained relatively quiet. It was the quiet of a savagely brutal police state in which any open expression of discontent by the natives would have been instantly punished by imprisonment, deportation or death. Leonard Ingalls, writing in the *New York Times* in 1960 had summarized the background situation in Mozambique by saying: "African nationalism simply does not get a chance to raise its head. For that matter, neither does any other type of nationalism except the one that is loyal to the Government in Lisbon." [19] At about the same time Cardinal Teodosio Clemente de Gouveia of Mozambique had defended the role of his Church in that colony by saying that the Catholic missions formed "the bulwark against anti-clericalism and consequent Communist infiltration." [20] The number of baptized Catholics, he declared, had risen from 85,000 in 1940 to 561,000 in 1960.

The Protestant and Catholic "Subversives"

It is not difficult to predict that the Church which has condoned and supported Portugal's inhuman colonial policies for all these centuries may go down in ruin in the Portuguese African colonies when the native peoples take over their continent. The unselfish contributions of countless Catholic missionaries and the occasional protest of a humane bishop are likely to be forgotten. Early in 1961 the hierarchy of Angola issued a pastoral letter deploring "social injustices," but it probably came too late. Perhaps the outcome would have been the same no matter what attitude the Church had taken. The Christian religion itself has been partially discredited in African native eyes by the history of white rule in Africa.

The Catholic Church, having participated in Portuguese rule for so many years, can still claim the nominal allegiance through baptism of millions of Africans—the claim includes 30 per cent of the population in Angola and 9 per cent in Mozambique. But these statistics are misleading. European national loyalties and European religious loyalties may not survive racial strife, as Belgian Catholics in the Congo can testify. And the capital of Angola is only three hundred miles from the capital of the Congo. The very union of church and state in the Portuguese colonies through the Missionary Agreement, which has kept the Church safe and the priests well fed, will be the Church's greatest handicap when the native tide has turned. As paid agents of the oppressing state, it is not likely that Catholic priests will have any substantial future in any emancipated Portuguese colony in Africa.

Meanwhile, there are serious Protestant *versus* Catholic tensions, particularly tensions between American-based Protestant missions and the Church. They have broken out in some localities into very savage warfare. The American Protestant missions in Angola, which have concentrated on medical and educational work, have automatically become foci of discontent. Hundreds of their native adherents were ruthlessly killed by Portuguese troops and police in the uprisings which began in 1961 after the *Santa Maria* incident. One non-Protestant African leader who had just left the Angolan border told me that at least four hundred native Protestants were killed in the first series of 1961 uprisings, partly because Protestants were being automatically rated by the Portuguese PIDE as potential subversives. In an April 1961 dispatch, Benjamin Welles of the *New York Times* reported:

Since rebellion broke out in north Angola on March 15, the regime-controlled newspapers have been permitted—some believe they have been inspired by local authorities—to wage a mounting campaign against "catequistas." These are Angolans who have been educated at Protestant missions, which have been in the territory since 1880. About 20,000 Angolans are receiving free education from Protestant missions.[21]

The Portuguese-controlled press in Angola published sensational articles attempting to show that rebel attacks almost always began where Protestant missions had functioned. Even a Catholic leader of mixed blood, the Apostolic Vicar-General in Angola, Monsignor Manuel Joaquim Mendes das Neves, was imprisoned for showing sympathy with "Communist terrorists." "From that moment on," says Gunnar Kumlein in the *Commonweal,* "a native priest or one with any Negro heritage at all was considered a practical traitor by the Portuguese police." [22]

Protestantism is, quite naturally, regarded with more hostility by the Angola police than Catholicism, since the Catholic Church is an arm of the Portuguese state and most Protestants tend to be both anti-Catholic and anti-Salazar because of their greater emphasis upon the values of self-government. Protestantism has been relatively successful in Angola, claiming at least 300,000 adherents.

American-based Methodist missions were particularly hard hit by Portuguese reprisals in the Angola uprisings of 1961. Many churches and schools were wrecked. One American missionary who had served the Board of Missions of the Methodist Church (U.S.A.) for three years in Angola, reported in September 1961 that, up to that month, 23 of the 164 Methodist pastors and teachers in the Luanda region alone had been killed, 30 were in prison, and the whereabouts of 77 was unknown. Only 10 of the 164 were still functioning in their work. Late in September, 4 white American Methodist missionaries were still in prison.[23] The black natives, of course, bore the brunt of Portuguese fury, a fury which expressed itself in wholesale slaughter of at least 30,000 men, women and children, often accompanied by torture and mutilation.

The leading American diocesan newspaper, the *Register,* summed up the situation from the Catholic point of view in a column by Father Paul Hallett: "We do not think any Catholic nation to be above criticism from other Catholics just on account of its religion, and this of course holds for Portugal. . . . Those who do the most to exaggerate conditions in Portuguese Africa are Baptist and Methodist missionaries, for whom the baiting of a Catholic country always seems profitable at home, and Leftists of all shades of Pink or Red. Those who instigate the Angolese trouble are Communist agents, who exploit native savagery in the same way they did in the Congo." [24]

If the Portuguese government were entirely free in the matter, it would probably exclude Protestant missionaries altogether from its African colonies. The exclusion could not legally be complete, because Portugal is a party to the Treaty of London of

1884 and the Berlin Act of 1885, which guaranteed to member states some freedom for missionary entrance into Africa. Some Protestant missions have been functioning in Portuguese Africa for eighty years.

Even before the 1961 Angola uprisings, Portuguese government administrators were cautiously non-cooperative with Protestant missions. The leaders of the Catholic Church did everything in their power short of actual physical violence to discourage Protestantism. Under Angola law, any Protestant missionary can be instantly deprived of his license to operate a school, hospital or church if the local governor or his representative, after an inquiry, finds that his conduct is "prejudicial to the interests of national sovereignty." For a time the Protestant missions were forbidden to train their students beyond the age of fourteen. The anti-Protestant discrimination has been particularly acute in Mozambique because of the presence there for many years of an anti-Protestant Catholic Archbishop, who has stated that of the two great dangers for Africa —Communism and Protestantism—the most dangerous is Protestantism.

14. THE FUTURE OF CLERICAL FASCISM

When we come to a discussion of the future of clerical fascism, the subject naturally divides itself into two parts: the prospects for clerical fascism within Spain and Portugal, and the prospects in other countries.

Although this book has been primarily concerned with state and church issues inside the Iberian peninsula and the American policy in dealing with the two Iberian dictatorships, our analysis would be incomplete if we did not make some attempt to connect the policies embodied in Spanish and Portuguese fascism with the policies pursued by other nations of the West. (We may leave Communist countries out of this discussion, although their forms of government often approximate a kind of inverted fascism without benefit of clergy.)

The issues to be faced include many difficult questions. Does clerical fascism pose a present threat to Western democracy? If so, how can it be met most intelligently? How much of the Iberian mixture is exportable? In what countries is clerical fascism most likely to develop, if at all? What part is Catholicism likely to play in the spread of the phenomenon, if there is to be any expansion?

Very Cautious Prophecy

The future of clerical fascism within Spain and Portugal is obviously a great gamble. The prospects in Spain seem to favor some kind of constitutional monarchy with Catholic leanings, but no one can tell how much of the present fascist system will be preserved in politics and industry after Franco goes. My inclination is to believe that Spain will not go far to the left even in the event of a sudden political revolution, because the Communist movement

254

is so small in Spain and the various Socialist and Christian Democratic groups are so uncertain in their strength. Also the memory of the Civil War horrors is still so much alive, and the army is so strong, that even without Franco it might be able to preserve Spain as the most reactionary nation in western Europe for a long time.

Portugal is in a somewhat different class. The nation is outwardly calmer but inwardly less stable than Spain. Its people are so ill-prepared for self-government that the nation has only a faint hope of a stable democracy in our time. It was profoundly shaken by the recent Angola explosion, but the shock treatment did not seem to produce any democratic sanity. The Portuguese reaction, in fact, seemed to strengthen the hands of the most extremist nationalists in the army and to indicate that Salazar may well be succeeded by rulers who have no more faith in democracy than he has. However, this surmise must be distinctly tentative and provisional. A nation whose people are so profoundly discontented might suddenly break loose from all restraint and produce left-wing chaos. In that event, the "model" church-state pattern would be even more completely destroyed than it was in the period from 1910 to 1926.

At the present time clerical fascism does not seem to be exportable by name to any country. The fascist label has lost its magic in the modern world. It is even shunned by its chief practitioners, Franco and Salazar. Most of the prestige in the word died when the body of Mussolini was strung up by the heels in a public square in Milan in 1944, and when Hitler committed suicide in the ruins of Berlin in 1945. The only other clerical fascist state besides Spain and Portugal died with Engelbert Dollfuss in Vienna in 1934.

The Catholic Church has read the handwriting on the wall of history and is backing away from the endorsement of fascist principles expressed by Pius XI in his 1930 encyclical, *Quadragesimo Anno.* The Church is even pretending that this endorsement was never given. When John XXIII issued the longest encyclical in Church history *Mater et Magistra,* in 1961, he sagaciously concealed all the embarrassing anti-democratic statements of Leo XIII and the pro-fascist statements of Pius XI and came out for the right of "socialization" in the modern welfare state. He reasserted the right of papal dictatorship over all "moral" areas for all Catholics throughout the world,[1] but he was careful not to make this dictum specific in the area of church-state union or the forms of political society. Although he did not repudiate Spanish and Portuguese clerical fascism in any way, his long encyclical represented a slight swing to the left in papal social policy.

Under the circumstances, this discarding of the fascist label by the Vatican and by Spain and Portugal, means little so long as the forces that create clerical fascism are alive in modern society. Even if the exact forms of social and ecclesiastical organization developed in Spain and Portugal are never duplicated elsewhere in the future, the familiar alignments are likely to appear wherever the familiar ingredients are present, a Catholic Church in league for practical reasons with a reactionary state, a corrupt and powerful aristocracy, a poverty-stricken and disillusioned lower class, a small and ineffective middle class, a weak and confused government and a consuming fear of Communism. In such situations a political Catholicism, in league with economic reaction, may succeed in imposing authoritarian limitations upon democracy in the name of morality and national security without making use of any of the specific slogans or exact forms of fascism.

Catholicism tends toward fascist forms of society because of certain inherent characteristics deeply rooted in pre-democratic history, going back to the days when all European governments were authoritarian and the Papacy was a kind of authoritarian supergovernment. This tendency is not apparent in the United States because there has never been any authoritarian political hierarchy in our nation with which a clerical hierarchy could make an alliance. The Catholic Church in the United States, like other churches in American society, has flourished under the blessings of tolerance, liberty and the separation of church and state. The great majority of the American Catholic people have come to accept this tolerant, democratic environment as a desirable one for Catholic growth, and they regard fascism and its various European subvarieties without enthusiasm.

But it should be remembered that Catholicism is primarily a European, not an American, phenomenon. Its all-powerful popes are always European and its College of Cardinals is overwhelmingly European in composition. All the important decisions concerning worldwide policy are made in Europe. Moreover, the Church is fascist in structural form, and this fascist form affects its political and economic ideology.

It will be worthwhile to examine this last statement in some detail, because the examination may throw some light on the nature of clerical fascism as well as its future.

Catholicism and the Nature of Fascism

At the beginning of this book is quoted a certain famous phrase from Count Coudenhove-Kalergi's *Crusade for Pan-Europe*: "Catholicism is the fascist form of Christianity. . . ." If the quotation stands alone, it should be reprinted with one word italicized— ". . . is the fascist *form* of Chrisianity. . . ." The Catholic Church is an institution whose structure of power follows the fascist form, not necessarily the fascist ideological content.

However, Count Coudenhove-Kalergi went far beyond this attack on Catholic form and pointed out that the authoritarian leadership form of Catholic power has an influence on its ideas and policies. The power structure creates a natural affinity with political systems of obedience and authority, rather than with systems of individual choice. He suggested that Catholicism accepts democracy quite gladly when it is a minority faith in a non-Catholic nation, and therefore needs the guarantees of civil liberties for survival. When it exists in a Catholic nation, it prefers "moderate fascism."

Coudenhove-Kalergi's analysis is important for those who would see Spanish and Portuguese Catholicism and fascism in world perspective. If his conclusions seem unduly pro-Protestant as well as anti-Catholic, it should be remembered that this distinguished leader of the Pan-European movement was not a Protestant, but one who had been born a Catholic. His analysis was written in defense of Pius XII, whom he greatly admired, after he had interviewed both Mussolini and the Pope on the same day in Rome in March 1938. Here is the whole passage from which I borrowed one phrase:

Critics of Pacelli [Pius XII] have reproached him for not taking a clear stand in favor of democracy and against fascism, although they excuse him with the fact that he is virtually a prisoner of Fascist Italy.

These critics start from the wrong premise. There is no reason for a basically anti-Fascist attitude on the part of Catholicism. Catholicism is the fascist form of Christianity of which Calvinism represents its democratic wing. The Catholic hierarchy rests fully and securely on the leadership principle with infallible pope in supreme command for a lifetime. Leadership is, of course, open to all classes of the Catholic society and so is leadership within the fascist state. But, like the Fascist party, its priesthood becomes a medium for an un-democratic minority rule by the hierarchy.

This constitutional—not moral—analogy between fascism and Catholicism offers the key to the fact that in Europe, as well as in America, Catholic nations follow fascist doctrines more willingly than Protestant nations, which are the main strongholds of democracy. Even in Germany the fascist movement did not come from the Protestant North but from the Catholic South, not from Berlin, but from Munich. Like Hitler himself, most other leaders of nazism have a Catholic and not a Protestant background.

It is obvious that the Catholic Church will prefer the democratic system in states where she forms a minority, because she depends on tolerance there. For a Catholic nation she seems to prefer a system of moderate fascism like that of Salazar in Portugal or of Dollfuss in Austria, based on authoritarian government, corporative representa-tion, and Christian ethics—uninfected, of course, by the paganism and anti-humanism of Hitler's racial doctrines.[2]

Such candid comment about the clerical underpinning of fas-cism is rare among modern writers. For the most part, their studies of fascism emphasize the physical and political steps by which a controlled and anti-democratic minority takes over a democratic society; or they specialize in the racial horrors of the Nazi regime, in respect to which Catholicism had a relatively clean record. Since stories about Blackshirts and Brownshirts and their murders and beatings are more dramatic and interesting than discussions of cultural and religious factors, the "shirt" stories absorb nearly all the attention of students in this field.

The "shirt" stories are not nearly as important as an under-standing of the way in which the areas of free choice in a demo-cratic society are whittled down by Catholic authoritarian control. The Catholic mind and the fascist mind are both created by author-itarian discipline from above, and their association in history is not accidental. One is called religious and the other is called political, but they both have political results.

Catholicism paves the way to fascism and thwarts the progress of society toward democracy by means of several basic policies. It conditions its people to accept non-democratic government because the Church itself has a completely non-democratic government; it weakens democracy's most important institution, the non-sectarian public school, by ordering its children to boycott that school whenever possible and to remain in a segregated Catholic environment; it parallels the fascist program of family control by attempting to assert monopoly power over the marriage of all Catholics, abolish divorce, outlaw birth control and capture for the Church the children of all mixed marriages; it limits freedom of thought for its people by denying them the right to read any literature directly attacking Catholic ideas; in some nations it organizes separate Catholic trade unions and political parties whose policies are partially under Vatican dictation—the political parties have scored notable successes in Italy, Germany, France, Belgium and the Netherlands; the trade unions in Belgium, France, the Netherlands and Switzerland, with some strength in Italy and Germany.

Catholicism has openly supported and still openly supports such fascist dictators as Franco and Salazar; it steadfastly refuses to endorse democracy as a form of government superior to dictatorship; it tends to develop anti-Communism into a fanatical religious crusade, quite justified in military terms but also quite unbalanced in its single-devil emphasis and therefore likely to induce tolerance for Catholic totalitarianism.

These are the basic policies of Catholicism which indicate that its alliance with Iberian reaction is not accidental or incidental. Of course, there are forces within Catholicism and in the world surrounding Catholicism which tend to counteract and weaken these anti-democratic factors. It is increasingly apparent that Catholic dictatorship with its system of control by clerical colonial agents is out of place in Western democratic society. This system of control is causing increasing resentment among educated Catholic laymen who have been trained to believe in the democratic way of life. Catholic censorship of literature, art and the theater has failed miserably in almost every Catholic country of the world except Spain, Portugal and the Irish Republic; the Catholic trade unions have been repudiated by the world's largest labor movements, and the vertical unions of Spain and Portugal have been rejected as fraudulent by both Catholic and secular labor leaders; the Catholic political parties of Europe, in order to acquire any power in coalition governments, have been compelled to repudiate clerical fascism and to accept both political democracy and a large part of the program of social democracy; the policies of the Church's hierarchy on contraception, divorce and mixed marriage are meeting with increasing resistance from educated Catholics and from nearly all non-Catholics.

On balance, the Catholic policies which tend to move society in the direction of clerical fascism seem to be on the defensive in every nation in Europe except Spain and Portugal; and in the United States they are embarrassing to an American Catholicism which would like to live in peace within a liberal democratic society.

The Future in America, North and South

But nothing in this summary should be taken as a justification for complacency, even in the United States. While no overt clerical fascism of the Spanish-Portuguese type is possible here, there is a very real possibility of the gradual growth of that creeping form of Catholic power which reduces the scope of freedom step by step in a process of erosion. The Catholic population is gaining on the non-Catholic population in the United States quite rapidly—some say in the ratio of 36 to 25.[3] The Catholic schools are growing faster absolutely and proportionately than the public schools,[4] and this growth is by no means without political significance in relation to clerical fascism. These schools are systematically promoting pro-Franco and pro-Salazar versions of Iberian history in their textbooks and attempting to make Catholic authoritarian forms of political dictatorship acceptable to American children in the name of anti-Communism. (I have elsewhere quoted at length pro-Franco passages from American Catholic textbooks.)[5] The great American newspapers, magazines and broadcasting companies usually avoid plain speaking concerning these domestic Catholic propaganda activities because of the mistaken—and carefully promoted—notion that critical analysis of a church's conduct is somehow equivalent to intolerance or bigotry.

Two events in 1960 and 1961 indicated that even on American soil the Catholic hierarchy is now ready to use its power in the style of European clerical politics. In the Puerto Rican election of 1960, the American-born bishops of the island's Church formed a Christian Action political party to destroy the career and the dominant political party of the popular Puerto Rican governor, Munoz Marin, because he had rejected a plan for released-time religious instruction in connection with Puerto Rico's public schools and because he had favored the right of birth control. It was announced that those Catholics who voted for Governor Munoz' party would be denied absolution in the confessional. Although the bishops were overwhelmingly defeated at the polls, and were severely criticized by some Catholic leaders in the United States, the reaction of the Vatican was distinctly bland. When Bishop James E. McManus of Ponce, chief political spokesman of the Puerto Rican Church, made his next personal report to Pope John XXIII after the 1960 election, he came away jubilant because he had not been "condemned or criticized." America's leading diocesan newspaper headed its story "Pontiff Not Critical of Puerto Rico Bishops." [6]

The other recent event that dramatized the American Catholic drive for political power in the European manner was the formal demand in January 1961 by the Catholic bishops of the United States for federal tax support for Catholic schools on a basis of equality with public schools. The demand was in flat opposition to an 8 to 1 decision by the United States Supreme Court which had interpreted the constitutional principle of the separation of church and state as forbidding the payment of any "tax in any amount" levied "to support any religious activities or institutions, whatever they may be called, or whatever form they may adopt to teach or practice religion." [7] The bishops attempted to form the Catholic population of the country into a Catholic political bloc in behalf of their educational program, and their subsidiary organizations conducted the greatest political pressure campaign in American history. The campaign was probably the determining factor in defeating President Kennedy's program for federal aid for public schools.

Although these developments of Catholic political policy on American soil are a far cry from full-blown clerical fascism, they show that the hierarchy is now ready to promote by political pressure in the United States that partial union of church and state which is the first demand of the Catholic political parties of Europe.

Latin American Variations

Although any detailed discussion of clerical fascism in Latin America is beyond the scope of this book, it would be unreasonable to ignore the possibilities south of the Rio Grande, since Spanish, Portuguese and Catholic influence have all played so large a part in shaping Latin America. All the twenty republics south of the Rio Grande are overwhelmingly Catholic in name—officially about 98 per cent—and they are all Spanish and Portuguese in cultural heritage except Haiti. To some extent Latin America is bound to be the battleground of the future between the church-state policies of Western democracy as exemplified in the United States and the church-state policies of Catholicism as exemplified in the "mother" countries of Spain and Portugal.

Not that any generalizations can safely be made about so complex and diversified an area as Latin America. The variations among Latin powers in respect to church and state policy are as great as the variations in Europe. The robust and free-swinging phenomenon known as Mexican anti-clericalism is as far removed from Colombian clerical reaction as Danish democracy is removed from Franco's dictatorship. Uruguay calls Christmas "Family Day" to avoid any state commitment to a Church holiday, while in Peru President Manuel Prado cancelled Protestant missionary activity among his native Indians with the declaration: "The Constitution protects the Catholic religion. The nation spends large sums for the development of Catholic missions and their activities should not be vitiated by diverse forms of religious propaganda." [8]

Mexico is probably the most anti-Franco nation in the world —unless Castro's Cuba cares to claim that distinction. Mexico will not even extend diplomatic recognition to the Spanish government, and it has refused to continue sending ambassadors to the Vatican. Colombia, at the other extreme, has for many years accepted and promoted Iberian policy in matters of church and state and has persecuted Protestants more severely than they have been persecuted in Spain. The exclusive 1953 Missionary Agreement which Colombia made with the Vatican is a direct parallel of the Portuguese Missionary Agreement.

The movement toward clerical fascism was quite strong in Latin America during the Spanish Civil War and during the early days of World War II, when it seemed likely that the Axis would win that war. Pictures of Franco and Salazar were conspicuously displayed on monastery walls, and the Latin American Church, ruled almost everywhere by Spanish-born prelates, became a propaganda instrument for Catholic fascism. Little caudillos rose to power in a number of nations, and sometimes they had the tacit or open support of the hierarchy. Falange parties of varying strength appeared in almost every Latin American country, although they never completely captured any nation.[9] Full-blown blackshirt parties were active in Chile in the late 1930s, and in the same period the Catholic clergy encouraged a similar movement in Mexico, the Sinarquista movement, which was patterned after the Spanish Falange and which created considerable turmoil in Mexico before it was suppressed by the government in 1949.

In Brazil there was an Integralist party with green shirts and the slogan "God, Country, Family," but it was finally absorbed by Dictator Vargas into his New State, which supposedly gained some inspiration from Salazar's New State. Dictator Rojas Pinilla tried to establish a corporative state in Colombia in 1956, but he was ousted before he could carry out his program. Until Peron turned against the Church in Argentina, his dictatorship had many of the earmarks of clerical fascism. Eva Peron received Spain's highest decoration, that of Isabella the Catholic, at about the same time her husband was receiving the Grand Cross of the Order of Pius IX from Pius XII.

Throughout Latin American history there has been the same kind of oscillation between anti-clerical liberalism and Church-supported conservatism that has characterized the history of Spain and Portugal. Until recently the Latin Church has richly earned the description of Professor Mecham, "a conservative institution always identified with privilege and vested interests." [10] As late as 1840 it held at least half the land in use in Mexico.

The Church clung to its privileged position in Latin America long after the Spanish and Portuguese colonies had been freed. It opposed the separation of church and state belligerently as long as it dared, and it still maintains partial church-state union in Argentina, Bolivia, Colombia, Peru and Venezuela.[11] There is nominal or real separation of church and state in Brazil, Chile, Ecuador, El Salvador, Guatemala, Honduras, Mexico, Nicaragua, Panama and Uruguay, but the phrase does not mean in Latin America what it means in the United States. Nineteen of the twenty republics south of the Rio Grande still send diplomatic representatives to the Holy See and ten of them have either full-blown concordats with the Vatican or some kind of informal agreements which usually confer some special privilege on the Catholic Church. In some countries, such as Colombia, the agreements give papal sanction to anti-Protestant policies. In Argentina and Paraguay the presidents must also be Catholic.

Although Protestantism is not dominant in any Latin American country, it is growing rapidly, particularly in Brazil, and Catholic authorities now estimate the total of Latin American Protestants at more than 6 million. Since most of the Protestant congregations get some support from people in the United States and since the leadership of Latin American Catholicism is still primarily Spanish, there are American-Iberian overtones in the conflict between Protestantism and Catholicism throughout Latin America.[12] Protestantism tends to be pro-American and anti-Spanish; Catholicism tends to reverse the formula. The contrasting philosophies of Protestantism and Catholicism concerning the separation of church and state are bound to provoke more conflict in the future.

The animosity is increased by the fact that Catholicism is fighting for its life in most of Latin America. While 98 per cent of the people nominally belong to the Church, only 7 per cent practice their faith. The intelligentsia, particularly the educated men, are almost all indifferent or hostile to the Church. Spain, which in spite of its own desperate need is sending four hundred priests a year to Latin America, has failed to check the anti-clerical trend. Latin America still has the smallest quota of priests of any so-called Catholic region of the world—4 per cent of the world's priests for 34 per cent of the world's Catholics—and Catholic leaders estimate that not more than one-third of Latin American Catholics ever receive communion at any time in their lives.[13]

The situation in Latin America has been greatly complicated by the rise of Fidel Castro's Communist-oriented regime in Cuba, the disastrous American sponsorship of the invasion of Cuba in 1961, and the crudely anti-Catholic policy of the Castro regime. Now the dangers of clerical fascism south of the Rio Grande are being obscured by the increased fear of Communism and the simultaneous Latin American apprehensions about blundering American policy. Will clerical fascism, on the rebound against a new Communist threat, gain new strength in Latin America by default? It must be remembered that fascism has always gained its initial impetus by exploiting anti-Communism.

In the 1961 struggle in Cuba it was revealed that the great majority of the priests of the island came from Spain. Castro deported them as "falangist traitors." Although his action was a gross violation of civil liberty, there was just enough truth in his description of the Spanish-born priests in his country to be painful to Catholic apologists. The leaders of Latin American Catholicism have been as consistently pro-Franco as Castro is now consistently pro-Communist. The recent tendency in the United States has been to forget this fact and to accept the image of the Latin American Church as a persecuted instrument of liberty facing the villains of Communist totalitarianism. This is exactly the kind of image of itself which the Church is attempting to promote in the United States. It represents approximately half of the truth. The other half is that the Spanish-Portuguese type of Catholicism which has been dominant in Latin America from the beginning is no more committed to liberty than is Communism. Its accomplishments in Spain and Portugal may be accepted as proof of this charge.

Some of the more progressive leaders of American and European Catholicism are beginning to realize that they cannot win or hold Latin America with the reactionary Iberian type of Catholicism. They are promoting large-scale movements for social reform and sponsoring a chain of Catholic political parties modeled after the Christian Democratic parties of Italy and Germany. An international convention of such Catholic political parties was held in Chile in July 1961 under the title of the Christian Democratic World Union. "Christian Democrats," said one leader at this convention, "must work to change a social and moral disorder that has denied the great majority of people the benefits of democracy, social progress and a fair share of the wealth." [14] It remains to be seen how much of this program will gain solid support from a Latin hierarchy which in the past has been "always identified with privilege and vested interests."

The American Responsibility

Meanwhile, American policy in regard to Spanish and Portuguese fascism has reached a crucial stage. The West is in mortal danger from Communist military aggression. It is not, at the present time, in mortal danger from fascist military aggression. In such a crisis, how far should we go in abandoning what George Kennan has called "the luxury of high moral attitudes" in order to welcome any military alliance which apparently strengthens us against Communism?

Perhaps the answer depends largely on one's definition of the word "strengthens." The concept should not be limited to purely military strength. We strengthened our nation immeasurably in moral terms when our representatives denounced Salazar's African imperialism at the United Nations in 1961. We proved to many new African nations that we may actually believe in a free world. Although we may have lost some potential military strength in the Portuguese Azores, even that is not certain.

The present struggle between the West and the East—we should keep reminding ourselves—is not only a struggle of intercontinental ballistic missiles but a struggle of ideas in which our moral prestige still has incalculable worth. In terms of moral prestige we have paid too high a price already for our alliance with Franco. The bases on Spanish soil, with their apparently official American approval of fascist dictatorship, are worth far more to Khrushchev than they are to us. They help him to "prove" that we condone fascism when it suits our military purposes. "In any case," says Norman Thomas, who has so often served as a useful conscience for the American people, "no nation's virtue is so potent as to sanctify any alliance with Franco."

Professor Arthur Whitaker suggests that the least we can do is to revert to the "cool and correct attitude of 1953," and let Spain know that we will no longer advocate Spanish admission to NATO "so long as the present contradiction persists between the character of the Spanish dictatorship and the declared purpose of NATO to defend freedom and democracy." Ultimately we should end the alliance with Franco altogether, at the first possible moment consistent with our treaty obligations.

Such a policy would bring agonized protests from both Pentagon and Catholic sources, accompanied by extravagant praise of Spain as a necessary and hospitable launching pad in a war for Western survival. But, to use the words of the *New York Times* editorial with which this book began; ". . . it is vital for Americans to keep in mind that the enemy in our century is totalitariansm, whether it take the form of communism or fascism. We fought the Second World War with communism as an ally, only to find at the end that the threat to world democracy was greater than ever. It would be extraordinarily shortsighted if now we fought communism with fascism as an ally."

APPENDIX

Key Provisions of the 1953 Concordat
between the Holy See and the Spanish Government

THE CONCORDAT

In the Name of the Most Holy Trinity

The Apostolic Holy See and the Spanish State, moved by the desire to secure a fruitful cooperation for the greater good of the religious and civil life of the Spanish nation, have decided to enter into a Concordat. . . .

ART. I. The Catholic Apostolic Roman religion will continue to be the sole religion of the Spanish nation and will enjoy the rights and prerogatives which are due it in conformity with the Divine Law and the Canon Law.

ART. II. 1. The Spanish State recognizes in the Catholic Church its character of a perfect society, and guarantees it the free and full exercise of its spiritual power as well as of its jurisdiction. It also guarantees the free and public worship of the Catholic religion. . . .

ART. III. 1. The Spanish State recognizes the juridical international status of the Holy See and the Vatican State.

2. In order to maintain in the traditional manner the friendly relations between the Holy See and the Spanish State, a Spanish ambassador to the Holy See, and an Apostolic Nuncio in Madrid, will continue to be permanently accredited in their respective posts. The Nuncio will be the dean of the diplomatic corps according to the rules set by traditional law.

ART. V. The state will have as holy days those established by the Church in the Code of Canon Law or in other particular regulations on local festivities, the State will also provide in its legislation the necessary facilities so that the faithful may comply during those days with their religious duties.

Civil authorities, both national and local, will see to it that these holidays are duly observed.

ART. VI. According to the concession of Popes Pius V and Gregory XIII, the Spanish priests will say daily prayers for Spain and for the

Chief of State, according to the traditional form and the prescriptions of the Sacred Liturgy.

ART. VII. For the appointment of the resident Archbishops and Bishops and their Coadjutors with the right of succession, will continue in force the rules of the agreement stipulated between the Holy See and the Spanish Government on June 7, 1941. [This means that when any vacancy occurs, the government, in consultation with the papal nuncio, submits six names to the Pope, who in turn selects three of these names from which the Spanish Government finally picks the person actually designated as archbishop or bishop.]

ART. IX. 2. In the establishment of a new diocese or ecclesiastical province, and in other changes in the diocesan boundaries which may be deemed necessary, the Holy See will seek first the agreement of the Spanish Government, unless the changes are of minor importance.

3. The Spanish State binds itself to provide the economic necessities of the diocese which will be established in the future, by increasing accordingly the funds established in Article XIX.

The Spanish State, also, per se, or through the local interested corporations, will contribute an extraordinary subsidy for initial expenses needed to organize the new dioceses; in particular, it will subsidize the construction of new cathedrals and those buildings necessary for the residence of the Prelate, offices of the chancery, and diocesan seminaries.

ART. XVI. 1. Prelates referred to in paragraph 2 of Canon 120 of the Code of Canon Law may not be summoned before a lay judge without having first obtained the required permission of the Holy See.

2. The Holy See agrees that litigation on ownership or temporal rights in which clergymen and members of religious orders are involved may be processed before civil tribunals. In such cases, the Ordinary [Bishop] concerned should receive prior notification of the place of the trial, and also be informed of the court's decision, on the same day it is handed down.

3. The state recognizes and respects the special authority of the tribunals of the Church in matters relating to crimes which exclusively violate an ecclesiastical law, in accordance with Canon 2,198 of the Code of Canon Law.

No appeal from sentences passed by these tribunals may be brought before civil courts.

4. The Holy See agrees that cases against clergymen or other members of religious Orders involving other, non-canonical crimes, which are covered by the penal laws of the state, may be judged by the tribunals of the state. Nevertheless, the judicial authority, before proceeding, should request, without prejudice to precautionary measures to be taken in the case, and with due reservation, the consent of the Ordinary concerned. In the event that the latter, for serious reasons, believes it

his duty to deny such consent, he will communicate in writing to the competent civil authority.

The necessary precautions will be taken to avoid all publicity during the course of lawsuits concerning ecclesiastics. The findings of the case, as well as the verdict, in the first as well as in the last instance, shall be made known to the Ordinary mentioned above.

5. In case of detention or arrest, clergymen and members of religious Orders shall be treated with the consideration due their position and rank.

Sentences involving incarceration shall be served in ecclesiastic or religious institutions which, in the judgment of the Ordinary concerned and of the state judicial authority, comply with the guarantees required; or, at least, in institutions other than secular, unless the competent ecclesiastical authority shall have reduced the prisoner to the lay status.

The rights of conditional liberty and other rights established under state law shall be applicable to imprisoned clergy.

ART. XIX. 1. The Church and the state shall study by common agreement means of creating an adequate Church fund which will provide for the maintenance of the clergy and of religious activities.

2. Meanwhile, the state, by way of indemnification for past confiscations of Church property, and as a contribution to the Church's work for the good of the nation, will provide the Church with an annual endowment. This will include, in particular, the apportionment of funds for diocesan Archbishops and Bishops, coadjutors, auxiliaries, general vicariates, cathedral chapters, collegiate churches, and parishes, as well as funds for seminaries and ecclesiastical universities and for the general practice of the [Catholic] religion. . . .

If, in the future, a marked change in the general economic situation should occur, the endowments will be adjusted to the new situation in such a manner that support of religion and the clergy will always be assured.

3. The state, ever faithful to the national tradition, will reward annual subsidies for the construction and repair of parish churches, rectories, and seminaries; the development of religious Orders, congregations and Church institutions devoted to missionary activities; and to the care of monasteries of historic value to Spain. It will also award subsidies toward the support of the Colegio Espanol de San Jose and the Spanish church and residence of Montserrat in Rome.

4. The state will collaborate with the Church in establishing and financing social institutions for the benefit of aged, feeble and invalid clergymen; also, the state will provide an adequate pension to resident Prelates who, for reasons of age or health, retire from their posts.

ART. XXIII. The Spanish state recognizes the full civil validity of marriages performed according to the norms of Canon Law.

ART. XXIV. 1. The Spanish state recognizes the exclusive competence of the ecclesiastical courts in cases involving the nullity of ecclesiastical marriage, in those where separation is sought, or in other cases involving the dispensation from marriages *"ratum non consummatum,"* or having to do with the Pauline privilege.

2. Once a demand of separation or of nullity has been established and admitted before the ecclesiastical tribunal, the civil court should dictate, at the request of the interested party, both precautionary norms and measures used to regulate the civil effects of the pending process.

3. When its sentences and decisions have been confirmed and have become enforceable, the ecclesiastical courts will notify the civil court in its jurisdiction. The civil court, in turn, will decree the necessary measures to give civil effect to the ecclesiastical court's decisions. The civil court will ordain, in the case of nullity, the *"super rato"* dispensations, or the application of the Pauline privilege, all these measures to be duly noted in the Civil Registry on the margin of the marriage certificate.

4. In general all sentences, decrees and decisions of an administrative nature issued by ecclesiastical authorities regarding any of the matters subject to their jurisdiction will have validity also in the civil order. Once they have been notified, the state authorities and civil officials will render the necessary assistance in carrying out these sentences, decisions and decrees.

ART. XXVI. In all institutions of learning—whatever their level and purpose and whether belonging to the State or not—education will be imparted in accordance with the dogmatic and moral principles of the Catholic Church.

Ordinaries will freely exercise their mission of vigilance regarding the integrity of Faith, good morals and religious teaching in these educational institutions.

Ordinaries may demand the banning and suppression of textbooks, publications and other teaching material which are contrary to Catholic dogma and morals.

ART. XXVII. 1. The Spanish State guarantees the teaching of the Catholic religion as a regular and compulsory subject in all educational institutions, whether state-controlled or not, and whatever their level and purpose.

Children of non-Catholic parents will be exempt from this teaching, upon the request of their parents or tutors.

2. In primary public schools, teachers themselves will impart religious instruction, except when the Ordinary objects to someone for reasons prescribed in Canon 1381, Article 3, of the Code of Canon Law. This instruction also will be periodically supplemented by Catechism lessons given by the parish priest or his delegate.

3. In public institutions of secondary education, religious instruction will be given by priests or religious, or instead by lay professors appointed by the competent civil authorities on recommendations of the Diocesan Ordinary. . . .

7. Professors of religion at non-state schools must have a certificate of aptitude issued by the Ordinary. Revocation of this certificate will instantly deprive the teacher of his functions.

8. The subject matter of courses in religion, both in public and non-public schools, will be prepared in accordance with the competent ecclesiastical authority. Only textbooks approved by the ecclesiastical authority can be used in the teaching of religion.

ART. XXVIII. 1. State universities may impart, by agreement with the ecclesiastical authorities, regular courses specializing in Scholastic Philosophy, Sacred Theology and Canon Law; programs and textbooks should be approved by the same ecclesiastical authorities. These courses may be given by priests, religious or lay teachers holding graduate degrees from a Catholic university, or the equivalent from the respective Order when a member of a religious order is concerned; all of them must have the Nihil Obstat of the diocesan Ordinary.

ART. XXIX. The state will assure that services and institutions which mold public opinion, and in particular radio and television, grant due attention to the explanation and defense of the religious truths, a task which will be trusted to priests and members of religious orders and in accordance with the Ordinary.

ART. XXX. 1. . . . The state will seek to render as much financial help as possible to institutions of religious orders and congregations, especially those devoted to the training of missionaries.

ART. XXXI. 1. The Church freely exercises its right, as established by Canon 1375 of the Code of Canon Law, to organize and operate its own schools, regardless of level or purpose, which are open for general registration—including lay students. In matters regarding recognition by the State of studies undertaken in such schools, civil authorities will act in agreement with the proper ecclesiastical authority.

ART. XXXII. 1. Religious care in the armed forces will conform to the regulations established by the agreement of August 5, 1950.

ART. XXXIII. The state, in agreement with the ecclesiastical authority, will provide the necessary means so that hospitals, sanitaria, penal establishments, orphanages and like institutions shall have the proper religious assistance for their inmates and the personnel in charge. By the same token, the state will seek the observance of these norms in similar establishments in private hands.

FINAL PROTOCOL. At the time of signing the Concordat, which is today being entered into between the Holy See and Spain, the plenipotentiaries signing the agreement have, by mutual agreement, made the following statements which will be an integral part of the Concordat itself: . . .

In Reference to Article I

In regard to the toleration of non-Catholic faiths, in territories under Spanish jurisdiction in Africa, the "status quo" observed up to now will continue in force. . . .

In Reference to Article XXIII

A. For recognition, by the state of the civil effects of canonical marriage, it will be sufficient for the marriage certificate to be transcribed in the corresponding Civil Registry. . . .

(1) Under no circumstances shall the presence of a state official during the celebration of a canonical marriage be considered as a required condition for acknowledgment of its civil effects. . . .

C. In the matter of acknowledgment of a mixed marriage between Catholic and non-Catholic persons, the State shall formulate its legislation so as to harmonize with Canon Law. . . .

Key Provisions of the 1940 Concordat and the Missionary Agreement Between the Holy See and Portugal.

THE CONCORDAT

In the Name of the Holy Trinity

His Holiness, the Supreme Pontiff Pius XII, and His Excellency the President of the Portuguese Republic, being disposed to regulate by mutual agreement and in a stable manner the juridical position of the Catholic Church in Portugal, for the peace and greater welfare of the Church and of the State,

Have decided to conclude among themselves a solemn Convention which recognizes and guarantees the liberty of the Church and safeguards the legitimate interests of the Portuguese Nation, also in regard to the Catholic Missions and the Patronage in the Orient. . . .

ART. I. The Portuguese Republic recognizes the juridical personality of the Catholic Church.

Friendly relations with the Holy See shall be assured in the traditional form in which historically they were formerly expressed, by means of an Apostolic Nuncio to the Republic of Portugal and an Ambassador of the Republic to the Holy See.

ART. II. The Catholic Church is guaranteed the free exercise of her authority: within the sphere of her competency she has the freedom to exercise acts of her powers of jurisdiction and of order without interference.

Hence the Holy See can freely publish any dispositions relative to the government of the Church, and, in everything that concerns the pastoral ministry, can communicate and correspond with the Prelates, the clergy, and all the Catholics of Portugal, and these with the Holy See, without the need of previous approval from the State in order that Bulls and any instructions or dispositions of the Holy See may be published and circulated in the Country. . . .

ART. X. The Holy See, before proceeding to the appointment of a resident Archbishop or Bishop, or of a Coadjutor with right of succession, without prejudice to the provisions made in regard to Patronage and Semi-Patronage, shall communicate the name of the person chosen to the Portuguese Government, to ascertain whether there are any objections of a general political character against the candidate. The silence of the Government, after thirty days from the aforesaid communication, shall be interpreted in the sense that there are no objections. All proceedings contemplated in this article shall remain secret.

ART. XI. In the exercise of their ministry, ecclesiastics enjoy the protection of the State in the same way as do the public authorities. . . .

ART. XVI. The Catholic Church is guaranteed the free exercise of all acts of worship, private and public, without prejudice to the exigencies of police and traffic control. . . .

ART. XX. The associations and organizations of the Church can freely erect and maintain private schools parallel to those of the State, which shall remain subject to State control according to the common law, and can, according to the same law, be subsidized and kept up to standards.

Religious instruction in private schools and courses does not depend on the authorization of the State, and can be freely imparted by the ecclesiastical Authority or its subordinates.

Seminaries or any other institutions for ecclesiastical education or higher training can be freely founded. Their internal government is not subject to the control of the State. But the State shall be informed of the books adopted for studies which are not philosophical or theological. The competent ecclesiastical Authorities shall see to it that, in the teaching of special branches, such as history, due consideration be given to the legitimate sentiment of Portuguese patriotism.

ART. XXI. The instruction imparted by the State in the public schools shall be guided by the principles of Christian doctrine and morality, which are traditional in the Country. Consequently the Catholic religion and morals shall be taught in the public elementary, complementary, and middle schools to those students whose parents or guardians shall have made no request for exemption.

In asylums, orphanages, official establishments, and institutions for the education of minors, and for correction and reform, which are dependent on the State, the Catholic religion shall be taught at the expense of the State itself and the practice of its precepts shall be assured.

The text for the teaching of the Catholic religion must be approved by the ecclesiastical Authority, and the teachers shall be appointed by the State upon agreement with it; in no case can the aforesaid instruction be imparted by persons whom the ecclesiastical Authority has not approved as fit.

ART. XXII. The Portuguese State recognizes the civil effects of marriages celebrated in conformity with canon law, on condition that the marriage be registered in the proper office of the civil state. . . .

ART. XXIV. In accordance with the essential properties of Catholic marriage, it is understood that, by the very fact of the celebration of a canonical marriage, the parties renounce the civil right of seeking a divorce, which accordingly cannot be applied by the civil tribunals to Catholic marriages.

ART. XXV. Cognizance of cases concerning the nullity of Catholic marriage and the dispensation from ratified and non-consummated marriage, is reserved to the competent ecclesiastical tribunals and departments.

The decisions and judgments of these departments and tribunals, when they have become definitive, shall be brought before the Supreme Tribunal of the Apostolic Signatura for review, and then, together with the respective decrees of the Supreme Tribunal of the Signatura, shall be transmitted through diplomatic channels to the Tribunal of Appeal of the State that is territorially competent, which shall put them into execution and order that they be noted in the registry of the civil State, in the margin of the registry of the marriage.

THE MISSIONARY AGREEMENT

The Holy See and the Portuguese Government have decided to strike an Accord intended to regulate more completely the relations between Church and State in regard to religious life in the Portuguese Colonies, without prejudice to what has been previously agreed upon regarding the Patronage of the Orient. . . .

ART. 7. Before proceeding to the appointment of a resident Archbishop or Bishop or of a Coadjutor with right of succession, the Holy See shall communicate the name of the person chosen to the Portuguese Government, in order to learn whether there are any objections of a general political character against him. Silence on the part of the Government, after thirty days from the aforesaid communication, shall be interpreted in the sense that there are no objections. All the proceedings contemplated in this article shall remain secret.

Whenever new missionary boards of administration are established within particular dioceses or missionary districts, the appointment of the respective directors, in cases where it cannot fall on a Portuguese citizen, shall be made only after consultation with the Portuguese Government.

ART. 9. Recognized missionary corporations of men and women, independently of the aid which they may receive from the Holy See, shall be subsidized according to their needs by the Government of the Mother-country and by the Government of the respective colony. In the apportionment of the aforesaid subsidies, not only the number of members of the houses of training and the number of missionaries in the colonies, but also the missionary works, including seminaries and other works for the native clergy, shall be taken into account. In the apportionment of the subsidies on the part of the colonies, dioceses shall be considered on a par with missionary districts.

ART. 10. Besides the subsidies referred to in the preceding article, the Government will continue to make gratuitous grants of allottable land to the Catholic missions, for their development and for new foundations. . . .

ART. 12. Besides the subsidies provided in Article 9, the Portuguese Government guarantees to the resident Bishops as Superiors of the missions of their respective dioceses, and to the Vicars and Prefects Apostolic, suitable salaries, and continues to acknowledge their right to a pension. But there will be no right to a special subsidy for travels or movements from place to place.

ART. 13. The Portuguese Government shall continue to make the pension proportionate to the number of missionaries actually in retirement, and for the future it shall make it proportionate also to the members of the secular missionary clergy, when they have completed the years of service necessary to this effect.

ART. 14. All the missionary personnel shall have a right to the payment of traveling expenses within and outside the colonies. . . .

ART. 15. The Catholic Portuguese missions can freely expand, in order to exercise the forms of activity proper to them, and in particular can found and direct schools for natives and Europeans, colleges of men and of women, elementary, secondary, and professional schools, seminaries, catechumenates, ambulances and hospitals. . . .

ART. 16. In the native missionary schools, the teaching of the Portuguese tongue is obligatory, but the use of the native tongue in the teaching of the Catholic religion remains entirely free in accordance with the principles of the Church.

ART. 18. The Prelates of the dioceses and missionary districts, and the superiors of the missionary corporations in the mother-country shall annually inform the Government regarding the missionary movement and the external activities of the missions.

ART. 19. The Holy See shall continue to use its authority to the end that the Portuguese missionary corporations intensify the evangelization of the natives and the missionary apostolate. . . .

NOTES

The titles and publishers of certain books and journals are listed in these Notes as follows:

America: Jesuit weekly, 920 Broadway, New York, 10, N.Y.

Brenan: Gerald Brenan, *The Spanish Labyrinth*, Macmillan, 1944.

Canon Law: T. Lincoln Bouscaren and Adam C. Ellis, *Canon Law: Text and Commentary*, Bruce Publishing Company, Milwaukee, 1948.

Cath. Alm.: National Catholic Almanac, 1961, St. Anthony's Guild, Paterson, N.J.

Cath. Enc.: Catholic Encyclopedia (and Supplement), Encyclopedia Press (various).

Delpech: Jacques Delpech, *The Oppression of Protestants in Spain*, Beacon Press, 1955.

Duffy: James Duffy, *Portuguese Africa*, Harvard University Press, 1959.

Ebenstein: William Ebenstein, *Church and State in Franco Spain*, Center of International Studies, Princeton University, 1960.

Ecclesia: Official journal of Spanish hierarchy, Cuesta de Santo Domingo 5, Madrid.

Fernsworth: Lawrence Fernsworth, *Spain's Struggle for Freedom*, Beacon Press, 1957.

Hughes: Emmet J. Hughes, *Report From Spain*, Henry Holt, 1947.

Hughey: John D. Hughey, *Religious Freedom in Spain*, Carey Kingsgate Press (London), 1955.

Iberica: liberal Spanish monthly, published in both Spanish and English, 112 East 19th St., New York 3, N.Y.

Livermore, *Spain:* Harold V. Livermore, *A History of Spain*, Allen and Unwin (London), 1958.

Livermore, *Portugal:* Harold V. Livermore, *A History of Portugal*, Cambridge University Press, 1947.

Madariaga: Salvador de Madariaga, *Spain, A Modern History*, Praeger, 1958.

Matthews: Herbert L. Matthews, *The Yoke and the Arrows*, Braziller, 1961.

277

N.Y.T.: New York Times.

Pattee, *Portugal:* Richard Pattee, *Portugal and the Portuguese World,* Bruce, 1957.

Pattee, *Spain:* Richard Pattee, *This Is Spain,* Bruce, 1951.

Peers, *Church:* E. Allison Peers, *Spain, The Church and the Orders,* Eyre and Spottiswoode (London), 1945.

Peers, *Eclipse:* E. Allison Peers, *Spain in Eclipse, 1937-1943,* Methuen (London), 1943.

Peers, *Tragedy:* E. Allison Peers, *The Spanish Tragedy,* Oxford (London), 1937.

Register: National Catholic diocesan chain weekly, Denver, Colorado.

Thomas: Hugh Thomas, *The Spanish Civil War,* Harper's, 1961.

Whitaker: Arthur Whitaker, *Spain and Defense of the West,* Harper's, 1961.

1. Personal Prologue: An American Issue

1. All general Catholic statistics in this volume are from the Catholic Almanac. All canon law citations are by number, and are so arranged in Canon Law. Several Catholic writers have indicated that more than half of the current contributed revenue of the Church comes from U.S. Catholic gifts. See, for this particular estimate, Bernard Wall, *The Vatican Story,* p. 127. U.S. Catholics contribute about 70 per cent of the total missionary funds of the Vatican according to Bishop Fulton J. Sheen, *Register,* July 22, 1956.

2. The details of this alliance will be described in Chapter X.

3. The multigraphed announcement of this picnic, of which I have a copy, as published in the Torrejon Air Base calendar, June 21, 1959, reads as follows: "Protestant Chapel Fellowship Picnic, 3-6 P.M., 27 June, Saturday, Casa del Campo Park. The Annual Family Style Picnic for all Protestants connected with the American Mission (Base) will be held at above date and place. It is sponsored by the Protestant Women's Chapel Guild. Bring enough food and silverware for your family, plus one, as single Air Force personnel are invited. Cold drinks, paper cups and plates will be furnished by the Protestant Chapel Fund. Games by age groups have been planned. You are urged and invited to come, visit old friends, and make new ones. In Park follow Picnic Signs."

2. From the Inquisition to Franco

1. Among general histories of Spain, Madariaga covers the whole sweep but concentrates more on recent events and social issues; Livermore, *Spain,* is authoritative but says little about church and state since the civil war; Hughey covers much church-state history, as well as contemporary conditions; Pattee states the Catholic interpretation, as does the *Cath. Enc.* Peers, in his three listed books, is scholarly

but very gentle in dealing with Catholic shortcomings. In a 1938 pamphlet, published originally in the London Catholic *Universe* during the Spanish Civil War, he said: "For the clergy and religious were, as they still are, the best friends of the Spanish people." Peers, *Church,* has a valuable date chart, "Two Centuries of Spanish Church History, 1737-1937."

2. See H. C. Lea's classics, *A History of the Inquisition in Spain* (4 vols.), Macmillan, 1906-7 (or the 1 vol. edition published in 1961); and *A History of the Inquisition in the Middle Ages* (3 vols.), 1888. Shorter treatments are G. G. Coulton, *Inquisition and Liberty,* Beacon Press, 1959; A. S. Turberville, *The Spanish Inquisition,* London, 1932; Cecil Roth, *The Spanish Inquisition,* London, 1937; and Chapter 3 of Hubert Herring, *A History of Latin America,* Knopf, 1961.

3. J. Lloyd Mecham, *Church and State in Latin America,* University of North Carolina Press, 1934, p. 12. Morelos facts, Ernest Gruening, *Mexico and Its Heritage,* Century, 1928, p. 267.

4. For Church income in sixteenth century and other financial facts, see Peers, *Church, passim* and Appendix; Pattee, pp. 82-86; and Will Durant, *The Age of Faith,* pp. 765ff.

5. Parts of the Philippine story are in Louis C. Cornish, *The Philippines Calling,* Dorrance, 1942; Herbert S. Duffy, *William Howard Taft;* and Henry Pringle, *The Life and Times of William Howard Taft,* vol. I, Farrar and Rinehart, 1939.

6. Hughey, p. 39.

7. Brenan, p. 47.

8. Segura's whole philosophy, anti-democratic, anti-Franco, anti-Protestant and anti-American, is best summed up in his suppressed volume of pastoral letters, *Por Unidad Catolica De Espana,* Seville, 1952. Brenan, p. 236, describes the reaction to the cardinal's letter. The Vatican rebuked him, *N.Y.T.,* March 17, 1955. Peers, *Tragedy,* p. 59, discusses Segura.

9. In Thomas, p. 40, it is estimated that anarchists numbered 1.5 million at the beginning of the Republic.

10. *Diario de Sesiones,* 13.10.31. Peers, *Tragedy,* discusses the debate at length, and Peers, *Church,* discusses the effects of Azana's program.

11. For discussion of American role, see Chapter X; also article on "Myth and Reality: How Red Were the Spanish Reds?" by Phil B. Taylor, *Michigan Alumnus,* Winter, 1956.

12. Matthews' estimates, p. 42. See also Foltz, p. 96 and Ebenstein, p. 6. Thomas, pp. 173 and 606, has documented estimate that total deaths in Civil War were about 600,000, of which perhaps 100,000 were by murder and execution. Father Antonio Moreno, director of *Ecclesia,* in his *History of the Religious Persecution,* as

cited in the Tablet, July 29, 1961, lists as victims 4,184 bishops and diocesan priests, 2,365 religious priests, and 2,283 other religious.

13. Madariaga, p. 495.

14. Foltz, p. 98.

15. Quoted in Fernsworth, p. 236.

16. *New Leader,* August 6, 1951, Foltz and Matthews have much personal material about Franco.

17. Matthews, p. 80.

18. Gunther, p. 139.

19. Madariaga, p. 596.

20. For accounts of 1947 referendum, *N.Y.T.,* June 15, 1947; and August 10, 1947, for post-election interview with cardinal primate.

21. *Ya,* July 18, 1959.

3. A Political Church at Work

1. *N.Y.T.,* February 14, 1951.

2. Ian Gilmour, editor of *The Spectator* of London, in a comprehensive article, "Spain Under Franco," in the *New Republic,* November 23, 1959, says: "The hierarchy consider the present form of government in Spain to be that which, in a well-ordered world, all Christians would have. . . . The political views of the average Spanish bishop are about as enlightened as those of Pio Nono and the Syllabus of Errors. To them democracy, anarchy, socialism and Communism are roughly synonymous, and equally anathema." For an analysis of the Spanish Church by a distinguished Catholic journalist, see Hughes, p. 59, and his article in *Esquire,* May 1959.

3. The praise of the Concordat, including that from *Ecclesia,* was summed up in a Madrid despatch in the Brooklyn *Tablet,* September 12, 1953.

4. *Canon Law,* p. 103.

5. Whitaker, p. 259.

6. Peers, *Eclipse,* p. 204.

7. For discussion of Mussolini-Vatican Concordat, see my *Communism, Democracy and Catholic Power.* Beacon Press, 1951.

8. Ebenstein, p. 44. The Franco speech was reported in *Tablet,* October 7, 1961.

9. Peers, *Church,* p. 18.

10. *Ibid.,* especially Appendix I.

11. Summarized, *Iberica,* May 5, 1958, p. 5. Ebenstein, pp. 26ff, is especially valuable in summarizing this and other religious surveys.

12. Brenan's excellent maps show distribution of anti-clerical strength.

13. *Ya,* July 12, 1959.

14. Summarized in *Register,* February 19, 1961. See also Eben-

stein; *Irish Ecclesiastical Record,* September, 1938, "Smoke Screen Over Spain"; and *La Vanguardia* (Barcelona), March 13, 1959.

15. *N.Y.T.,* June 15, 1960. Papal Nuncio statement, *ibid.,* November 6, 1960; Bishop of San Sebastian statement, December 4, 1960; *Tablet* comment, July 16, 1960.

16. Basque priest story, *Iberica,* June 15, 1958. See also issue of March 15, 1959, for article by Jorge Tamarit, "The Catholics Against Franco."

17. Church leaders in West Germany in 1961 also supported Adenauer by condemning the principles of his opponents. In 1957 (*Register,* June 16, 1957) German workers were told that a vote for Social Democrats was morally unjustified. Basil Davidson said in *The Nation,* February 17, 1951: "The West German state is in the most practical sense a Catholic base in Europe, in every way as self-conscious and proselytizing as, for instance, Franco's Spain."

18. *Theological Studies,* June and September, 1949. Father Murray's general position is stated in his book, *We Hold These Truths,* Sheed and Ward, 1960. Father Murray attacked and quoted Guerrero in *Razon y Fe,* 1948, pp. 518-39. His position was repudiated by the Vatican through Cardinal Ottaviani, *N.Y.T.,* July 23, 1953. Cardinal Ottaviani deplored what he called "liberal Catholicism" as expressed by some circles in the United States, and said: "The Church, too, recognizes the necessity with which rulers in some Catholic countries may be faced of granting—because of grave reasons—a degree of tolerance to the other cults. But tolerance is not a synonym for freedom of propaganda which foments religious discord and alters the secure and unanimous possession of truth and of religious practice in countries such as Italy, Spain and others." A Madrid dispatch in the same issue (*N.Y.T.,* July 23, 1953) said: "Spanish ecclesiastical circles said today that the doctrinal stand taken by the Roman Catholic Episcopacy of Spain on what it considered the duties and obligations of a Catholic state toward religion in general and the Protestant minorities in particular had been confirmed by the Vatican."

19. *Razon y Fe,* 1946, pp. 148-71.

4. The Protestants

1. The address of the closed church is Calle Madre de Dios 4, Barrio de Usera, Madrid.

2. *The Christian Century,* September 30, 1959.

3. The estimate of 11,000 Protestants came from leaders of the Protestant Defense Commission in Madrid in 1959. The standard pre-Civil War work by C. Araujo Garcia and Kenneth G. Grubb, *Religion in the Republic of Spain,* World Dominion Press, 1933, estimated 6,259 Protestant communicants in 166 local churches. Recent Catholic estimates put the number nearer 20,000.

4. *Cath. Alm.*, pp. 443-5 estimates 40,871,302 American Catholics in a population of 171,238,845 in 1960.

5. Valuable background historical material on Protestantism in Spain is contained in Hughey; Delpech, with a powerful Introduction by John A. Mackay; Araujo and Grubb, *op. cit.*, *Religious Liberty in Peril* (pamphlet), Paris, Pro Hispania, 1948; annual reports, British and Foreign Bible Society, London; M. Searle Bates, *Religious Liberty: An Inquiry*, International Missionary Council, New York, 1945; Pattee; a series of articles by W. E. Garrison, "Religious Liberty in Spain," *Christian Century*, fall of 1950; Bjorn Hallstrom, *Secret Journey Through Spain*, Latterworth Press, London, 1948; Richard Pattee, *The Religious Question in Spain* (pamphlet), National Council of Catholic Men, Washington, 1950.

6. Quoted, Hughey, p. 39.

7. T. Lincoln Bouscaren, *The Canon Law Digest*, vol. I, p. 607.

8. Hughey, p. 39.

9. *Ibid.*, p. 104.

10. The Charter in Spanish, together with the Spanish version of the Charter of Labor, the Law of Succession, and Principles of the (Falange) Movement are available at low cost in one pamphlet, *Leyes Fundamentales*, from Editorial Garcia Enciso, Pasaje de la Alhambra 4, Madrid.

11. Delpech, p. 56.

12. Homer Bigart's four articles on Spain were published in the *New York Herald Tribune* in February 1949, and attacked by the Spanish Press Attache in Washington in the issue of March 20, 1949. Following *Ecclesia* quote from Bigart.

13. For Segura's letter against Protestants, dated September 20, 1947, see *Information Bulletin*, Federal Council of Churches, October 29, 1949.

14. Dated December 22, 1947, quoted by Hughey, p. 150.

15. *Christian Century*, April 15, 1950.

16. Welles' two articles on Protestants in Spain were in *N.Y.T.*, May 2 and 3, 1959. See also *Time*, March 30, 1959.

17. My exchange of letters on church architecture in Spain with Father Thurston Davis, editor of *America*, was in *N.Y.T.*, March 31, April 13 and April 22, 1960.

18. The address of Rev. Cardona is Trafalgar 32, 2, Madrid 10.

5. The Masons and The Jews

1. I have described Father Fahey's activities in *The Irish and Catholic Power*, pp. 197-8.

2. Peers, *Eclipse*, p. 90.

3. Published by Editorial Vilamala, Valencia 246, Barcelona.

Yo soy espanol is published by Editorial Escuela Espanola, Calle Maya 4, Madrid.

4. The conditions for absolution for Catholics who have been Masons are summarized in *Canon Law,* p. 904.

5. The *Register,* July 4, 1955, declared that "there is a heavy blight of Masonry in Latin America, and Masonry is always violently anticlerical in Latin lands."

6. *Ya,* as cited in *N.Y.T.,* February 5, 1961.

7. Madariaga, *Fall of the Spanish Empire,* p. 254.

8. Thomas Hamilton in *Appeasement's Child,* p. 96, comments on Franco's 1939 decree against Masons. See also Brenan, p. 234.

9. *Register,* July 22, 1956.

10. Peers, *Eclipse,* p. 203.

11. *Arriba,* May 3, 1939, quoted by Hughey, p. 233. For a defense of Franco's policies in dealing with Jews, see *N.Y.T.,* May 13, 1961, letter by Spanish delegate at U.N.

12. Roth's chapter on "The Marranos" is especially valuable. See also Livermore, *Spain;* and for the history of anti-Semitism in Europe, Malcolm Hay, *Europe and the Jews,* Beacon Press, 1960.

13. G. G. Coulton, *Inquisition and Liberty,* Beacon Press, 1959, p. 289.

14. *N.Y.T.,* November 5, 1950.

6. Sex, Marriage and Burial

1. The student who wishes to explore Catholic marriage practices in detail will find valuable the nearly 200 pages of Part V of *Canon Law;* the cases recorded under these canons in T. Lincoln Bouscaren, *The Canon Law Digest,* vol. II, Bruce, 1943; and William J. Doheny, *Canonical Procedure in Matrimonial Cases,* Bruce, 1943. Hughey, Chapter IV, has historical background facts, with references, on the development of Spanish marriage law; and Delpech covers some aspects. A standard Spanish text is *El Matrimonio y las Causas Matrimoniales* by Eloy Montero y Gutierrez, Madrid, 1950. The important criminal statutes on marriage are in the Spanish *Codigo Penal,* sections 471-479. Article 42 of the Civil Code is the most important for mixed marriage. *Ecclesia,* October 3, 1953, reprinted a Bulletin of Information of the Ministry of Justice covering civil marriage and non-Catholics.

2. For discussion of position of wife in marriage, see "Women's Rights in Spain" by Beverly Berghaus, *America,* January 31, 1950.

3. *Time,* October 24, 1955. The decree abolishing prostitution was described by Religious News Service, March 12, 1956.

4. Richard Wright, *Pagan Spain,* Harpers, 1957, p. 154.

5. Brenan, p. 49. Coulton, *op. cit.,* p. 290, says of 15th century Spain: "Among the ordinary clergy concubinage was even more com-

mon than elsewhere in Europe." Gruening, *op. cit.*, p. 267, says of early Mexico: "Celibacy among the clergy was at all times at least as much honored in the breach as in the observance."

6. *N.Y.T.*, July 11, 1959.

7. *Ya*, July 16, 1959.

8. The trial was in Madrid's criminal court, July 4, 1959; the verdict was dated July 8. My brief description of the trial was in the *Christian Century*, September 23, 1959.

9. Quoted with interpretation by Ministry of Justice, Delpech, p. 72. See also *Information Service Bulletin*, National Council of Churches, January 13, 1951.

10. *N.Y.T.*, December 26, 1954.

11. *Time*, January 10, 1955.

12. *America*, March 26, 1955.

13. *Register*, May 10, 1959.

14. Published by the National Union of Protestants, 55 Gloucester Road, Kensington, London, S.W., 7.

7. Education in the Shadow of the Church

1. The indoctrination begins in the earliest grades. See, for example, *Primeras Lecturas, Grado Preparatorio,* Editorial Magistero Espano, Calle de Quevedo 5, Madrid.

2. *Five Encyclicals,* Paulist Press, New York, 1939, p. 40.

3. McCluskey, *America,* July 31, 1954.

4. Most Spanish statistics in this chapter were secured personally from Spain's Education Department in Madrid. They are not guaranteed, since educational statistics in Spain are in a rather primitive condition. I have used both the annual statistical yearbook of Spain and the condensed *Anuario Estadistico de Espana,* 1959. Office of Education figures in the United States were summarized in *N.Y.T.*, August 14 and September 4, 1960, estimating total school and college enrollment at 48,650,000, with nearly 4,000,000 in college. See also Ebenstein, p. 46.

5. Peers, *Church,* p. 150. Thomas, p. 35, estimates that in Madrid in 1930 there were 80,000 children who did not go to school.

6. Hitler-Vatican Concordat, Appendix B in *The Struggle for Religious Freedom in Germany,* A.S. Duncan-Jones, Gollancz (London), 1938. The general German situation is well described in Guy Stanton Ford, *Dictatorship in the Modern World,* University of Miami Press, 1939.

7. Delpech, p. 79, gives key paragraphs of both the Law of Primary Education of July 17, 1945, from the *Oficial Boletin,* and the Law of Secondary Education of April 12, 1952.

8. For example, Pius XI, *Christian Education of Youth* in *Five Encyclicals,* p. 56.

9. *Iberica,* May 15, 1960, and November 15, 1958.

10. *N.Y.T.* October 7, 1954.

11. *Pueblo,* April 21, 1959.

12. Statistics on U.S. education from Office of Education. Comparison between 1960 and 1890 summarized, *N.Y.T.,* July 8, 1960.

13. Peers, *Church,* p. 150.

14. *Tablet,* December 6, 1958.

15. *Iberica,* June 15, 1959.

16. *America,* December 6, 1958.

17. Ebenstein's discussion of Opus Dei is notable. For Catholic interpretations see "A Look at Opus Dei" by Father Thurston Davis, *America,* April 1, 1961; and official statement of the Secretarial of Opus Dei in Chicago, *America,* May 20, 1961. For critical analysis by Spanish writer see *Iberica,* September 15, 1957, "Behind the Cross, the Devil." A 1957 summary by Benjamin Welles was in *N.Y.T.,* March 7, 1957.

18. The *Register,* April 3, 1960, lists four classes of Opus Dei members; (1) Numeraries; (2) Oblates; (3) Supernumeraries; and (4) Co-operators. The Co-operators are not actual members in the ordinary sense of that word. The first two classes take oaths of poverty, chastity and obedience.

8. How The Censorship Works

1. Spain's censorship system goes back to the Inquisition, and is described in the *Encyclopedia Britannica,* "Inquisition." Roth, *op. cit.,* describes the extra censorship by Spanish ecclesiastics beyond the *Index Librorum Prohibitorum.* For estimate of Catholic dailies in Spain see *America,* July 22, 1961.

2. *N.Y.T.,* December 17, 1960.

3. A good summary of censorship operation is in *Iberica,* July-August, 1959. See also Alastair Reed, "Letter from Madrid," *The New Yorker,* November 12, 1960.

4. Mussolini's press law is described by Peter Odegard in *Dictatorship in the Modern World,* edited by Guy Stanton Ford, pp. 237ff.

5. Ambassador Areilza in Washington protested the *N.Y.T.* editorial of June 23rd in a letter published June 26, 1959, as "hardly consistent with the traditions of a great newspaper." In Madrid Ambassador John Davis Lodge attempted no parallel protest.

6. *Life* story, *N.Y.T.,* July 3, 1960.

7. *Iberica,* March 15, 1961. *Life,* in a Spanish edition, sells more than 6,000 copies in Spain.

8. The ban includes "all translations of Sacred Scripture into any language, made or published by non-Catholics," Canon Law, p. 726.

9. *Ecclesia* summary, *N.Y.T.*, November 9, 1954. *Ecclesia*, May 23, 1958, also complained very mildly about too much censorship by the state.

10. Santander story in *N.Y.T.*, June 19, 1960; and *America*, November 12, 1960.

11. I have described the American operations of the Legion of Decency and the National Organization for Decent Literature in *The Right to Read*, Beacon Press, 1955.

12. *Ecclesia*, March 21, 1959. For more general facts see *Ecclesia*, January 18, 1958. *Iberica*, September 15, 1960, describes the very extensive Church ownership of cinemas.

9. The Labor-Capital Strait Jacket

1. Full text of encyclical, *Five Encyclicals*, Paulist Press, 1939.

2. Claim contained in summary by U.S. Department of Labor, June 1, 1961. Also see *Tablet*, July 15, 1961; and for Catholic general interpretation, Chapter III of *Church and Society*, edited by Joseph N. Moody. The CISC originally claimed a 10 per cent Protestant membership.

3. *N.Y.T.*, May 8, 1960, p. 14, Sec. 10.

4. *Iberica*, April 15, 1958.

5. The Statistical Office of the U.N. reports annual average per capita income in U.S. dollars for 1957-59 as follows: Portugal, 200-299; Spain, 300-399; Italy, 400-499; West Germany, 800-899; France, 900-999; Great Britain, 900-999 and the U.S., 2100-2199.

6. *Conclusiones*, Consejo Social de la Organizacion Sindical Espanola, Madrid, April 26, 1959. For Falange history see Brenan, 308ff; Pattee, Chapter 13; Madariaga, *passim;* and Hughes, Chapter 5.

7. *N.Y.T.*, September 2, 1956, article on "Franco's Spain Twenty Years Later."

8. *N.Y.T.*, January 1, 1961.

9. See *Iberica*, June 15, 1960, "Organic Democracy" by "Steparius."

10. A favorable, pro-Franco description, especially of family benefits, was in the *Tablet*, April 14, 1951.

11. *Iberica*, June 15, 1960.

12. *Ibid.*, February 15, 1960.

13. *America*, December 18, 1954.

14. Vicente Girbau Leon, *Iberica*, December 15, 1958.

10. Unholy Alliance

1. Our American ambassadors in recent years have cooperated in pro-Franco propaganda in many ways. For example, Stanton Griffis, who became Ambassador in 1951, wrote a partisan and pro-Franco introduction to *Highlights* of *Spanish History* by his former

associate, Colonel Richard C. Harris, Saragossa, 1955, which denounced as "utterly stupid" the decision of the major powers (adhered to by the U.S.) that Spain should be "outside the pale of polite society."

2. See Charles C. Griffin, *The United States and the Disruption of the Spanish Empire, 1810-1822,* Columbia University Press, 1937, p. 66.

3. Quotes from Anson P. Stokes, *Church and State in the United States,* Harpers, 1950, Vol. II, p. 312.

4. Pius XI's Mexican encyclicals were in 1926, 1932 and 1937. For accounts of the Mexican church-state struggle, see J. Lloyd Mecham, *Church and State in Latin America,* University of North Carolina Press, 1934, Chapter XVI; Hubert Herring, *A History of Latin America,* Knopf, 1961, *passim;* and Gruening, *op. cit.* Chapter 4.

5. *America,* August 20, 1938.

6. See F. Jay Taylor, *The United States and the Spanish Civil War,* New York, 1956, Chapters 7 and 8; and Thomas.

7. *The Secret Diary of Harold Ickes,* Simon and Schuster, 1953, vol. II, p. 390; Thomas, p. 536.

8. Ebenstein, p. 20, from Mildred Strunk, *Public Opinion,* p. 808.

9. See Thomas J. Hamilton, *Appeasement's Child;* and Chapter VI, "Franco Invades Latin America," in Carleton Beals, *The Coming Struggle for Latin America,* Lippincott, 1938.

10. *Time,* January 9, 1942.

11. The economic side of the picture is presented in Herbert Feis, *The Spanish Story: Franco and the Nations At War,* Knopf, 1948.

12. The U.N. Assembly condemned Franco 45 to 0, *N.Y.T.,* February 10, 1946. The U.N. subcommittee's resolution is reprinted in part in Foltz, p. 308.

13. Bases agreement text in Department of State release 519, September 26, 1953.

14. Our economic aid program for Spain, according to State Department figures, totalled $1,004,000,000 to September 1, 1960; our military assistance program from 1950 to 1961 totaled $454,250,000; our base installations cost approximately $350,000,000. *N.Y.T.* estimate December 30, 1960 by Benjamin Welles put total at not less than two billion.

15. *N.Y.T.,* March 12, 1961. Testimony concerning misplaced bases summarized, *Iberica,* February 15, 1958.

16. *New York Daily News,* October 8, 1959; *Iberica,* October, 1959. Kowalski said that all countries in Western Europe allow the American flag to be flown from U.S. military installations, but in Franco's country this is denied.

17. See Hanson Baldwin, *N.Y.T. Magazine,* October 19, 1960.

18. *Washington Post,* December 20, 1959. See also issues of December 12 and 31, 1959, for events of Eisenhower trip.

19. *N.Y.T.,* February 28, 1960.

20. *Iberica,* January 15, 1961.

21. May 28, 1949.

22. *This Is Spain,* p. 378.

23. *The Religious Question in Spain,* p. 17.

24. *Ibid.,* p. 37.

25. *This Is Spain,* p. 390.

26. *The Religious Question in Spain,* p. 43.

27. Religious News Service, April 13, 1956.

28. From *N.Y.T.* profile of Castiella, March 25, 1960.

29. *Congressional Record,* March 23, 1960, p. 6917.

30. Religious News Service, March 5, 1956.

31. *Tablet,* June 18, 1960.

32. *Ibid.,* December 2, 1961.

11. From the Inquisition to Salazar

1. The State Department estimated the per capita annual income of Portugal at $238 in 1961. The U.S. Commerce Department (*N.Y.T.,* August 21, 1961) estimated 1960 U.S. per capita income at $2,223. Illiteracy in Portugal was estimated at "nearly one half" in *N.Y.T.,* January 29, 1961. UNESCO's *World Illiteracy at Mid-Century* estimated Spanish illiteracy in 1950 at 17.3 per cent for those ten years old and older; Portuguese illiteracy at 44 per cent for those fifteen years old and older.

2. See essays by C. R. Boxer, H. V. Livermore, and William J. Entwistle in *Portugal and Brazil,* ed. Harold V. Livermore, Oxford (London), 1953; Livermore, *Portugal;* Pattee, *Portugal;* and Edgar Prestage, *Portugal, a Pioneer of Christianity,* London, 1945. For eighteenth- and nineteenth-century developments within Portugal see *Cath. Enc.,* "Portugal."

3. P. 21, *The Significance of Portugal,* World Dominion Press, 1933. Although this work is now out of date, it is the most useful older work about religious minorities.

4. Encyclical, *Jamdudum in Lusitania,* issued in 1911. The Portuguese government's story in English of the anti-clerical Republic is in *Portugal* (government review), March-April, 1959, together with a general description of the Church.

5. Oliveira Salazar, *Centro Catolico,* 1922.

6. Pattee, *Portugal,* pp. 220 and 222.

7. *Doctrine and Action,* Faber and Faber, London, 1939.

8. *The Great Encyclical Letters of Leo XIII,* p. 123.

9. Two pro-Salazar books are Christine Garnier, *Salazar, An Intimate Portrait,* Farrar, Straus and Young, 1954, and F.C.C. Egerton,

Salazar, Rebuilder of Portugal, London, 1943. *N.Y.T.* profile, May 21, 1960; *Time* summary, November 16, 1953; *Saturday Evening Post,* April 9, 1960, "The World's Most Durable Dictator" by Toni Howard.

10. *U.S. News and World Report,* May 30, 1960.

11. In an address published as a pamphlet, *The Reality of National Unity.*

12. *The Nation,* January 9, 1960.

13. *Iberica,* April 15, 1960.

14. *Political Constitution of the Portuguese Republic,* S.N.I., Lisbon, 1957. A non-critical factual description of the political and educational systems under Salazar is that of William C. Atkinson, pp. 87ff, *Portugal and Brazil, op. cit.*

15. *Atlantic Monthly,* October, 1961, and *N.Y.T.,* April 14, 1961. The various Portuguese factions in 1955 are described in *Iberica,* September 15, 1955.

16. *America,* April 1, 1961.

12. Catholics, Protestants and Fatima

1. The series began in the *Catholic News* (New York) October 16, 1948.

2. *Commonweal,* September 22, 1961. This magazine also condemned Salazar's policy in Angola, June 23, 1961.

3. Parts of the story of the Bishop of Oporto were told in *Iberica,* April 15, 1959; earlier statements were discussed in *Tablet,* December 27, 1958. The bishop's 8-page letter, dated July 13, 1958 and numbered Official 271/58, was privately printed in Portuguese but never officially translated or distributed.

4. Summarized, *Tablet,* January 24, 1959.

5. *Lumen,* January, 1958.

6. August 25, 1959.

7. There is no good recent book on Protestantism in Portugal, but see Eduardo Moreira, *op. cit.*

8. *Christian Century,* July 13, 1949.

9. A statue of Our Lady of Fatima, 53 inches in height, can be purchased from *Soul* magazine, official organ of the Blue Army, for $195. The bi-monthly magazine, published under the Imprimatur of the Bishop of Trenton at the Ave Maria Institute, Washington, New Jersey, can be secured for $1 a year. The Blue Army's English edition of *Voz da Fatima,* a propaganda newspaper describing miracles, is published by the Grafica de Leiria, Leiria, Portugal. Catholic descriptions in English are contained in *Cath. Enc. Supplement; Our Lady of Fatima* by Father William T. Walsh; *Vision of Fatima* by Thomas McGlynn, etc. Probably the most important early authoritative description in Portuguese is the 1927 work, *As Grandes Maravillias*

de Fatima by Viscount de Montelo (pen name of a priest), published under the Imprimatur of the Bishop of Leiria, who governed the Fatima ecclesiastical district, by Unaiao Grafica, Lisbon. It carries two alleged pictures of the solar phenomena of October 13, 1917, both looking like ordinary near-eclipses. On pp. 99 and 109 are the definite October 13 statements that the war would end that day. The Vatican has repudiated the authenticity of two alleged pictures of the sun at Fatima, as pictures taken earlier, but I am not certain that the above pictures were those repudiated. Gilbert F. Santos admitted to me that he was not present on July 13, 1917, when the Virgin Mary is alleged to have discussed Russia with Lucia. The exposure of the miracle, *Fatima,* by Tomaz da Fonseca, Editoria Germinal, Caixa Postal 142, Agencia Postal da Lapa, Rio de Janeiro, Brazil, is in the Library of Congress. It was smuggled into Portugal under a false title, and sold 4,000 copies before the government and Church censors caught up with it. For details of the La Salette story see *Larousse du XXe Siecle,* vol. 6 (Salette); and the *Cath. Enc.,* "La Salette." When some skeptical priests accused a French girl of playing the part of the Virgin for the credulous peasant children at La Salette, she sued them for damages and lost.

10. Many independent political figures, acting in good faith, have been drawn into the Blue Army anti-Communist television programs, apparently without realizing that they are being used for the promotion of an essentially McCarthyite organization which also condones and promotes clerical fascism. The Blue Army's "Zero 1960" series on television included Henry Cabot Lodge, Alfred M. Gruenther, James Mitchell, Hubert Humphrey, John Sherman Cooper and John F. Kennedy. (*New York Herald-Tribune,* March 8, 1960). The "Zero 1960" series was promoted on the assumption that 1960 was "the zero hour for the opening of the last part of the message of Fatima" from Lucia. Fourteen anti-Communist films, described in *Soul* for November-December, 1960, are available for "interested groups" at $5 per film from Blue Army Television, Ave Maria Institute, Washington, N.J. What they say against Communism is, for the most part, true. What they do not say is that the Blue Army is also being used to promote confidence in Catholic totalitarianism in the Iberian peninsula.

13. America, Portugal and the African Explosion

1. *N.Y.T.,* March 28, 1961; *Iberica,* April 15, 1961. The *Washington Post,* March 29, 1961 had an editorial reply to Portugal. For U.S. vote in U.N. Security Council, and Stevenson statement, *N.Y.T.,* March 16, 1961. Salazar interview on Angola, *N.Y.T.,* May 31, 1961. Earlier U.N. discussion, *N.Y.T.,* November 13, 28 and 30, 1960.

2. *Congressional Record*, September 26, 1961. All American economic aid since 1951 has come under the program of PL 480, Title III (Voluntary Relief Agencies).

3. Eisenhower address in Lisbon, *N.Y.T.*, May 21, 1960.

4. *Santa Maria* stories, *N.Y.T.*, January 23 to February 5, 1961.

5. Krishna Menon statement, *Hispanic America Reports*, July, 1957, p. 400.

6. Galvao record, Duffy, p. 327; *Iberica*, February 15, 1961.

7. *N.Y.T.*, January 31, 1961.

8. *Tablet*, June 17, 1961. *America*, June 17, 1961.

9. *Iberica*, April 15, 1961.

10. For 1960 and 1961 territorial dispute between Spain and Morocco, *N.Y.T.*, December 19, 1960, April 16, 1961, and September 1, 1961; and *Iberica*, February 15, 1961.

11. *Voz da Fatima*, February 13, 1961.

12. Basil Davidson's work is *The African Awakening*, London, 1955.

13. *N.Y.T.*, November 13, 1960.

14. Portuguese native policy summarized, Duffy, Chapter XII; recent Angola policy (Welles), *N.Y.T.*, February 12, 1961, and March 19 and 21, 1961.

15. Repeal of the native statutes was announced by the government (*Time*, September 8, 1961), but the head tax and the literacy test will still deny citizenship rights to the majority of natives.

16. Duffy, p. 315.

17. Marvin Harris, *Portugal's African "Wards,"* American Committee on Africa, 4 West 40th St., New York 18, 1958.

18. Harris, *op. cit.*, p. 13.

19. *N.Y.T.*, July 10, 1960.

20. *Register*, May 15, 1960, and *Tablet*, July 22, 1961.

21. *N.Y.T.*, April 23, 1961. Earlier valuable treatments of Protestantism in Portuguese Africa are to be found in Eduardo Moreira, *Portuguese East Africa*, London, 1936; and John T. Tucker, *Angola, Land of the Blacksmith Prince*, London, 1933.

22. *Commonweal*, September 22, 1961. See also *The Progressive*, October 1961, for article "Revolution in Angola" by Russell Howe.

23. Personal communication from Rev. Malcolm McVeigh. The address of the Board of Missions of the Methodist Church is 475 Riverside Drive, New York 27. The description of Angola events by a Baptist leader was in *N.Y.T.*, May 3, 1961. A summary of the situation in 1961 was written by Ronald Chilcote, "Politics in Portugal and Her Empire," *World Today* (London), September, 1961. See also Religious News Service, August 16 and October 18, 1961.

24. *Register*, July 22, 1961.

14. The Future of Clerical Fascism

1. *N.Y.T.*, July 15, 1961. The Pope said: "It is clear, however, that when the hierarchy has made a decision on the point at issue, Catholics are bound to obey their directives because the Church has the right and obligation not merely to guard ethical and religious principles but also to intervene authoritatively in the temporal sphere when it is a matter of judging the application of these principles to concrete cases."

2. P. 173; published by Putnam's, 1943.

3. *The Humanist*, No. 1, 1961; and Dudley Kirk, "Recent Trends of Catholic Fertility in the U.S.," in Report of Annual Conference, Millbank Fund, 1955.

4. Roger A. Freeman, author of *Taxes for the Schools*, is cited in *America*, February 25, 1961, as estimating that public school enrollment has increased 42 per cent since 1940, and private school enrollment 147 per cent. But the private school figures include some non-Catholic private schools.

5. *American Freedom and Catholic Power*, rev. ed., p. 272.

6. *Register*, August 20, 1961. The bishops' pastoral letters condemning the Popular Democratic Party as "anti-Christian" and "anti-Catholic," which were read in all Catholic churches in Puerto Rico on October 23 and October 30, 1960, are summarized in Cath. Alm., pp. 84-6.

7. *Everson vs. Board of Education*, 330 U.S. 1, as quoted and approved in *McCollum vs. Board of Education*, 333 U.S. 203. Catholic demands were voiced by Cardinal Spellman on January 17, 1961 and by Archbishop Karl Alter, in behalf of all the bishops, on March 3, 1961.

8. John J. Considine, *New Horizons in Latin America*, Dodd, Mead, 1958, p. 254. This valuable work is the approved Catholic description of Latin American religious conditions by the head of the Latin American Bureau of the U.S. Bishops' Committee on Latin America. The best independent scholarly work in this field is *Church and State in Latin America*, by J. Lloyd Mecham, University of North Carolina Press, 1934.

9. There is a short description of semi-fascist political parties in Harold E. Davis, *Government and Politics in Latin America*, Ronald Press, 1958, p. 200. Carleton Beals has a vivid account in his *The Coming Struggle for Latin America*, Lippincott, 1938. See also the essay by William S. Stokes in *Freedom and Reform in Latin America*, edited by Frederick B. Pike, University of Notre Dame Press, 1959. Hubert Herring's *A History of Latin America*, Knopf, 1961, is standard and indispensable. Stokes concludes that "it is the author's firm impression that 'leftist' and 'rightist' political ideologies

will continue to enjoy in the forseeable future greater popularity and success, in the sense of acquiring political power in most of the Latin American countries, than political ideologies which emphasize in any basic or fundamental way the principles of individualism, democracy and liberalism." Concerning Communism he says that "there are many more Communists in Latin America than in the United States, their present influence is considerable, and their potential effectiveness is great indeed." There is also an interesting discussion of liberal and conservative parties in *The Struggle for Democracy in Latin America* by Charles O. Porter and Robert Alexander, Macmillan, 1961.

10. Mecham, *op. cit.*, p. 506. Mecham, pp. 164ff, shows how Church censorship in Colombia parallels that of Spain, although anti-clericals captured government for a time.

11. Father Considine, *op. cit.*, p. 215, says: "There is union of Church and state in Argentina, Bolivia, Colombia, Peru and Venezuela and varying degrees of separation in other nations." The facts about diplomatic representation are from *Vatican Diplomacy* by Robert A. Graham S.J., Princeton University Press, 1959, pp. 19-21.

12. Much of the Protestant story is told by W. Stanley Rycroft in *Religion and Faith in Latin America*, Westminster, 1958, and by George F. Howard, *Religious Liberty in Latin America*, Westminster, 1944. A blistering and biased attack on Protestant missions by a Catholic writer is John W. White, *Our Good Neighbor Hurdle*, Bruce, 1943.

13. *Cath. Alm.*, p. 370; and *America*, October 7, 1961, p. 9.

14. *N.Y.T.*, August 6, 1961.

INDEX